More Murder in East Anglia

Robert Church served for almost twenty-six years in the Metropolitan Police before retiring in 1978 to train as a probation officer. He now lives and works in Lowestoft numbering among his interests not only criminology but also military history, genealogy and flying.

Also by Robert Church

Murder in East Anglia
Accidents of Murder

More Murder in East Anglia

A New Look at Notorious Cases

ROBERT CHURCH

ROBERT HALE · LONDON

© *Robert Church 1990*
First published in Great Britain 1990

ISBN 0 7090 4031 8

Robert Hale Limited
Clerkenwell House
Clerkenwell Green
London EC1R 0HT

Photoset in Palatino by
Derek Doyle & Associates, Mold, Clwyd.
Printed in Great Britain by
St Edmundsbury Press, Bury St Edmunds, Suffolk.
Bound by Woolnough Limited.

Contents

To
Mum and Dad

Acknowledgements

I have pleasure in acknowledging the help of the following individuals without whose co-operation and courtesy this book could not have been written. The names are not given in any order of priority.

Mrs Ruth Crabtree, Polstead, Suffolk; office of the judge advocate general, Department of the Air Force, Washington, DC; military personnel records, St Louis, Missouri, USA; Headquarters Third Air Force (USAFE), RAF Mildenhall, Suffolk; Barbara Green and the staff of the archaeological department, Norwich Castle Museum; Mr B.R. Cole, Framingham Earl; P.Y. Domaingue, Lowestoft; David Wright and the staff of Suffolk Record Office (Lowestoft); Catherine Clinton, information services librarian, Central Library, Great Yarmouth; Inspector Goffin, community relations officer, Great Yarmouth police station; Detective Chief Inspector Alan Hill, Essex police; Derek Wyatt, Colchester; Kenneth Runicles, editor, and Rita Hills, librarian, *Colchester Evening Gazette*; ex-Superintendent C.J. Fuller, Newmarket; Alan Holzer, assistant secretary, Halesworth Museum; PC David Fayers, Lowestoft police station; the staff of the local studies library (Cambridge Collection), Central Library, Cambridge; my wife Dorothy for her continuing support and encouragement.

Finally, the anonymous reporters of *The Times*, *The Cambridge Chronicle and University Journal*, *Ipswich Journal and Suffolk, Norfolk, Essex and Cambridgeshire Advertiser*, *Colchester Evening Gazette*, *The Norfolk News (Eastern Counties Journal)*, *Eastern Daily Press*, *Lowestoft Journal* and *East Anglian Daily Times*, whose contemporaneous accounts of several cases supplemented other research.

MORE MURDER IN EAST ANGLIA

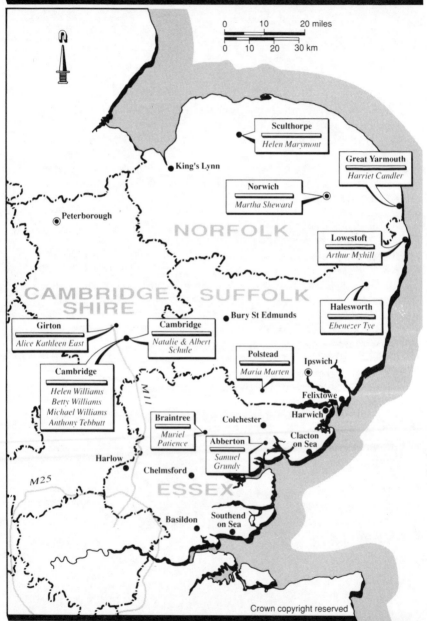

0   10   20 miles
0   10   20   30 km

Sculthorpe
Helen Marymont

Great Yarmouth
Harriet Candler

King's Lynn

Norwich
Martha Sheward

Peterborough

NORFOLK

Lowestoft
Arthur Myhill

CAMBRIDGE
SHIRE

SUFFOLK

Bury St Edmunds

Halesworth
Ebenezer Tye

Girton
Alice Kathleen East

Cambridge
Natalie & Albert Schule

Cambridge
*Helen Williams
Betty Williams
Michael Williams
Anthony Tebbutt*

Polstead
Maria Marten

Ipswich

M11

Braintree
Muriel Patience

Colchester

Felixtowe

Harwich

Abberton
Samuel Grundy

Clacton on Sea

Harlow

Chelmsford

M25

ESSEX

Basildon

Southend on Sea

Crown copyright reserved

THE NAMES OF THE VICTIMS ARE SHOWN IN ITALIC BELOW THE PLACE NAMES

Introduction

In the introduction to my first book, *Murder in East Anglia*, in which I reconstructed eleven regional murders committed during the past 140 years, I apologized for any obvious omissions. In *More Murder in East Anglia* I have written about eleven other homicide cases that for various reasons were not included in my earlier book.

From the well-documented 'Red Barn' case in 1827 to the more recent death of Mary Helen Marymont at the USAF base at Sculthorpe and the callous shooting of Mrs Muriel Patience in her Braintree home in 1972, I have attempted to recapture the horror and drama surrounding the crimes. It should be noted that the direct/indirect speech variations in the text stem from the various styles used in newspapers and other sources from which the speech has been obtained.

This second book of East Anglian murder cases has, like the first, resulted from facts and information gathered from a variety of sources. I hope that like its predecessor it will provoke thought, stimulate debate and act as a cogent reminder that violent death in our society is by no means a recent phenomenon but has been lurking for many years in even the most attractive corners of our land.

R.C.

– 1 –
The Polstead Slaying
1827

Anyone passing within earshot of the Red Barn in the Suffolk village of Polstead just before midday on Friday 18 May 1827 may have paused momentarily to listen to the raised voices of a wrangling couple within. Had they lingered a few moments longer, they would have heard the sound of a pistol-shot which brought the quarrel to an abrupt end.

The murder of Maria Marten, and the subsequent trial and execution of William Corder, has since been the subject of countless books, plays and even ballads. 'The Red Barn Murder', which is still referred to briefly in some local guide-books, has passed into Suffolk folklore.

What attracted Maria, a mole-catcher's daughter, to the wealthy farmer's son in the spring of 1826 is hard to say. Physically he failed to measure up to many of the village lads; his reputation as a ne'er-do-well was no secret, and it was his brother who had first seduced and then deserted her. Maybe the wealth and prestige associated with the Corder family were sufficient to counterbalance his other shortcomings. Maria's appeal was more obvious. Attractive, vivacious and worldly wise (she had already had two illegitimate children, one of whom had died, while the other lived with her and her parents), she held out to Corder the promise of a relationship well suited to one with his established reputation for licentiousness.

The romance flourished, and after a few months Maria again became pregnant, a condition that seemed at first not to worry her lover unduly. However, the death of his father and older brother Thomas, together with the serious ill-health that dogged his other brothers John and James and killed them both within the year, threw a different light on the situation. The responsibility for running the farm devolved upon William; in addition, he was trying to placate his mother, who disapproved of Maria, and to reassure Maria's family, who were hoping to engineer the couple's marriage. For William Corder, faced with his new-found responsibility, together with the conflicting interests of the two families, the early months of 1827 were a time for serious thinking and decision-making.

As tenant farmer of some 300 acres, William's father had met the challenge of the Agrarian Revolution and had coped well with the fundamental changes to farming methods it had brought. Progressive but thrifty, highly respected by his neighbours, by the time of his death John Corder had become a wealthy man. The men who had worked for him on the land seem to have been reasonably content with their lot; he was regarded as strict but fair, with a reputation for paying a fair day's wage for a fair day's work.

It was this situation that William took over in February 1827. In that month, possibly to gain some respite from the pressures being applied by his mother and Maria's family, he arranged for Maria to move into lodgings at Sudbury until after the birth of the baby. Sadly the infant survived for only two weeks, dying from an unknown cause after Maria had returned home to Polstead. At Corder's instigation it was decided that the birth should be kept secret from all but her family. To facilitate this, a couple of nights later the couple stole out, carrying the dead baby in a cardboard box, and buried it in a field. After Maria's death there was speculation as to the cause of her baby's death and the location of its final resting-place.

Despite her complicity in disposing of her child's body, Maria was beginning to have serious misgivings about her relationship and future with Corder. These were not assuaged following the interception by Corder of a £5 note sent to her by her former lover as maintenance for her young son. This act shocked Maria, so much so that, despite her father's continuing enthusiasm for the idea, she now had serious doubts about marrying William.

Although Corder was not entirely averse to the idea of marrying Maria, the pressure from her family precipitated matters. The last week in her life was for Maria one of some apprehension: she became alarmed on Sunday when Corder told her that he had heard that the village constable held a warrant for her arrest on a charge of having given birth to illegitimate children. When he suggested that they immediately regularize the situation by travelling to Ipswich the next day to get married, despite her reservations she agreed to the proposition. It so happened that Maria had four more days to dwell on the prospect, as for various reasons Corder delayed their departure until the end of the week.

On Friday 18 May 1827 he called at the Martens' cottage about midday and told Maria to prepare to leave with him immediately. As it was broad daylight, she demurred, concerned lest she be spotted leaving the village and summarily arrested. Corder reassured her and prevailed upon her to disguise herself in the men's clothing that he had brought with him. Whilst she was so engaged, he took her other clothing to the Red Barn, after telling her that they would pause there long enough for her to change back into her own clothes.

Maria's progress from her cottage to the barn was not accomplished without some discomfort. The brown jacket, blue trousers and striped waistcoat, all surmounted by a red-and-green neckerchief, had been dragged over the flannel petticoat, Irish linen chemise and boned stays that she was already wearing. As she waddled across the fields to meet her lover, she hardly looked her most ravishing.

He met her before she reached the barn, and according to his later confession they started quarrelling about the burial of their infant son. The quarrel extended to other matters and grew more heated after they arrived at the barn.

'A scuffle ensued,' said Corder, 'and during the scuffle, and at the time I think she had hold of me, I took the pistol from the side-pocket of my velveteen jacket, and fired. She fell and died in an instant. I never saw even a struggle ...'

Although Corder insisted that he had killed Maria with a single pistol-shot, later medical evidence proved that she had been stabbed and possibly also strangled. However she had died, her assailant lost no time in burying her in a shallow, hastily dug grave in the floor of the barn.

Two days after Mrs Marten had seen him depart with her stepdaughter for Ipswich, she was surprised to meet Corder back in Polstead. He explained that he had left Maria in Ipswich, but soon she would be going to stay with a former schoolfriend's sister at the seaside. Corder meantime remained in Polstead to live and work on the farm, regularly visiting the Martens during the next few months to reassure them about their daughter, from whom they received no word.

However, by September 1827, maintaining the pretence was becoming too much for Corder, who was running the farm and being assailed from all sides by enquiries about Maria – this persuaded him to leave Polstead again. He called on the Martens before he left and told them that, after going first to a health spa, he intended going on to London, where he and Maria were to be married.

Taking with him £400, he travelled to the Isle of Wight, where by accident he met the young woman he was destined to marry.

After that first casual meeting they were surprised to meet again by chance in London. Again the couple made no arrangements to further their acquaintanceship.

Corder meanwhile wrote several letters to Maria's father, two of which were later produced in court. The first, sent from London, informed Tom Marten that William and Maria were now man and wife and then went on to censure him for not having replied to Maria's letter. This fiction provoked an immediate reply from Marten, informing Corder that he had not heard from his daughter. In the same letter he asked Corder for some money to help him to look after Thomas Henry – Maria's surviving child, whose father, he explained, was no longer supporting him. A few days later Tom Marten received another letter from Corder enclosing a sovereign and expressing concern and bewilderment at the non-delivery of Maria's letter. Corder urged him to write to Thomas Henry's father asking for some financial support for the child.

These letters temporarily allayed the family's concern over Maria. However, as weeks and months passed without further word from either their daughter or Corder, the worry and doubt returned, fuelled by the speculations and suspicions of their neighbours, who all had theories as to the couple's fate.

Eventually, in April 1828, eleven months after Maria had left home, her stepmother, after a succession of dreams about Maria's disappearance, persuaded her sceptical husband to investigate the interior of the Red Barn. Thus it was that on 19 April 1828, accompanied by William Pryke, a local bailiff, Tom Marten tentatively poked his mole spike into the floor of the barn. It emerged smelling abominably and with what appeared to be flesh clinging to it. It was enough to prompt the two men to go and fetch a third villager; the three of them then set about digging up the floor of the barn. Soon afterwards their efforts were rewarded when revealed before their horrified gaze was what appeared to be the remains of a human body.

William Corder had decided that it was time to marry and settle down. Alone in London he felt the desire for matrimony more urgently than he had in Polstead. Having so decided, he did not waste time. To contact as many young, eligible women as quickly as possible, he inserted an advertisement in the *Morning Herald* on 13 November 1827, and in the *Sunday Times* twelve days later.

MATRIMONY – A Private Gentleman, aged 24, entirely independent, whose disposition is not to be exceeded, has lately lost the chief of his family by the hand of Providence, which has occasioned discord among the remainder, under circumstances most disagreeable to relate. To any female of respectability, who would study for domestic comfort, and willing to confide her future happiness in one every way qualified to render the marriage state desirable, as the advertiser is in affluence (the lady must have the power of some property, which may remain in her own possession). Many very happy marriages have taken place through means similar to this now resorted to, and it is hoped no one will answer this through impertinent curiosity; but should this meet the eye of any agreeable lady, who feels desirous of meeting with a sociable, tender, kind, and sympathising companion, they will find this advertisement worthy of notice. Honour and secrecy may be relied on. As some little security against idle applications, it is requested that letters may be addressed (post-paid) to A.Z., care of Mr. Foster, stationer, No. 68, Leadenhall-street, which will meet with the most respectful attention.

Corder was surprised and gratified at the response he received to his extraordinary advertisement. So overwhelmed was he that he took the trouble to read only about half of the ninety-five replies he received.

'Sir ... myself being disengaged, and of domestic habits, and having nothing but youth to recommend me, I take this opportunity to offer myself ....' 'Sir ... In person I am considered a pretty little figure. Hair nut-brown, blue eyes, not generally considered plain, my age nearly twenty-five. My married friends have often told me, I am calculated to make an amiable man truly happy ....' 'Sir ... I am one who possesses *every* qualification calculated to render the object of my choice happy. You will excuse, sir, my not being explicit, but at present I consider it quite unnecessary ....' These are typical of the letters sent in reply.

By an amazing coincidence, for like the others she was unaware of the advertiser's identity, Mary Moore, the young woman whom Corder had met briefly on the Isle of Wight and then later in London, was one of those who wrote to him, and it was to her letter that he responded. Within a week the couple were married.

Mary's impetuosity initially dismayed her mother and brother, but their concern seems to have been allayed by the apparent devotion and solicitude displayed towards her by her husband. While her brother continued to live and work as a jeweller in London, Mary and William moved with her mother to Ealing Lane, Brentford, where Mary opened a girls' school. There Corder remained in the background, leaving his wife to run the establishment. His mother-in-law was nevertheless disturbed by his unsettled behaviour, particularly at night, when his unfortunate habit of talking and moaning loudly in his sleep alarmed many of the school's young boarders.

The morning after Maria's body was found, it was disinterred from its makeshift grave in the presence of the coroner's jury, who then immediately adjourned to the Cock Inn in Polstead for the inquest. After evidence of identification had been given by Maria's sister Ann, her distressed father told of his daughter's departure with Corder the previous May. After a similar account had been given by her stepmother, the coroner, John Wayman, adjourned the inquest and suggested that, in the light of what had been said, someone should travel to London to trace and apprehend Corder and bring him back for the remainder of the hearing.

Following the adjournment the jury and the rest of Polstead's inhabitants attended the burial service and final laying-to-rest in St Mary's Churchyard of the young woman who for twenty-six years had lived amongst them.

Meanwhile a local constable named Ayres was dispatched to London to seek out William Corder. Before leaving he spoke to a friend of Corder's who was able to give him a lead to the wanted man's whereabouts. In London Ayres first went to the Lambeth Street police office, where he conferred with Constable James Lea. Further enquiries were then made by the two men which led them eventually to the Grove House Academy at Ealing Lane, Brentford.

On the morning of Tuesday 22 April, four days after the discovery of Maria's remains, Ayres and Lea travelled out to Brentford. Leaving Ayres in a local inn, Lea continued to the school, where he was taken in to meet Corder, who was eating his breakfast in the company of his wife and another lady. After introducing himself and explaining the reason for his visit, Lea told Corder that he was arresting him on a very serious charge and that he must consider himself his prisoner. Corder replied, 'Very well,' after which he confined himself to denying any knowledge of Maria Marten. Before leaving, Lea found in Corder's dressing-room a small bag containing two pistols, bullets, powder and a bullet-mould.

Back in London Corder was detained overnight. The next morning the three men boarded a stage-coach that was to convey them to Colchester on the first lap of their journey back to Suffolk. The party eventually arrived in Polstead during the early hours of Friday 25 April, in time for the resumed inquest due to reopen a few hours later.

By this time news of the inquest and Corder's apprehension had spread far and wide. When the proceedings recommenced, villagers and strangers alike caroused on the green while Mr Gordon, keeper of the Cock Inn, tried vainly to quell the animated conversation and noisy laughing and singing that rang out from a room close to that in which the inquiry was being held.

A succession of villagers spoke of Corder's behaviour before and after Maria had disappeared. Constable Lea told of his arrest, and a cutler, Robert Offord, described how a year before Corder had gone to him with a small sword to be ground, asking that it be made 'as sharp as a carving knife'. Finally John Lawton, a surgeon, described how he had examined Maria's body immediately after it had been disinterred. He said that a green handkerchief around the neck '... was drawn tight enough to have caused death ...'. Underneath the handkerchief '... was the appearance of a wound from a sharp instrument ...', while a bone of the right eye was fractured '... as if a pointed instrument had been thrust into it ...'. The surgeon oddly made no mention of pistol-shot wounds.

Before the jury returned their verdict, Corder, who had been in another room, was summoned. Handcuffed and wearing a cloak, he appeared nervous as some of the depositions were read out. He declined Mr Wayman's invitation to respond and returned to the other room while the jury foreman announced a verdict of wilful murder against him. Mr Wayman immediately issued a warrant committing Corder to Bury St Edmunds gaol to await his trial at the next Suffolk assizes.

Before leaving, Corder was visited by several of his neighbours, including members of the jury, who bade him farewell. A large crowd also watched him depart, and several people ran with the post-chaise until it had left the village. Similarly, as it passed through other villages where he was known, groups of people had gathered in the hope of catching a glimpse of him. Corder was escorted to the gaol by Constable Lea, with whom by now he was on quite friendly terms. Before they parted, Corder gave Lea a silk purse embroidered by his wife as a keepsake.

On most days whilst awaiting trial Corder was visited by his wife Mary. When not with him, she was either hastening back to London to consult with Mr Humphrey, the solicitor who was arranging her husband's defence, or travelling across to Polstead to console her distraught mother-in-law.

William meanwhile was adapting as best he could to life in prison. His request to be allowed to have his wife to live with him having been summarily rejected by the governor, he turned to religion. This scarcely offered him the solace he had hoped for. On the Sunday before his trial the prison chaplain, the Reverend Mr Stocking, chose as the text for his sermon the sixth commandment, 'Thou shalt not kill.' Corder was dumbfounded to hear the chaplain tell the congregation that, '... having carefully searched the annals of crime, I am unable to find a case where a criminal was ever charged with so diabolical a murder as one in the congregation stood charged with'. Corder showed commendable restraint in confining his comments to a fellow inmate, to whom he muttered as they left the chapel, 'Ah! that text was a slap at me.'

There had been more drama back in Polstead. Five weeks after Maria's funeral, the coroner, after consultation with two local surgeons, decided to have her body disinterred. Mr Wayman wanted to investigate a suggestion that Maria had been stabbed in the side of her head in addition to the other wounds that had been inflicted. The exhumation took place during the early hours of one morning and revealed irrefutable evidence of a stab wound to Maria's left side which had pierced her heart. With only flickering lamplight as illumination at the graveside, the gruesome task was performed of removing Maria's heart and two of her ribs for later production at the trial.

Confusion reigned in Bury St Edmunds on the morning of Thursday 7 August 1829, the opening day of William Corder's trial. The Suffolk market town had been crowded since the first day of the assizes on the Monday, but during Wednesday night hundreds more people arrived in the hope of gaining entry to the court. Every inn and lodging-house was full, and many opted for sleeping in the open rather than forfeit a chance of catching a distant glimpse of Corder. Torrential rain added to the discomfort of those who by five in the morning were assembling outside the front and back doors of the Shire Hall.

Corder was the first to appear, being driven up in a chaise cart. Upon his arrival the crowd surged around so closely that it was only with difficulty that the vehicle reached the back door to enable him to alight. There followed the judge, counsel, magistrates and jurors, all of them dishevelled, soaked and agitated after having negotiated a way through the mob outside. Women of all ranks seemed particularly anxious to catch a sight of the accused man. They were partly frustrated in their objective on the first day, when the trial judge banned them from entering the court. Undeterred, they hitched their skirts and clambered onto walls alongside the men to gaze through the courtroom windows. Even a drenching thunderstorm failed to deter them. The judge, Lord Baron Alexander, may have found their presence distracting on that first day, as the following morning he relaxed his ban and allowed both men and women to be admitted to the court.

Eventually order was restored in the courtroom on the first morning. Apart from those perched on ledges and walls outside the building, other daring souls had clambered onto the roof, from where they peered down through a dusty window. The fortunate reporters and members of the public who had succeeded in gaining entry to the building settled down to await the start of the proceedings.

William Corder's appearance at the bar drew appreciative murmurs from the spectators. A new frock coat with a velvet collar, worn with a black waistcoat, was complemented by blue breeches and silk stockings. Around his neck he wore a spotless white neckerchief. His stay in Bury gaol seemed not to have affected him adversely; a short beard enhanced his appearance, and he exuded an air of confidence.

There was a total of ten indictments alleging murder by a variety of methods, including shooting, stabbing, strangulation, burying alive and a combination of all four. After pleading 'not guilty', Corder settled himself comfortably as Mr Andrews rose to open the Crown case.

The Crown prosecutor first described to the court the backgrounds of Corder and Maria before telling of their meeting, subsequent intimacy and William's promise of marriage. He related how the accused had persuaded Maria suddenly to accompany him to Ipswich to get married by playing upon her fear of being arrested for having given birth to bastard children. Their departure on 18 May was the last to be seen of Maria, said Mr Andrews.

The court listened intently as he went on to tell of the conversations Corder had had with various people, and the letters he had written to Tom Marten, all with the object of allaying suspicion. The prosecutor ended his opening address by describing the finding of Maria's remains and Corder's subsequent arrest.

The first prosecution witness was Maria's stepmother, Ann Marten, described at the time as 'a decently dressed countrywoman'. She told of Corder's relationship with her stepdaughter, his frequent visits to their cottage, and the birth and early death of the couple's baby. On the morning Corder and Maria had departed for Ipswich, Ann had remarked to him, 'Oh, William, if you had but married Maria as I wished you, all this would have been settled.'

'Well,' he had replied, 'I am going to Ipswich to marry her tomorrow morning.'

Ann had been unconvinced. 'William, what will you do if that cannot be done?' she had asked.

His reply had been an attempt to reassure her: 'Don't make yourself unhappy. She shall be my lawful wife before my return, or I will get her a place until such time as we can be married.'

With this Ann Marten had had to be satisfied. During the following months, whenever the two met, Corder never failed to reassure her of Maria's well-being.

Ann Marten stood up well to Mr Broderick's cross-examination, which concentrated upon Maria and William's disposal of their baby after its death, and the quarrel they had had over the missing £5 note.

Tom Marten and his younger daughter, Ann, were next to give evidence. Marten described how he had found Maria's body in the Red Barn: 'When I had poked with my mole spike about four inches, I found something come out with it like flesh.' He had returned to the barn later and with two other men had continued where he had left off: 'We then took up part of the earth until we came to the body .... The legs were drawn up and the head bent down ....'

Ann told of Maria's departure from home, and of subsequently identifying her sister's body: 'I have seen a dead body since which was found in the Red Barn, which I know to be my sister's ....'

Before George Marten, Maria's young brother testified, there was a brief exchange between him and the judge.

'How old are you, my little fellow?' asked the Lord Baron.

'About ten years old,' was the reply.

'Do you know the nature of an oath? What will become of you when you die, if you swear falsely and state the things which are not true?'

'God would send me to hell, sir,' responded George.

'Let him be sworn,' said the judge.

Corder sat eating a snack while the lad spoke of seeing him leave with Maria on 18 May and then seeing him again later the same day: 'On the day they left our house, I saw him again coming from the barn with a pickaxe on his shoulder .... He was then going from the Red Barn homewards .... I am quite sure he is the person I saw with the pickaxe ....' Probably due to his age, George was not cross-examined. Corder meanwhile seemed to have lost his appetite as he sat listening to the damaging testimony.

After a succession of Polstead villagers had given evidence of conversations and contact they had had with Corder since Maria's disappearance, Tom Marten was recalled to the witness-box to identify two letters he had received from Corder the previous October, the first telling him of the marriage and censuring him for not having replied to Maria's letter, the second urging him to write to Peter Matthews (the father of Maria's surviving illegitimate child), to ask for financial support for the boy.

It was Matthews who was next called upon to give evidence. He gave his account of the conversations he had had with Corder regarding the missing £5 note, Maria's whereabouts and his intentions. The witness made clear the doubt he had felt as to the truth of Corder's explanations.

After Constable Lea had told of Corder's arrest, the day's final witness, surgeon John Lawton, described his findings when first he had examined Maria's remains. He considered that she had been shot, stabbed and strangled. 'It appeared to me as if a ball had passed through the left cheek, removing the two last grinders .... I do not think that a ball passing through as I have stated would have produced death. Not instant death of itself; but strangulation, and the stab in the neck, together with the ball, would, if all concurring together.'

While Lawton was speaking, Corder seemed all but overcome, sitting with his head lowered, and beads of perspiration on his forehead.

The witness continued: '... there was a stab in the heart which exactly corresponded with the wound in the ribs. It appeared to have been inflicted with a sharp instrument, and that injury alone would have been, in my opinion, sufficient of itself to produce death .... There is a short sword which I have fitted into the wound. It exactly corresponds with it ... it must have penetrated two or three inches ....'

Near the end of his testimony the surgeon gave a macabre demonstration. To a gasp from those in court, he produced Maria's skull and lower jaw bone, announcing, 'I have the head here and produce it. This is the jaw, and there are two teeth gone ....' The exhibits were passed around the court for examination, all the while Corder remaining seemingly unaffected by what was taking place. After briefly clarifying some points in answer to Mr Broderick's questions, Lawton stepped down. At this point the Lord Baron Alexander decided that everybody had had enough for one day and adjourned the proceedings until nine o'clock the next morning.

On Friday the crowd was as large as ever but was more orderly than on the previous day. When proceedings got underway, the first part of the morning was taken up by the evidence of two surgeons, John Nairn and Henry Chaplin, who confirmed Maria's injuries, and identification of her clothing by her sister and stepmother. Their evidence ended the prosecution case. Lord Baron Alexander then called upon William Corder to present his defence.

Corder spoke first. He and his friends had overruled the advice of his counsel, Mr Broderick, who had advised him to remain silent, leaving counsel to advance a defence of provocation in the hope of having a verdict of manslaughter returned. Instead Corder considered that his best chance lay in his saying that Maria had committed suicide.

For thirty-two minutes William Corder nervously stammered his way through a prepared script. He opened by attacking the newspapers, which, he said, had described him as 'the most depraved of human monsters', thus stigmatizing and prejudging him. He went on to criticize Mr Wayman, the coroner, for having conducted the inquest in his absence. It was later pointed out by the judge in his summing-up that, by having had the witnesses' depositions read out to him, Corder had received his legal entitlement.

After referring to the deaths of his father and brothers, Corder admitted that by withholding his version of the events surrounding Maria's death until his trial he had jeopardized his position. He explained that, after having disposed of the body of their baby, Maria had returned to stay with him secretly for a couple of days, so as to keep her presence concealed from his family and other villagers. It was whilst she was with him, he said, that she gained possession of a pair of pistols that were in his room.

Corder went on to say that after eventually returning home Maria had later prevailed upon him to marry her. To prevent his mother's finding out, it was arranged that the marriage should take place at Ipswich. It was whilst they were making their way to the Red Barn on 18 May that an argument started between them. It continued after they had arrived at the barn, where, according to Corder, '... whilst she was changing her dress, she flew into a passion; told me that she did not care anything about me ...'. This tirade, he said, prompted him to cancel the arrangements they had made and to leave the barn to return home. He had no sooner left her than he heard the sound of a pistol-shot. Running back into the barn, he had been horrified to find Maria lying on the floor, apparently dead.

The remainder of his speech was taken up mainly with his ill-fated decision to say nothing of what had taken place but instead to bury Maria's body in the barn. The stab wounds found on her body, he insisted, must have been inflicted by the mole spike or other implements used by Tom Marten and his friends when searching for the body. Corder ended by pointing out to the jury what he considered to be the improbability of his having shot Maria at a time and place when discovery was likely. His subsequent behaviour, he told them, was also indicative of his innocence. He had remained in Polstead for several months and then on medical advice had spent a few weeks in Portsmouth and on the Isle of Wight before moving with his wife to Brentford. Before he sat down, he agreed that, although suspicion against him was justified, it had been brought about through his own default. At the end of his speech William slumped back into his seat, seemingly exhausted by his effort.

His witnesses contributed little to the proceedings. William and Mary Goodwin said that Corder had visited Maria during her stay with them at Sudbury in 1826. Two other witnesses testified as to Corder's having had pistols in his possession, and implied that Maria would have had access to them. Dr Edward Living told the court that he had frequently attended Corder and that during the previous year he had been concerned over his health and had recommended that he visit the south coast. The remaining six witnesses unanimously agreed that he was a 'kind, humane, good-tempered young man'.

Lord Baron Alexander summed up for almost two hours, during which time Corder seemed to experience a gamut of emotions. After first appearing eager not to miss a word, he adopted an obsequious attitude, repeatedly bowing towards the bench as the judge advised the jury to disregard rumours and reports that were circulating regarding the prisoner's guilt.

When the Lord Baron referred to the ploy Corder had adopted to persuade Maria to leave home, and later mentioned his having had his sword sharpened, the accused man seemed about to faint. He revived when reference was made to Constable Lea's testimony, only to relapse dejectedly when the judge made little comment about his defence speech. It was a fascinating spectacle: on the one hand the Lord Baron's quiet and deliberate summing-up before a hushed court, while opposite him Corder reacted silently and theatrically to what was being said.

The judge pointed out that during his speech Corder had admitted that the body found in the Red Barn had been that of Maria Marten, therefore the question of identity had already been established, rendering it unnecessary for him to dwell on that aspect of the case. Before referring to the testimony of Constable Lea, he reviewed the evidence of Tom and Ann Marten regarding events on the day Maria had left home, and later upon the discovery of her body.

It was apparent from his comments that the Lord Baron considered the surgeon John Lawton's testimony, refuting Corder's submission that Maria had committed suicide, to be the most damaging to his case: 'Gentlemen, you have heard it asserted this day, that this truly ill-fated girl had committed suicide; but if that be so, it appears exceedingly strange that, immediately on the prisoner abruptly quitting the barn and leaving her alone, she should have used such various instruments in order to destroy herself; for it appears that she must have fired a pistol, and, either before or after she discharged it, must have stabbed herself, in various parts of the body, with some sharp instrument.' After these damning remarks the remainder of the Lord Baron's summing-up seemed anticlimactic.

He referred to Corder's version of the events on 18 May 1827 culminating in Maria's death. Although the judge refrained from giving his direct opinion on the veracity of the prisoner's story, his scepticism was apparent when, in referring to Corder's character witnesses, he said, '... character, however good it may have been, can be of no avail where it comes into opposition to direct and conclusive evidence ...'.

The Lord Baron concluded by asking the jury again to assess the credibility of the medical evidence, '... to consider how far it was possible, or whether possible at all, that all these multifarious wounds could have been inflicted by her own hands .... Are the representations made by the prisoner today true or false?'

The jury took only thirty-five minutes to decide; at twenty-five minutes past two they returned to their box, from which the foreman nervously announced that they had unanimously found William Corder guilty.

Corder appeared stunned; he recovered to hear the Lord Baron express his agreement with the verdict before urging him to make his peace with the Almighty – a concession that he had not made available to his victim, the judge reminded him. At the end of the Lord Baron's peroration, when he was sentencing him to be hanged and his body to be then dissected and anatomized, Corder's self-control wavered, and he appeared to be near to collapse.

He had recovered by the time he emerged from the Shire Hall to be conveyed back to gaol. It seemed that half the population of Bury St Edmunds was anxious to catch a sight of the condemned man. Hundreds of people were awaiting his appearance, and it was only with difficulty that the chaise was able to start its journey. Spectators clung to the vehicle, trying to impede its progress, while others hung from windows and climbed every possible vantage-point to monitor Corder's progress. The prisoner himself remained outwardly calm, but it was probably with some relief that he entered the relative peace of the gaol.

Nineteenth-century prisons were not overly concerned with the well-being of their inmates. Squalid conditions, atrocious food, brutality and drunkenness among both the custodians and their charges were the common denominators at most gaols. Attempts at penal reform received little sympathy either in or out of Parliament, and over half a century was to elapse before the improvements urged by the great prison reformer John Howard were introduced.

So it was that Corder was fortunate in that the governor of Bury St Edmunds gaol in 1828 was one of the more humane and enlightened of his kind. John Orridge had accompanied Corder throughout the trial, escorting him to and from the court and remaining with him during the proceedings. He had been on hand to prevent him from collapsing as he was sentenced, and had later offered consolation. It was therefore not surprising that a rapport had grown between them, and that it was in Orridge that Corder should initially confide after he had returned to the gaol.

For several hours the two men conversed, mainly about the trial. Corder was unhappy with much of the prosecution testimony, but, as John Orridge pointed out, there was nothing that could be done about it, so he should prepare himself spiritually for the fate awaiting him.

Corder had little time to himself during his last weekend. On Saturday morning he was woken at six o'clock by the Reverend Mr Stocking, who, alive to his responsibility, spent the next two hours ministering to him spiritually and vainly urging him to confess. Corder had decided views on the desirability of such a course; he told John Orridge later: '… confession to God is all that is necessary, confession to man is popery and I will never do it.'

On Saturday afternoon he received a visit from his wife. It was reported as being an unbearably distressing occasion; the couple had been married for only nine months, four of which William had spent in gaol following his arrest. After the Corders had tearfully parted, William spent some time in the gaol chapel before returning to his cell. There he was again joined by the Reverend Mr Stocking, who stayed with him until the late evening.

Sunday morning saw Corder join the other convicts for morning service. Probably aware that the governor had granted permission for reporters to be admitted to the service, the Reverend Mr Stocking seemed inspired. Constant oblique references to him soon had Corder weeping bitterly. During his sermon the chaplain dramatically called upon Corder to prepare himself to meet his executioner the following day. While the other prisoners listened in awe, Corder was further overcome as he was adjured '... to acknowledge the justice of his sentence, and that the judgement of the Lord is right ...' under the threat that '... his doom would be fixed – it would be too late – and that irrevocable doom would be eternal torture ...'. Not surprisingly, at the conclusion of the service Corder had to be assisted by John Orridge back to his cell, where he collapsed in a fit of convulsive sobbing.

By this time his appearance also was reported to have changed: '... his cheeks were considerably collapsed, and his eyes appeared much swollen as if from weeping, indeed he looked like a ghastly image of despair'.

In the afternoon a final harrowing visit from his wife, during which Mary urged her husband to repent, was to be Corder's last contact with the outside world before stepping onto the scaffold the next day. Meanwhile the chaplain and the governor spent several hours trying to persuade him to confess. Finally, late that evening, Corder submitted to their pleadings and made a statement which was written down by Orridge. In it he said that he had shot Maria following an argument over the burial of their dead baby, and had then buried her in the barn. He emphatically denied having inflicted any other injury on his victim but at one point said, 'I think I dragged the body by the handkerchief that was tied round her neck ....' This may have resulted in the tightening of the handkerchief as described by the surgeon, John Lawton.

By five o'clock on Monday morning hundreds of people were gathered outside the prison to witness the execution scheduled to take place at noon. The number of spectators grew during the morning until almost 10,000 were thronging the concourse outside the gaol. Men and women of all classes arrived in Bury from around the county, including some from Polstead, intent on being present during the final moments of their former neighbour.

Corder meanwhile was preparing himself for the ordeal

ahead. Although much of his remaining time was spent with the Reverend Mr Stocking, he made a point of bidding farewell to each of his fellow prisoners individually, and writing a last, brief note to his wife – 'My life's loved Companion', as he addressed her.

A few minutes before noon Corder stepped out through a gate in the wall of the prison and ascended the scaffold, dressed in the clothes he had worn at his trial. He gazed over thousands of upturned faces at the undulating, tree-studded countryside beyond. His last moments were to be agonizingly prolonged as, capped and bound, he waited while one of the officials present and the executioner briefly discussed the length of the drop. Then all was ready. The hangman descended the steps to the ground and with one swift movement sliced through the rope supporting the platform. The silence was broken only by the Reverend Mr Stocking, intoning a final prayer. William Corder was dead.

As the crowd drifted away and Corder's body was removed for later dissection, questions were being asked. What had been William Corder's real motive for slaying Maria? Apart from his statement that the murder had been the culmination of an argument about their dead baby, no convincing reason had emerged.

It was later suggested that Maria had been blackmailing Corder into marrying her, under threat of exposing the true circumstances of their infant's death – the manner of its demise and the reason for its shameful burial in a field were never fully explained. Did Corder kill the mite with Maria's knowledge, or even with her connivance? If so, and if later she threatened him with exposure, it would have been imperative that she be silenced.

His motive may have been less dramatic. It is conceivable that he had simply changed his mind about going through with the marriage. Although his mother was opposed to the union and would doubtless have welcomed an end to the betrothal, he was under increasing pressure from Maria's family to marry her. This, added to the responsibility for running the farm, may have decided him to plot the scheme whereby the Marten family were deceived into believing that Maria was married but living away. At the same time it would have enabled him to leave Polstead and start life afresh elsewhere.

Another question was whether Corder had been solely responsible for Maria's death; had he an accomplice, or had someone else even killed her? Corder's acquaintanceship with the disreputable character 'Beauty Smith' who remained a shadowy figure throughout the case led some people to suggest that he may have been involved in Maria's death.

Smith had earlier injudiciously remarked to a fellow convict in prison that he knew Corder, but when later questioned he denied any knowledge of the circumstances surrounding Maria's death, and indeed there does not seem to have been a credible reason for Smith to have been involved, or to have been in the vicinity of the Red Barn at the time Maria died.

The questions, the theories, even the facts surrounding the events at Polstead on that spring day over 160 years ago will continue to be debated. One thing is certain: the exact circumstances which led up to the deaths of Maria Marten and William Corder will remain clouded and be the subject of conjecture.

– 2 –
Only One Would Hang
1844

'Twas all for worldly sordid wealth,
That tempted me to sin;
And horrid murder's dreadful crime,
My guilty soul brought in.

A poor defenceless woman was
By me deprived of life;
To hide my guilt her throat I cut,
All with the fatal knife.

From a penny broadsheet, 1845

Early on the morning of Saturday 14 April 1846, a group of workmen were engaged in erecting barriers around the concourse fronting onto Norwich Castle. It was Fair Day, and a larger crowd than usual was expected, as an extra attraction, the public hanging of the Yarmouth murderer, was to take place.

During the morning town- and countryfolk, including horse-traders, farmers, craftsmen, servant girls and gentlemen, congregated opposite the scaffold until, as twelve o'clock approached, 20,000 people were jostling, pushing, arguing and occasionally fighting. Street entertainers, musicians and vendors of cakes and pies helped to relieve the tedium of waiting.

Inside the castle the condemned man had risen early and had spent most of the morning with the gaol chaplain. The previous afternoon he had been visited for the last time by his friends and relatives, including his distraught young wife, to whom he had bid a poignant farewell.

Suddenly his cell door opened and the black-clad executioner and his assistant entered, followed by the governor and the sheriff. The prisoner shook hands with the governor and thanked him for his consideration before being led to the pinioning-room, from which soon afterwards a solemn procession, headed by the chaplain intoning the burial service, wended its way along the castle passages.

The tolling of the gaol bell had indicated to the waiting crowd the imminence of the execution, and as the condemned man emerged into the open and unaided ascended the steps onto the scaffold, the shouting, booing and hissing which had greeted his appearance gradually subsided. He took a final glance round before the white cap was placed over his head and the noose adjusted; a pause, and then, as the executioner released the bolts allowing the trap to fall open, the prisoner dropped from sight. The hubbub recommenced.

The *Norfolk News* carried a brief, disparaging denunciation of the spectacle: 'Last Saturday was a memorable day for the inhabitants of Norwich and its neighbourhood .... A hanging and a fair, death and buffoonery, the functions of the executioner, and the freaks of the Harlequin, were the sights then furnished in immediate succession, and on the same spot, for the edification and amusement of the multitude ....'

Constable William Johnson of Yarmouth police had twice passed 79 Howard Street South during the night of Monday 18/Tuesday 19 November 1844, without noticing anything amiss. Admittedly he had not tried the front door of the small general store, so he was unable to say later whether it had been locked.

Shortly before two o'clock on the Tuesday morning, Johnson again arrived outside the shop, this time accompanied by Police Constable Samuel Waller. It was Waller who tried the front door, which to his surprise he found to be unlocked. Together the policemen entered the darkened premises and moved cautiously around the interior. As they were retracing their steps, Johnson stopped short and stared down behind the counter. On the floor in a squatting position was the body of the shop's proprietor, 46-year-old Harriet Candler; by the dim glow cast by their oil-lamps, Johnson and Waller could see that she had been savagely beaten about the head. As they stooped to examine her more closely, they saw also a hideous gash slicing deep into the shopkeeper's throat. With Harriet Candler obviously beyond all help, Johnson hastened from the shop to fetch assistance, leaving Waller to watch over the scene.

Crime during the first decade of Victoria's reign was peaking to unacceptable heights. Sir Robert Peel's Tory administration and the public alike were becoming increasingly alarmed as offences against property and the person escalated. The introduction of the new-style police forces did not have any appreciable effect until the 1860s, and the crime wave meanwhile only gradually receded. Although transportation to the colonies was being phased out, public executions survived until 1868, serving – many people believed – as a deterrent. It seemed, however, that the person or persons responsible for the death of Harriet Candler had not baulked at the prospect, if caught, of being strung up in front of their fellows.

Half an hour after she had been discovered, a group of people assembled in Mrs Candler's front room. Constables Johnson and Waller now had with them their immediate superior, Sergeant John Williment, Mr Henry Worship, a surgeon, and the mayor, all three of whom had hurried to the scene in response to Johnson's urgent summons. Also present were William Catchpole, a solicitor who owned the property and lived upstairs, and Samuel Yarham, who also lived on the premises, with his wife, who was employed as Catchpole's housekeeper.

Catchpole and Yarham, who had been roused by Sergeant Williment, had immediately denied any knowledge of the murder. The solicitor had been out to dinner and had not returned home until about half-past one. He had been greeted by Yarham and had then gone straight to bed, only to be awoken soon afterwards and told that something had happened to Mrs Candler. Yarham said he had been indoors all evening, awaiting Mr Catchpole's return, and had heard nothing untoward. Sergeant Williment thought this strange as there were only thin partitioning walls separating Yarham's room from the shop, and it seemed unlikely that the premises could have been entered and the murder committed without his having heard something.

Mr Worship, the surgeon, carried out a preliminary examination of the dead woman, and Sergeant Williment took possession of a blood-stained knife and a small packet of tobacco found at the scene. Finally before the group of men dispersed, arrangements were made for the body to be removed from the shop.

Next morning news of the murder quickly spread through Yarmouth. A rumour – later confirmed – that Mrs Candler had had a large sum of money delivered from Norwich a day or two earlier suggested robbery as the likely motive for the crime. Also during the morning Police Constable George Layton reported that in the early hours he had seen Yarham heading away from his home towards the south end of the town and soon afterwards had noticed a man he knew to be John Hall loitering near the market-place only a short distance from Harriet Candler's shop.

Another man, John Sayer, walked into the station house that same morning and stated that, soon after leaving his place of work in Black Swan Row at eleven the previous evening and after passing the time of night with Police Constable Sam Waller, he had seen three men, whom he recognized as John Hall, Robert Royal and James Mapes, crossing the market-place. Sayer described the clothing the three men had been wearing, and seemed a convincing witness, although his testimony was later to be vigorously disputed.

Sergeant Williment meanwhile had been thinking about Samuel Yarham. The more he pondered on the explanation the shoemaker had given of his movements during the evening of the murder, the more certain Williment became that Yarham knew far more about Harriet Candler's death than he had revealed. The policeman decided to have another talk with him and was confounded when Yarham broke down and admitted being implicated, along with Hall, Royal and Mapes.

The same afternoon a small group of people called at the station. Sergeant John Dick, a soldier stationed at one of the Yarmouth artillery batteries, was accompanied by his wife and 14-year-old daughter; with them was Robert Royal. Sergeant Dick deposited two canvas bags containing cash on the station counter, while Royal followed suit with a third bag.

Mrs Dick then told Sergeant Williment a story that was to help complete the pattern of information the policeman already had regarding the murder. She said that an hour earlier, as she was walking home with her daughter across Yarmouth Denes, she noticed that the sand had been more than usually disturbed on one of the dunes. Curiosity had prompted closer investigation, whereupon the couple to their surprise discovered the money bags buried just beneath the surface. They had then been joined by her husband, who had come to meet them, and by Royal, a local beachcomber. A brief examination of the bags had revealed that they contained coins of various denominations, while on the largest bag was attached a small tag bearing the inscription 'Mrs Harriet Candler by Rail.' Seeing this, the small party had hastened with their find to the station house.

Williment, although astute, was also an impulsive policeman. With only the word of Samuel Yarham, a sighting by John Sayer, and his presence nearby when the money bags were recovered, he nevertheless decided to detain Royal. Mrs Dick and her daughter then mentioned a series of clearly defined footprints they had noticed in the vicinity of the money bags' hideaway. The sergeant and other officers immediately left to examine these marks for themselves. Incredibly, weeks later mother and daughter were to testify that the footmarks in the sand matched the sole patterns of several pairs of boots and shoes they were shown in court: '... the impression made by the shoes now produced is the same as made in the sand ...,' Mrs Dick was to say.

On Wednesday, within forty-eight hours of the murder and after further discussion among themselves, the local policemen decided, on only flimsy evidence, to arrest Hall and Mapes in connection with its commission. Viewed in the light of the painstaking and often lengthy investigations that nowadays precede an arrest and the charging of a suspect with a major crime, the precipitate action on the part of the Yarmouth police in 1844 seems difficult to comprehend. It should, however, be borne in mind that it was only eight years since the borough police force had been formed and that, lacking today's sophisticated equipment and advanced investigative techniques, decisions tended to be made more intuitively than they would today. In the case of the Yarmouth murder, despite evidential deficiencies, it was decided nonetheless to charge all four men with the murder of Harriet Candler.

News of the arrest and charging of the four – all in their twenties and well known in Yarmouth – generated a wave of interest and speculation among the townsfolk and beyond. As time for their committal for trial drew near, in early 1845, people from around the region converged on Yarmouth for the hearing.

This was dominated by the testimony of Yarham. After John Sayer had identified Hall, Royal and Mapes as the men he had seen just after eleven o'clock on the night of the murder, walking in the market-place in the direction of Mrs Candler's shop, Yarham told the court that sometime after eleven o'clock on the same night he had heard what he thought were two or three people in the shop downstairs. A few minutes later he had seen two men, the first crossing the street outside the shop, the second, whom he identified as Royal, emerging from the front door of the premises. He said he had challenged Royal and asked the whereabouts of Mrs Candler.

Royal at first denied having seen her but then admitted that he had knocked her down behind the counter. This revelation drew forth some animated whispering among the spectators in court, while the other three defendants glared at Yarham. Unabashed, he related a brief conversation between himself and Royal, before describing his finding of Harriet Candler behind the shop counter. Yarham maintained that he had been intimidated by Royal into keeping quiet about their encounter that evening. As he rejoined his fellow accused in the dock, Royal made no attempt to conceal his hostility towards him.

After Sarah Dick had told of finding the money bags and seeing the footprints in the sand, it was the turn of Hall, Royal and Mapes. Each called a succession of witnesses who spoke of seeing them in various taverns during the evening Mrs Candler was attacked. Before being committed for trial, Royal told the packed courtroom: '... all Yarham has said is false, and all the other witnesses, particularly Sayer's evidence. I am perfectly innocent of this crime ....'

Before the trial there was to be a dramatic development, one that was to prove a gross misjudgement by Samuel Yarham. He approached the prosecution and offered to turn Queen's Evidence against his fellow accused, on the mistaken assumption that by so doing he was rendering himself immune from future prosecution in connection with the murder. The prosecution lawyers, while happily accepting his offer, kept him in ignorance of the true legal position.

During the first week of April 1845 Sergeant Williment and his men were called upon to quell a disturbance at Yarmouth dockside. Seamen on strike over a wages dispute with their employers tried to prevent a ship crewed by non-strikers from sailing. The Yarmouth docks dispute had petered out so allowing Williment, Johnson and Waller to go unhindered to Norwich for the trial on Monday 7 April at the Norfolk Lent Assizes of the three men accused of Harriet Candler's murder.

A sizeable contingent of Yarmouth's citizenry also travelled to Norwich that Monday morning, including several young men anxious not only to witness the proceedings but also to avoid the 'gaudy trappings of the recruiting soldiery' (*Norfolk News*), who were in Great Yarmouth endeavouring to entice susceptible youths into accepting the 'Queen's shilling'.

In the temporary absence of Mr Palmer, who should have led the prosecution case, Mr O'Malley, the junior counsel, opened for the Crown. Although the testimony of Samuel Yarham was essential to his case, Mr O'Malley seemed to be under no illusion regarding his chief witness, referring to him early in his opening address as a 'most depraved character'.

The prosecution case was virtually a repeat of that at the committal hearing, the main difference being that Yarham now gave evidence for the Crown instead of on his own behalf. After going to bed on the night of the murder, he said, he had soon afterwards gone downstairs, where he heard a 'scuffling noise as if some people were walking about'. After telling of seeing

Royal emerge from Mrs Candler's front door, he said he had challenged him – 'Royal, what are you about?' to which the other had replied, '... blast your eyes, if you say anything I'll serve you the same.' The witness went on to say that, after then admitting having knocked Mrs Candler down, Royal offered him a sovereign to keep quiet, pleading, 'Don't blow off an old playfellow. You shall have a share when we dole.' Yarham said he had considered the matter for a couple of hours but, fearful of retribution from Royal, had decided to say nothing. It was principally regarding this last assertion that Yarham was searchingly cross-examined by Mr Prendergast, the counsel representing Hall and Royal.

Asked to repeat why he had not at the time told Sergeant Williment what he was now asking the court to believe, Yarham replied, 'It was on account of Royal's intimidation that I said nothing ....' This answer failed to satisfy Mr Prendergast, who pressed him further on the point. 'I went to a magistrate on 1 December. I was in custody a week before I said anything ...,' Yarham continued. 'After I was indoors, I considered I had been previously in trouble and somebody also might find it out ....' This was different: now he was suggesting that he was concerned lest his criminal record be held against him if he spoke to the police. 'It was not on account of Royal, but having been in trouble before that, I said nothing about it ...,' he persisted.

As Mr Prendergast pressed on with his questioning, Yarham became uncomfortable and confused, reverting to his original explanation for not having told the police the truth: 'I had fear of Royal; that was the principal reason. When Royal was in custody I did not expect any harm from him then. I cannot tell why I did not tell of it then ...,' he ended lamely.

Yarham was trembling as he left the witness-box, avoiding the contemptuous gaze of Royal. His uncertain and contradictory testimony had to an extent embraced Hall and Mapes, who consequently had cause also to feel satisfied with the day's hearing. Many of the spectators in court were already in no doubt that Yarham had lied to save his own skin, and as he left at the end of the first day he was subjected to the invective that was to pursue him through the ensuing months.

The second and final day of the trial was taken up by defence witnesses called to provide alibis for Hall, Royal and Mapes.

Samuel Davis and his wife Elizabeth said they had been in the Half Moon tavern between 8.30 p.m. and 12.45 a.m. on the night of the murder. 'Royal was in the public house all that time ...,' said Mr Davis.

Similarly for Mapes: Mr Crouch, his counsel, called Charles and Sarah Bullen, who explained that they had been in the Queen's Head public house during the evening of 18 November 1844 and that Mapes, apparently on a pub-crawl, was there during the late evening. Other witnesses stated that they had seen him drinking elsewhere that night.

Hall produced witnesses who swore that he had been drinking in his father's hostelry, the Feather's Tap, during the material time.

Mr O'Malley vainly counter-attacked: 'His learned friends Mr Prendergast and Mr Crouch,' he said, 'had endeavoured all along to throw the charge upon Yarham. It was undoubted that two persons must have committed the murder ....'

However, after his summing-up during which Mr Justice (Sir John) Patteson pointed out that, 'Yarham had most foully perjured himself if he had anything to do with the transaction ...,' the jury took only ten minutes to find the three accused men 'not guilty'.

'Thank you, gentlemen,' said Royal after hearing the verdict.

As Yarham left the Shire Hall, an angry crowd tried first to mob him and then chased him as he raced away. After succeeding in outdistancing his pursuers, he made his way to the railway station. For Samuel Yarham the result of the trial was a disaster. Instead of its ending as he had hoped in the conviction of Hall, Royal and Mapes, they had been acquitted, and suspicion was now firmly directed towards himself. His situation was manifestly worse than had he stood trial with the other three, when he would at least have stood a chance of being acquitted with them, whereas now – although still erroneously believing that he was immune from prosecution – his perfidy would, he knew, lead to almost universal condemnation.

According to Mrs Sarah Dick later, it was on the train returning to Great Yarmouth after the trial that she had the first of two remarkable encounters with Yarham. Anticipating the reaction of his neighbours following his appearance at the trial, he advised Mrs Dick and her husband against talking about it – surely a forlorn hope? He then asked whether in their opinion his remaining in Yarmouth was more likely to persuade the townsfolk of his guilt than if he left. Three weeks later he again saw Mrs Dick, on this occasion in the market-place. This time he complained of the harassment and condemnation to which he had been subjected since the trial; then, being still under the delusion that he was immune from prosecution, he admitted to her his complicity in the murder. The soldier's wife was stunned by the revelation, but when later she told her husband, he forbade her from informing the authorities.

For the Yarhams the disapprobation of their former friends and neighbours continued unabated. Samuel was obliged to seek police protection, but although this deterred physical assaults, it did nothing to stop the verbal abuse and vilification directed towards the couple as soon as they stepped outside their front door. Eventually they could endure it no longer, so in the early summer of 1845, to escape the persecution, they moved to Gloucestershire, their rail fare paid by the town's guardians.

Their departure spurred Mrs Dick into action. She confided in her 14-year-old daughter her recent conversation with Yarham in which he had admitted his participation in Mrs Candler's murder. Sarah junior, realizing the significance of what her mother had told her, prevailed upon her to go immediately to Mr William Yates, a town magistrate, and tell him of Yarham's confession. After listening to Mrs Dick, Yates lost no time in informing the police.

By now it was July 1845, but another five months were to elapse before Samuel Yarham was arrested and returned to Great Yarmouth. The delay may have been attributable to difficulty experienced by the police in tracing the Yarhams. More likely it was due to a reluctance on the part of the local constabulary to act too hastily. The disappointment resulting from their precipitate action thirteen months earlier still lingered, so, despite the evidence of Mrs Dick, it is probable that they decided to investigate the matter more thoroughly and act with greater circumspection.

After returning to Yarmouth in December, the prisoner was lodged in the town gaol house; it was there that a full hearing of the case against him was heard in private on 5 January 1846. This lasted all day, and it seemed that much of the testimony given at the trial of Hall, Royal and Mapes was to be repeated and that Yarham's evidence on that occasion would this time be largely used against him.

News of his arrest had aroused both interest and jubilation in the town, so much so that at times the prosecuting solicitor, Mr Tolver, and Mr Sheringham, representing Yarham, had difficulty making themselves heard above the commotion outside the gaol. Among the crowd was Robert Royal, gloating at Yarham's arrest and basking in his notoriety. At half-past five in the afternoon the hearing ended with the prisoner's being committed to stand trial at the Norfolk spring assizes.

The growth of the railway system, which had reached Great

Yarmouth the year before, enabled many to travel the twenty miles to Norwich for the trial who would otherwise have been unable to make the journey. The spring assizes at the Shire Hall opened on Tuesday 24 March 1846, but Yarham was not due to step into the dock until the Friday. Meanwhile frantic efforts were being made to obtain the services of a lawyer prepared to defend him. It seems that in the mid-nineteenth century advocates were not inclined to represent a man who was regarded with abhorrence and whose guilt was by many already assumed – an attitude which nowadays would be quite unacceptable.

It was not until nine o'clock on the morning of the trial that a barrister was found who would accept the brief. Meanwhile the crowd, anxious to gain admittance to the public gallery in the Shire Hall, had to curb their impatience until the afternoon, to allow Mr Dasent a few hours in which to prepare his case. Aware of the prejudice which rendered his task all but hopeless, he was nevertheless to defend Yarham skilfully, cross-examining hostile witnesses shrewdly and making an impassioned final speech.

By two o'clock on that spring afternoon the courtroom was packed to suffocation. Women predominated among the spectators, the more influential among them having secured a seat on the magistrates' bench, while their less fortunate sisters had to be content with sitting packed shoulder to shoulder in the gallery.

The court stood as Sir William Henry Moule, the 57-year-old judge, entered. Mr Justice Moule had a well-earned reputation as a knowledgeable, down-to-earth arbiter; unfailingly courteous and good-humoured, he had the ability to circumvent technicalities that might otherwise unnecessarily prolong or complicate the proceedings.

Facing him was Mr Dasent, representing Yarham, while Mr Palmer and Mr O'Malley again prosecuted. The continuity the Crown team thus enjoyed, following on from the earlier trial, gave them an incalculable advantage over their opponent.

Stolidly watching the ritualistic preliminaries were the jurymen. Ten of them were farmers, the rustic representation varied only by the presence of Mr Henry Bridges, a gentleman from the village of Brooke, and a Caister miller named William Blythe.

Finally Yarham himself. Dressed for the occasion in his Sunday best, the young prisoner, pale-faced after his sojourn in Yarmouth gaol, nonetheless appeared confident as he surveyed the courtroom.

Mr Palmer opened the prosecution case by recounting again the circumstances surrounding Mrs Candler's murder – how at 11.30 on the night she died she had gone to the Black Swan public house opposite her shop and bought her usual half-pint of porter. Later, Mr Palmer alleged, the accused had let three other men into her shop, and they had then acted together in slaying her. (Here Mr Palmer was presumably referring to Hall, Royal and Mapes, who had already been acquitted of any such involvement!)

Police Constable Johnson gave evidence: 'On going behind the counter I saw the poor woman there with her throat cut ...,' then Sergeant Williment: 'The first thing I saw was the body of the woman ... near her was a knife .... I saw that her throat was cut .... I took up the knife ... it was covered with blood and quite wet. There was a quantity of blood on the floor.'

They were followed into the witness-box by friends of the dead woman. Mrs Lydia Cozens told the court: 'I used to clean her knives, the one produced was the one she used to cut the lard with ...,' and Margaret Edwards said that on the day before her death Mrs Candler had confided in her that she had recently been sent a large sum of money.

A murmur of anticipation greeted the calling of the next witness. Henry Worship, the surgeon who had attended Mrs Candler's shop on the night she died and who had carried out a detailed, on-the-spot examination of her body, told the court: 'My attention was called to a body behind the counter in a squatting position. There was a large wound six inches long in the neck. The wind pipe was not cut through, nor were any large veins. The wounds in the head were five in number. The first was on the upper and right side of the head, about an inch long, and one in the scalp and driven in a part of the brain.' Worship paused to allow the scene to imprint itself on the minds of his listeners before continuing: 'The next wound, I observed, was on the top of the nose, and three other wounds on the top of the left eye. Great violence appeared to have been used .... There was blood behind the counter ... which came from the wound in the neck.'

Although in no doubt that the injuries had led to Mrs Candler's death, the witness qualified this by saying that death might not have resulted instantaneously from the head wounds and that she might even have survived the neck wound alone. In reply to a query from Mr Justice Moule, Mr Worship told him, 'My opinion is that the wound in the head was given first.'

There was little to dispute in the surgeon's evidence, so Mr Dasent confined his cross-examination to seeking clarification on certain points.

'It was impossible that she could have survived more than an hour or two .... The wounds were inflicted with an instrument of weight with a flat surface. The wounds were quite through the skull,' Worship replied to Yarham's counsel.

The next person to testify, although a prosecution witness, offered some cheer to the defence. William Catchpole was the solicitor who owned the property which included Mrs Candler's shop and accommodation. After describing his movements earlier on the evening of 18 November, and his later being roused from slumber following the police arrival, he told Mr Dasent during cross-examination that the Yarhams had been living in his house since June or July 1844. They had been recommended by a local tradesman, and '... he had always found him [Yarham] strictly honest and industrious ....' This comment by the softly spoken, white-haired lawyer was one of the few remarks made that were favourable to Samuel Yarham.

George Layton, keeper of the King's Head public house, had not been called at the trial of Hall, Royal and Mapes. He told the court that in November 1844 he had been a policeman in Yarmouth and that on the night of the murder he had seen the accused heading towards the Denes. Layton's testimony was not in itself particularly significant, but his subsequent admission that he had been discharged from the police force as a consequence of '... some difference between me and the superintendent. I was charged with leaving my beat ...' caused slight amusement among the spectators and eased the tension in court.

The prosecution case effectively closed with the evidence of the Dick family, of whom Mrs Sarah Dick was to give the most damning testimony. She was seemingly overawed by the occasion, and her inarticulateness as she told of her encounters with Yarham seemed to emphasize her words.

After describing how she and her husband had met the Yarhams on the train going home from the earlier trial, Mrs Dick went on to tell how two or three weeks later she accidentally met Yarham in the town market. She said that, after bemoaning the problems he was having with people in the town, as a consequence of which he was thinking of moving away, he had astounded her by suddenly admitting his involvement in the murder. After telling her that he had let his three accomplices into Mrs Candler's shop, he had gone on to blame them for what had followed: 'I made a bargain with them not to hurt the old woman ...,' Yarham had insisted; '... they had time enough to get the money in the time she was getting the beer, as she was generally a quarter of an hour gone.'

The court listened spellbound as Mrs Dick continued: 'He let them in at the back door .... He told them to go into the bedroom, for that was where she kept her money. While they were there the woman came in sooner than usual ....' According to Yarham, Mrs Candler had seen Royal and had asked him what he wanted; upon his replying that he wanted tobacco, she had turned her back, whereupon 'Royal and Hall knocked her down with the pincers. They thought she was dead ....' All three men had then run away, leaving him with the severely injured shopkeeper. 'She turned her eyes on him, and he, seeing a lard knife lying by her, he took it and cut her throat ...,' Mrs Dick told the court. She said that when she had accused Yarham of being the murderer, he had replied, 'No, she could not live, she had been beaten so by Royal and Hall ....'

A hush had fallen on the courtroom while Mrs Dick had been speaking; when she finished, most of those listening were alive to the conclusions to be drawn if she had told the truth and had accurately recalled her conversation with Yarham. Not only did it point to him as a major participant in the crime but it rekindled the suspicion that perhaps, after all, the earlier trial had ended with three not-so-innocent men walking free.

Aware of the devastating effect her evidence would have on his client's case, Mr Dasent subjected Sarah Dick to a gruelling cross-examination, in particular concentrating his attack on the market discussion. The length of time they had been talking, the presence of other people in the vicinity, and other probing questions were aimed at either discrediting her or casting doubt on the entire conversation.

'I thought it was very strange that he should tell me ...,' Mrs Dick said at one point. She had thought it her duty to mention the conversation to someone, but her husband had forbidden it: '... he would not even allow me to tell him. It was my duty to mention it; I ought to have done it ...,' she plaintively admitted.

Mrs Dick's daughter spoke of having persuaded her mother to tell a magistrate of her conversation with Yarham, while John Dick, resplendent in his army uniform, shamefacedly admitted that, 'Some time after [the first trial], my wife was going to tell me some conversation with Yarham about it [the murder], but I refused to listen to her.' Sergeant Dick stepped out of the witness-box a subdued and discredited man.

After admitting to his own shortcomings and to the reservations he had felt about taking on a case that had attracted such widespread renown, Mr Dasent went on to tell the jury, in his closing speech, 'I trust that I shall discharge the duty that has been imposed upon me, in the best way that the weakness of my ability will allow me .... This was one of the most extraordinary investigations of which they had ever heard ....'

Mr Dasent's defence case centred more on a procedural attack on the prosecution than on attempting to nullify the witnesses' testimony. He maintained that, as a consequence of Yarham's having turned Queen's Evidence at the first trial, much of the evidence against him then had been withheld. The acquittal of Hall, Royal and Mapes, and the subsequent arrest of Yarham, entailed building an entirely new prosecution case against his client, based on resurrected evidence that his legal opponents had long been aware of but for reasons of expediency had chosen not to use. It was an ingenious argument, challenging the ethical issue rather than the evidence that had been given.

Yarham's advocate went on to criticize the methods adopted by examining magistrates, who, he said, with the object of extracting a confession, had several times visited and interrogated the accused while he had been in gaol awaiting trial. The defending lawyer's most disparaging comments were reserved for Mrs Dick. He dwelt at length on her market-place conversation with Yarham, telling the jury that it must be a fabrication and that '... no reliance could be placed upon her evidence .... If they [the jury] did not place reliance upon it, there was no case against the prisoner.'

Finally Mr Dasent cautioned the jury not to be influenced by feelings they might have after having read reports of the case or heard alleged confessions. It was an eloquent speech based on a flimsy defence. Yarham was entitled to feel that, despite the almost universal condemnation he had attracted, his case, such as it was, had been put across forcefully and effectively.

Likewise Mr Justice Moule's summing-up. This was a splendid example of dispassionate judicial objectivity. After agreeing with Mr Dasent that the magistrates' examination of Yarham in gaol had been 'highly improper', the judge moved on to the evidence of Mrs Dick. After pointing out that it was not unknown for prisoners on occasion to make strange statements, he confessed that he could see no reason why Mrs Dick should have attended court to perjure herself, thereby taking away the prisoner's life without accruing any advantage to herself. Such a crime, Mr Justice Moule said, while being far worse than the prisoner's, would subject her only to transportation.

He told the jury that, if they thought that Mrs Dick's evidence had been corroborated – as indeed some of it had been by other witnesses and circumstances, he added – it would be enough to convict. However, he reminded them of defence counsel's assertion that Mrs Dick could have obtained all the facts she had related either from the earlier trial or from newspaper reports. Mr Justice Moule concluded by asking the jury to allow '… the good character he [Yarham] had received from Mr Catchpole to have some weight in their minds'.

The judge's closing words may have been listened to by the jury, but they certainly did not influence them in Yarham's favour. After a ten-minute absence they re-entered the stifling courtroom to announce that they had found the prisoner guilty.

'I am innocent, so help me God,' replied Yarham when asked why sentence of death should not be passed. He then stood impassively as Sir John Moule entered into the lengthy diatribe which was customary in the nineteenth century before the passing of a death sentence. After being solemnly told that he could hold out no hope of a remission of sentence and being advised to prepare himself for the hereafter, Samuel Yarham listened as the judge made a significant comment: '… it appears upon the evidence, which must be taken to be established by the verdict, that you, *in conjunction with others* [author's italics] committed the most deliberate crime of murder upon a most harmless and inoffensive person ….' With those words, Mr Justice Moule seemingly confirmed that a miscarriage of justice had resulted from the first trial.

After sentence had finally been pronounced, Yarham, with a last glance round the court, disappeared from view. In two weeks time it would be the day of Norwich Fair.

Although on his own admission Samuel Yarham had participated in the murder of Harriet Candler, he could with some justification feel aggrieved at the way in which a perfidious fate had singled him out to pay the supreme penalty. Many people were convinced that more than one person had been involved, and although there was no doubt of Yarham's guilt, the question remained as to the degree of culpability of John Hall, Robert Royal and James Mapes.

All three men had been acquitted at their trial, but could not this have been a reaction on the part of the jury to Yarham's *volte face* in turning Queen's Evidence? Yarham, by his treachery, had brought upon himself the rancour of the entire community, so was it not conceivable that this animosity had been reflected in the jury's verdict?

What about the alibi evidence? Hall, Royal and Mapes had each produced witnesses prepared to swear that they had been drinking in public houses at, or very near, the time Mrs Candler was killed. Without wishing to impugn upon the integrity of people long since dead, it is reasonable to point out that the witnesses themselves had also been drinking during the evening. Could not this have affected them, resulting in mistaken identification or clouding their recollection of the time or date?

Again, the public houses in which the three men were supposedly seen were in the vicinity of Mrs Candler's shop. Would their absence necessarily have been noticed during the few minutes it would have taken them to reach her premises, commit the murder during the hurried and abortive search for her money and return to their drinking?

Finally it may be assumed that the witnesses were friendly with the accused men. Is it not possible that they had been prevailed upon to testify falsely?

These questions, by themselves, without the revealing comment made by Mr Justice Moule during his summing-up of the Yarham trial, raise doubts as to the correctness of the verdict at the first trial.

The ultimate irony is that Yarham should have turned Queen's Evidence in the mistaken belief that by so doing he was rendering himself immune from prosecution. That momentous decision, coupled with his subsequent loquaciousness in his conversations with Mrs Dick, were fatal and irretrievable miscalculations. Had he made even a perfunctory inquiry into the legal position before acting as he did, he might well have avoided contributing to the 'edification and amusement' of the Norwich citizens on their Fair Day.

– 3 –
Killer with a Conscience
1851

Charlie Johnson recoiled in horror when his dog emerged from a small wood at Trowse, his home near Norwich, holding in its mouth the remains of a human hand. That find – on the afternoon of Saturday 21 June 1851 – started a series of events that rapidly escalated before as quickly losing momentum, only to be revived after nearly two decades had passed.

The hand found by Johnson's dog was taken straight away by him and his father to the police station, where they laid it before Inspector Stewart. The policeman immediately returned with them to the wood to seek other remains. Their efforts were rewarded by their finding several pieces of flesh, which they took back to the station. The activity of the three had not gone unnoticed, and when the nature of their find was made known, the news spread rapidly. An appeal for assistance – when it was announced that the search was to continue the following day – resulted in dozens of people presenting themselves at the police station on Sunday morning, expressing their willingness to help.

The search, which continued for a month, unearthed a considerable quantity of human remains. A foot and a pelvis, recovered early on, were followed a couple of days later by arm and leg bones found by searching constables on the Hellesdon road. It fell upon Police Sergeant Peck, a former butcher, together with the three doctors called in, to determine the origin of several pieces of human and animal flesh that were found. The doctors later testified under oath before examining magistrates that the flesh and bones recovered were those of a woman aged between sixteen and twenty-six.

Meanwhile pieces of the body were still coming to light. Intestines were recovered from a sewer near the city centre; part of a female breast was found on the last day of June; a left foot

45

was uncovered in a churchyard by a schoolboy on 12 July; and finally, eight days later the search ended where it had begun, another schoolboy, Bobby Field, found another hand, minus a severed third finger.

Interest in the case then inexplicably waned. It may have been that public interest was directed more to the Great Exhibition which had opened in Hyde Park in May and which by July was in full swing. Many local people had probably taken advantage of the railway excursions to the exhibition on days when the admission charge was reduced for the working class from the usual £1 to one shilling. A murder committed at about this time at Holkham in north Norfolk may also have occupied the public's attention to the exclusion of the gruesome finds at Norwich.

The flagging interest extended to the authorities. The police investigation petered out, and exceptionally no inquest was held on those parts of the body that had been found. Possibly the rumour circulating that the remains were those of a corpse illicitly obtained and dissected by medical students, who then as a macabre joke distributed them throughout the city, was given more credence than it merited. Be that as it may, the final scene of the first act of the drama took place around Christmas 1851, when the unidentified parts that had been recovered were buried and then covered in lime by Sergeant Peck in the basement of the Guildhall at Norwich.

The Sheward tragedy extended altogether for thirty-three years. It started on 29 October 1836, at Greenwich, London, when William Sheward, a 24-year-old pawnbroker's assistant married Martha Francis, a domestic servant fourteen years older than himself. They were an ill-matched couple: Sheward, an outwardly respectable, hard-working young man, his wife a woman who, according to contemporary accounts, had a disreputable background. This may have accounted partly for the increasing disharmony between the couple during the years that followed.

Soon after they married William and Martha moved to Wymondham, her Norfolk birthplace, where they lodged with her married twin, Mary Bunn. They did not long remain there before moving to Norwich, where there were better employment prospects for William.

During the next few years the Shewards lived at a succession of different addresses in and around Norwich, while William resumed his former occupation as a tailor. He worked for several employers before deciding to start up his own business.

This proved disastrous for William and Martha's marriage, which until then had been tolerable despite rumours of William's occasional philandering with other, younger women. The situation deteriorated as the couple increasingly argued over their worsening financial situation. By 1849 this had reached a stage at which Sheward was forced to declare himself bankrupt. In November of that year, probably in an attempt to frustrate the demands of the bankruptcy commissioner, he deposited the sum of £400 with a man named Christie with whom he had obtained employment as a pawnbroker. Although Sheward had subsequently returned to him upon demand a total of £150, the arrangement was a constant source of irritation to Martha, due to Christie also having access to the money for his own use.

Matters came to a head during the summer of 1851, by which time they were living at 7 Tabernacle Street (now Bishopgate), close by the cathedral.

On Saturday 14 June, Christie asked Sheward to go to Great Yarmouth the next day and there give £10 to the captain of a merchant ship to enable him to pay his unloading fee on Monday. As he prepared to set out on his errand on Sunday morning, an argument erupted between Sheward and his wife. While he insisted that he *had* to go to Great Yarmouth, Martha was equally determined that he should remain at home. When she informed him further that she proposed visiting Christie to retrieve the £400, as Sheward later wrote in his confession, '... a slight altercation ensued ....' It is more likely that all the pent-up frustration and suppressed verbal and physical aggression that existed between them exploded in a violent outburst. Again quoting Sheward's confession, written dispassionately a few days before his execution, '... I ran a razor into her throat. She never spoke after ...' – another passage that understated the ferocity of what had taken place. It later became evident that, provoked beyond endurance and incensed by his wife's obduracy, he had grabbed his razor and slashed deeply into her throat.

It was a particularly bloody method of execution. Not only does death follow very quickly, as the severing of the carotid arteries denies the brain its blood supply, but a powerful jet of blood spurts over everything within range. Thus Sheward would almost certainly have had to have washed and then changed his clothes before setting out on the delayed trip to Yarmouth. Later in the day, when he returned home, he would have been faced with the task of disposing of Martha's body.

*

During the hours and days following Martha's death, Sheward seems to have succeeded in banishing from his mind thoughts of the nightmarish task that daily awaited him. According to his own account, he had continued to go to work each day, returning home at four in the afternoon to get on with the dismemberment.

Not surprisingly, in view of the time of year, he had noticed that on the Monday after returning home from work, 'The house began to smell ....' He had therefore lit a fire in his bedroom before starting on his labour. The horror of the scene on that Monday evening and during the succeeding days beggars description: Sheward, completely unversed in surgical skills, hacking, sawing and carving his wife's body into small, manageable pieces which he then took out in a pail to distribute in and around Norwich.

The cold-blooded resolve Sheward displayed by continuing to go to work each day, knowing what faced him upon his return home, surely ranks with that of his more notorious counterparts, the 'Brides in the Bath' killer, George Joseph Smith; Doctor Buck Ruxton, who killed and dismembered his common-law wife and their servant girl, and more recently Dennis Nilsen, the compulsive slayer of over a dozen young men.

By Sunday the job was almost completed. Martha's head, most of which was never found, and her hands and feet had been boiled in a saucepan in the futile hope that they would disintegrate before being deposited around the city, while her entrails had been disposed of down a drain. Even her hair was cut into small pieces and scattered to the wind, although remnants were later found still adhering to small pieces of flesh. The final task remaining on the Sunday morning was for the house to be cleaned, and the bedclothes and other blood-stained items burned.

Three months after ridding himself of Martha, Sheward moved from Tabernacle Street into three rooms in nearby King Street. Meanwhile he continued working for Mr Christie.

Notwithstanding the recovery of some of his late wife's remains a mere week after he had distributed them about Norwich, he kept his nerve and betrayed no sign of his awful secret. That came later.

As interest in the case declined, so Sheward's confidence increased.

Few people seemed to notice Martha's sudden disappearance. The Shewards' next-door neighbours, Potter and Sarah Batson, were able many years later to recall the couple, but neither of them seems to have attached any particular significance to her abrupt departure. Martha's family made no immediate enquiries, a lack of interest probably stemming from the coolness that had existed between her husband and themselves. However, a few weeks later a confrontation did take place between Sheward and Martha's twin sister, Mary Bunn, when, together with her husband, she paid him a visit. Her main purpose was to try to establish the whereabouts of her sister but, as might be expected, her brother-in-law was not very helpful. He told Mrs Bunn that before seeing his wife off in a train he had appealed to her to write to her sisters even if she wished to have no further contact with him. According to Sheward, his wife's response had been a terse, 'No, never.' With that, for the time being, the dead woman's sister had to be content, though as far as she was concerned, Martha might have gone but she was by no means forgotten. Sheward told the one or two other people who took the trouble to enquire after Martha that she had left suddenly for either Australia or New Zealand in search of a former paramour called Worseldine who had been transported.

In November 1851, following the death of a sister-in-law, Mrs Francis, Sheward received a letter from her son Thomas inviting both himself and Martha to the funeral. He declined the invitation on their behalf, while feeling reassured in the knowledge that Martha's family still assumed her to be alive.

As the months passed, Sheward took to visiting local taverns more frequently, and was not averse to entertaining the occasional young woman in his rooms. One of them, Charlotte Maria Buck, a local nursemaid, became a frequent visitor, so much so that in February 1853 Sheward's landlord, John Bird, in a fit of self-righteousness over Charlotte's presence in his young lodger's rooms, gave him notice to quit. Sheward apparently left without demur and moved to another address in King Street where, together with Charlotte, he remained until 1868.

For nine years the couple cohabited, and it was not until 1862, by which time they had three children, that they decided to legitimize the situation. So it was that on 13 February that year, at Norwich registry office, William Sheward married for the second time. To the registrar, Mr I.O. Taylor, he described himself as a widower.

All now seemed well for Sheward: married, with three children, a comfortable home and a steady job, the horror of the events back in the summer of 1851 had receded into the innermost recesses of his mind. They had receded but not disappeared; the process of physical and mental deterioration was so gradual that at first Sheward probably did not appreciate what was happening. His visits to local hostelries became even more frequent, and he also had a cask of ale in a back room at the place where he worked. Not only did his drinking adversely affect his working performance but he became subject to fits of tearful depression. His physical appearance degenerated and he started to age prematurely. Most worrying of all, as far as he was concerned, was his increasing tendency to talk in his sleep.

The effect on his wife of these changes is not recorded. Preoccupied no doubt in looking after their children, who by now had increased to four, it is possible that she did not fully recognize or understand her husband's gradual decline.

Sheward tried to counter the malign influences afflicting him. He left Mr Christie's employ, with its constant reminders of all that had taken place so many years before, to start his own pawnbroking business. The venture was not a success; business slumped and in the winter of 1868 he sold out to a rival. Sheward, whose alcoholism was by this time severely affecting him physiologically, displayed a sad lack of judgement by moving with his family to Oak Street, where he became the landlord of the Key and Castle Inn. For one in his ravaged state, the responsibility of running such an establishment soon proved too much: on Tuesday 29 December 1868, after a Christmas spent with his wife, children and merrymaking customers, Sheward armed himself with a razor and caught the London train, intending to end once and for all the hell that had by now driven him to the brink of madness.

Inspector James Davis was bored. At Carter Street police station in the South London district of Walworth, he had been on duty for only half an hour on the evening of Friday 1 January 1869 but already he was feeling a sense of anticlimax after the activity that had accompanied the Christmas and New Year's Eve celebrations. He looked up as the door leading on to the street opened and a man entered. Elderly, slightly built and of below-average height, the newcomer was respectably dressed and looked tired.

'I want to speak to you. I have a charge to make against myself.' The man paused. 'What is it?' asked Davis.

'For the wilful murder of my first wife at Norwich,' came the reply.

Davis looked more closely at the man. Was he telling the truth, or was he just a harmless crackpot hoping to attract attention to himself? The policeman felt instinctively that he was genuine.

'Have you given due consideration to the very serious nature of the charge?' he asked.

'Yes, I have. I have kept the secret for years and can keep it no longer …. I left home on Tuesday with the intention of destroying myself. I intended to cut my throat with a razor …. I wish you to make a charge in writing,' the man ended.

Davis, no longer bored and all but certain that the stranger before him was telling the truth, complied with the request and wrote down at his dictation, 'I, William Sheward, of Norwich, charge myself with the wilful murder of my wife.' Little more could be done that night, so Sheward was detained until enquiries to verify his claim could be made the following day.

The next morning he enlarged on his confession. After describing to Inspector Davis the murder and the disposal of Martha's remains, he moved to more recent events: 'Last night I went to a house in Richmond Street, Walworth, where I first saw my first wife. That brought it so forcibly to my mind that I was obliged to come to you to give myself up ….'

What had induced Sheward to return to Richmond Street after so many years can only be conjecture. Perhaps, after three days spent wandering around London trying to summon up enough courage either to kill himself or to surrender to the police, he had first had an urge to return to Martha's old home. This had finally prompted him to walk into the nearest police station.

On the strength of only his confession, later on the Saturday morning Sheward appeared before Mr Woolrych, the magistrate at Lambeth police court, who remanded him in custody until the following Thursday. In the meantime Inspector Davis wrote to the chief constable at Norwich explaining what had taken place and asking for '… enquiry to be made to ascertain whether there is any truth in his statement'. A reply came a few days later, informing Davis '… that there is no doubt about the truth of Sheward's statement ….' The letter confirmed that in 1851 portions of a female body had been found in the city, and ended by asking what further action was now deemed appropriate.

There was little question as to what the next step should be. As the alleged crime appeared to have been committed in Norwich, Sheward would have to be transferred to within the jurisdiction of the local assizes. Accordingly, when he reappeared before Mr Woolrych on 7 January, police gave additional information to the magistrate, whereupon he accepted a formal application that Sheward be transferred to Norwich.

No time was wasted: later the same day, escorted by Inspector Davis, Sheward was taken by rail to Norwich. At Trowse, just outside the city, the train was halted and the prisoner was given into the charge of Robert Hitchman, the chief constable, who took him by cab straight to the police station to avoid the crowd that had assembled at Norwich's Thorpe station to meet the train from London.

The next morning Sheward made the first of his five appearances before the magistrates in the Sword Room at the Guildhall. During the next three weeks over twenty-five prosecution witnesses were to testify, a tribute to those charged with tracing and interviewing them after a lapse of eighteen years.

Two significant events occurred while the preliminary hearings were taking place. Probably on the advice of his solicitor, Joseph Stanley, who had been engaged by some of his friends to represent him, Sheward retracted the written admission he had made to Inspector Davis, explaining that at the time he had been in a deluded state through drink. Then, on Tuesday 12 January, the remains that had been interred in the basement of the Guildhall eighteen years before by Sergeant Peck, were exhumed. Present (in what was by now the Guildhall's coal cellar) were Peck, by now an inspector, Mr Hitchman, the chief constable, Mr Stanley and two of the doctors, Dalrymple and Nichols, who had originally examined the remains with Peck. The bones were still identifiable as such, but all traces of the flesh and tissue had long since disappeared.

On Monday 1 February the prosecution concluded its case at the lower court. Sheward reserved his defence and before a packed assembly was committed to the Norwich Spring Assizes to stand trial.

Monday 29 March 1869 would have been Martha Sheward's seventy-second birthday. It is doubtful if many in the large crowd that gathered that morning outside the Shire Hall in Norwich, hoping to gain admittance to the trial of her former husband, were aware of the fact. The case had aroused widespread interest, and there was some sympathy for the prisoner, notwithstanding the horrific details that had been disclosed at the preliminary hearings. Such feelings probably sprang from an awareness of the anguish born of guilt that Sheward had suffered over the years and which had eventually compelled him to go to the police. Sight of him in the Assize Court may well have aroused even more compassion: an undersized, insignificant man, prematurely aged, Sheward was a picture of dejection as he was carried to the dock by two warders and there given a seat – necessary concessions to the incapacitating rheumatism he suffered in both ankles.

The hearing of *The Queen v. Sheward* lasted only two days. The prosecution was in the hands of Mr O'Malley QC, Mr Carlos Cooper and Mr E. Tillett, assisted by Mr Mayd, while the defence had been entrusted to Mr Metcalfe and Mr Simms Reeve, with Sheward's solicitor, Joseph Stanley, hovering in the background. Mr Baron Piggott was the judge.

On the first morning the crowded courtroom listened as Mr O'Malley outlined the prosecution case, from the finding of the human remains scattered in and around Norwich in 1851 until Sheward had given himself up to the police in London eighteen years later. From the commencement of the trial some of the ladies in court appeared to be near fainting as counsel described the recovery and the condition of the remains; worse was soon to follow.

After Inspector Davis had told of Sheward's arrival at Carter Street police station on New Year's Day, there followed a succession of witnesses who spoke of having found what appeared to be human remains during the summer of 1851: Charles Johnson, whose dog had found the hand that had sparked off the search; Harry Layton, who had discovered a foot lying in a churchyard, and James Palmer, who had come upon a thigh bone in a field. Constable James Flaxman, who had been on duty at the police station when some portions of the body had been deposited, told how later he had joined the search for other remains. A description by Charlie Sales, who in 1851 had been a sewerman, of how he had recovered entrails and other human parts in a drain not far from where the Shewards lived, was particularly gruesome and had most of the female audience in court hastily reaching for their smelling-salts. Only slightly less harrowing was the testimony of Richard Fryer, a stationmaster at Sevenoaks in Kent, who had been a schoolboy in 1851. He told the court that on a Sunday in July that year he had found in a neighbour's garden a badly decomposed left hand minus its third finger.

Another policeman, William Futter, provided a further tenuous link between Martha Sheward and the remains that had been found, by telling how he had given to Sergeant Peck pieces of flesh he had recovered, with traces of golden-coloured hair attached. In turn Edward Peck, the one-time butcher turned policeman, recalled that in June 1851 a quantity of human female remains and some blood-stained clothing had been brought to the police station. The former had been preserved in glass and earthenware vessels for about a month before being buried under the basement floor of the Guildhall. He had been present when the remains had been exhumed, and testified that they were those that had been interred in 1851.

The public in court listening to the evidence may have thought that they were to be allowed a brief respite from the horror as Peck stepped out of the witness-box; if so, they were to be disappointed. It was the turn now of Doctors Nichols and Dalrymple to tell of their examination of the remains, and the conclusions they had arrived at eighteen years earlier.

William Peter Nichols, a surgeon, told how on 21 June 1851, assisted by Dr Dalrymple and the late Dr Norgate, he had carried out an examination of human remains that he had concluded were those of an adult female aged about twenty-six or twenty-seven. He had noted at the time, however, that the condition of the flesh and skin was not inconsistent with being that of a woman of about fifty-four. The feet, hands and pelvis appeared to have been immersed in hot water. The pelvis had been '... rudely sawn through, first in one direction and then in another in two pieces which did not meet, and then it was broken up, which was certainly not the work of any student in a dissecting room ....' Thus did Nichols, in advance, effectively dispose of a line of defence that Mr Metcalfe was later to put forward. He was not shaken under cross-examination, insisting at one point that the remains he had examined had been those of a woman, and not a man, as Mr Metcalfe suggested.

Dr Donald Dalrymple's evidence largely corroborated that of his colleague, although under cross-examination he too was imprecise. When asked by Mr Metcalfe to assess the age of the woman whose remains he had assisted in examining, he replied unhelpfully, 'I shall state no more than that she was a full-grown adult.'

The evidence so far had been targeted largely on the recovery and examination of what remained of Martha Sheward. When relatives and friends of the couple testified, the emphasis was more on William's movements and behaviour before and after the death of his wife.

Hannah Lane told the court that Sheward had been married to her Aunt Martha and that she had visited them when a child. She had last seen her aunt just before the 1851 Exhibition. Several years later she visited Sheward in King Street, Norwich, by which time he was living with the woman who was now his second wife. On that occasion there had been no mention of her aunt.

One of Martha's sisters, Dorothy Hewitt, followed Hannah into the witness-box. Now, at the time of the trial, she was an old woman. She remembered having last seen the couple together '... about eighteen years ago .... And I have not heard from her [Martha] since'. She further demonstrated her powers of recollection when she stated that, during a visit to King Street some years later, she had said to Sheward, 'I shall be very much obliged, Mr Sheward, if you will tell me where my sister is.' The formally phrased request had merely elicited the ambiguous reply, 'Mrs Hewitt, she can write to you if she likes.'

During his cross-examination of Dorothy Hewitt, Mr Metcalfe suggested that at one time, prior to her marriage, Martha had been living in London with the man called Worseldine, who, according to Sheward had later been deported. It was a liaison of which the witness denied all knowledge. Worseldine was to be mentioned again later.

As the trial progressed, the spectators in court found it increasingly difficult to reconcile the inoffensive and unhappy-looking man sitting in the dock with the cold-blooded wife slaying of which he was accused. For his part, Sheward sat listening miserably, at times uncomprehendingly, as a succession of people, with most of whom he had not had contact for years, stepped into the witness-box to tell of long-forgotten meetings and of conversations which now seemed to have assumed a new significance.

The family evidence continued on Tuesday. William Bunn, Martha's brother-in-law, whose wife Mary had been dead for several years, said that after hearing rumours that the Shewards had separated, he had visited King Street. There William had told him that Martha had remarked as her train was about to depart, 'I will not write to you or my sister, never!'

During his cross-examination Mr Metcalfe harked back to the man called Worseldine. Bunn admitted that he had heard his wife mention the name while Martha was still living alone in London. He added that he had understood Worseldine to have been a carpenter, but he had no knowledge of his having been transported.

The last important prosecution witness was Eva Hewitt, the daughter of Dorothy Hewitt who had already given evidence. Eva recalled having regularly visited Sheward and his second wife while they were living in King Street, and remembered particularly an occasion in 1862 when Sheward had called at her home. Present also had been her aunt, the astringent Mrs Bunn, who had asked Sheward outright, 'What have you done with my sister?' Apparently somewhat irritated by the question, he had replied, 'I have done nothing with your sister; she went away and left me penniless.'

The witness told Mr Metcalfe during cross-examination of the time in 1853 when her great-aunt, Elizabeth Fisher, died, leaving a modest legacy to be divided among her nephews and nieces, including Eva's mother and her aunts Mary Bunn and Martha Sheward. Mrs Bunn had written to Sheward to inform him of the windfall due to his wife, but Sheward had written back in a letter dated 24 March 1853 saying, 'Mrs Bunn. I am sorry to hear of Mrs Fisher's death, but your sister not being in Norwich at the present time, I shall not take any part in arranging affairs; therefore you need not expect me, nor send to me any more about it. William Sheward.' Dorothy Hewitt and one of Elizabeth Fisher's nephews had been equally unsuccessful in enlisting Sheward's co-operation in the share-out of the estate, so eventually it was distributed among the legatees, with Martha's entitlement being held in trust by the testator's solicitor, Mr John Stevenson Cann.*

After Eva Hewitt had left the witness-box, the remaining witnesses called by Mr O'Malley testified to the second Mrs Sheward's former modest lifestyle, her meeting with her future husband, and their subsequent courtship and cohabitation. It may have been that the testimony of these witnesses was introduced to promote the theory that the couple's ripening association had provided a motive for killing Martha. If so, the tactic misfired, for at least two of the witnesses said that Sheward and Charlotte Buck had not met until after 1851.

Mr Metcalfe did not call any defence witnesses, so it remained only for the respective advocates to make their closing speeches, and for Mr Baron Piggott to sum up, before the jury retired to consider their verdict.

In view of what had been said by some of the witnesses, Mr O'Malley did not dwell very long on the suggestion that the prisoner's liaison with Charlotte Buck had been the motive for his killing his wife. Instead he concentrated on the confession Sheward had made to Inspector Davis. Although it had later been retracted, Mr O'Malley declared that the details contained in the statement were still consistent with the facts uncovered about Martha's disappearance.

Mr Metcalfe in turn drew attention to several matters that in his view pointed to his client's innocence. He said that, as Sheward was living in Norwich at the time the remains had been found, he could well have recalled sufficient of the published details to have made a statement of admission, and that later there was nothing inconsistent with his reason for having retracted it. He continued by pointing out the lack of evidence showing where Sheward had supposedly dismembered

---

* John Stevenson Cann had appeared as a witness for James Blomfield Rush during his trial in 1849 for the murder of Isaac Jermy and his son at Stanfield Hall near Wymondham. See *Murder in East Anglia* by Robert Church (Robert Hale, 1987).

his wife. If he had murdered her, as the prosecution said, it would seem that he had done so at his home near the city centre, without there being any audible protest from his wife.

Mr Metcalfe went on to stretch the credulity of all those in court, with the possible exception of his client, by advancing the hypothesis that the body had been illegally obtained from he-knew-not-where, by an unknown person or persons who for whatever reason had then crudely dismembered it before hurriedly disposing of the various pieces. The medical evidence, said counsel, pointed to the remains being those of a young woman; if such was the case, it admitted the possibility that Martha had left her husband for the man Worseldine.

Towards the end of his address Mr Metcalfe put forward what may be considered his most telling submission. There was no proof of his client's alleged misconduct when married to Martha, he said; furthermore, by waiting nine years before remarrying, Sheward was surely demonstrating his belief in his first wife's being alive and his desire to avoid being indicted for bigamy.

Mr Metcalfe had done his best; he had countered with varying degrees of conviction the points made by the prosecution. It now remained only for the judge to sum up.

Was Martha Sheward dead? Had she been murdered? Were the remains found in 1851 hers? Finally, did the jury believe that Sheward's confession to Inspector Davis was true? The answers to these questions, said Baron Piggott, would help them reach their verdict. The judge took his time over his summing-up, pointing out among other things that not all the witnesses had agreed and that the doctors had qualified their original opinions over the age of the woman whose remains they had examined. He gave full weight to the submissions of Mr Metcalfe – some thought that his summing-up was tilted in favour of the accused. It was strange, he said, that although the butchery was alleged to have taken place at the Shewards' home in Tabernacle Street, no traces of it remained. He also pointedly remarked that, although eighteen years had elapsed since most of the events of which they had heard had taken place and although many of the witnesses were now of advancing years, they had been remarkably sure of their facts and dates.

Sheward watched indifferently as the jury retired to consider their verdict; he seemed already resigned to the judgement's going against him. After an hour and a quarter the jury re-entered the courtroom. The man in the dock listened without emotion as the 'guilty' verdict was announced, and he remained impassive as Baron Piggott sentenced him to death. On account of the prisoner's age, frailty and the interval that had elapsed between the commission of the crime and his being brought to trial, some observers had expected the jury to add a rider recommending mercy. No such recommendation was made, and as he was carried from the court to return to St Giles Gaol, Sheward knew that there was scant hope of his escaping the gallows.

Although the prospect for Sheward was grim, his solicitor, Joseph Stanley, was determined to do everything possible in the time remaining to save his client. The first task was to organize a petition. Considerable sympathy still existed for Sheward among the people of Norwich, and soon over 500 of the city's most prominent citizens had signed a petition for his reprieve. At the same time his counsel, Mr Metcalfe, was objecting on technical grounds to the legality of the trial. His submissions were laid before the attorney general, who, after due consideration, rejected his arguments.

As was invariably the case in capital charges, dozens of letters were sent to Sheward's lawyers and the press expressing views on the trial and its outcome, particularly on the rectitude of executing a man who had suffered deeply from remorse over the years and who had voluntarily gone to the police. Other letters served to hinder rather than help those still involved in the matter. One intriguing example, sent to *The Times*, purported to verify the former existence of Worseldine, now said to be dead, who, the writer alleged, had associated with a woman in London many years before. The writer suggested that Mr Stanley contact Worseldine's son, who would confirm the matter one way or the other. The suggestion was not followed.

What of the object of all this activity and correspondence? The verdict seemed to have had the opposite effect upon Sheward to that which might have been expected. His general health improved, and he ate and slept well, and received regular visits from his wife and Mr Stanley. It seems that he was enjoying greater peace of mind during the last three weeks of his life than he had for many years.

His execution was fixed for the morning of Monday 19 April, but as Calcroft, the executioner, already had another 'engagement' at Gloucester Prison that day, his appointment with Sheward was put back to eight o'clock the next morning. Following the recent abolition of public hangings, Sheward was to be executed in the privacy of the gaol.

Although efforts to secure a reprieve continued until the eve of his execution, Sheward seems to have resigned himself to his fate. On the afternoon of Thursday 13 April he sent a request from the infirmary, to which he had been taken on account of his rheumatism, asking to see the governor, Mr John Howarth, and his principal warder (now called a chief officer). When they arrived, Sheward announced that he wanted to make a written confession to the crime. Accordingly the statement, in all its detail, was written down at his dictation.

After describing how he had killed Martha and mutilated her body, he went on to tell how he had disposed of the remains: 'I carried some portions in a frail basket to another part of the city ....' After putting a saucepan containing Martha's head on the fire, 'to keep the stench away,' he continued, 'I then broke it up and distributed it about Thorpe ... emptied the pail in Bishopgate Street with the entrails etc ... I then put the hands and feet into the same saucepan in hopes they might boil to pieces.' He concluded by telling his ashen-faced listeners that on the Sunday (a week after the murder) he had burned all the blood-stained bedclothes and Martha's nightgown and had cut up her hair, which '... blew away as I walked along ....'

A visiting justice, Mr J. Godwin Johnson, and the Reverend Robert Wade, the prison chaplain, arrived in time to witness Sheward's signature to the document, and it was Mr Johnson who, much to the chagrin of the governor, departed with it in his possession. Sheward had agreed to the statement's being shown to the home secretary and to the trial judge but asked that it not be made public until after the execution had taken place, a request that was readily acceded to.

His fate was finally confirmed at four o'clock on the Monday afternoon. He had had a last emotionally charged visit from his wife, when the governor received a brief communication from the Home Office: 'HOME SECRETARY WILL NOT INTERFERE.'

According to contemporary reports, Sheward went to his death bravely. After a final night's rest he seemed to be at peace and calmly awaited the arrival of eight o'clock. Shortly before the appointed hour, with the melancholy tolling of the prison bell as accompaniment, he was carried out by two warders, Messrs Hall and Base, to the pinioning-room. A few minutes later a sombre procession emerged for the short walk to the scaffold; a portable structure, this had arrived the day before and had been erected in a corner of the gaol yard, within sound of the large and noisy crowd that had gathered outside the gate. Leading the procession were the under-sheriff and the surgeon, followed by the governor, John Howarth, and then the chaplain intoning the burial service. Sheward came next, carried between the two warders, while bringing up the rear were Calcroft and several reporters, the latter presumably invited so that they could describe the dreadful ritual from which the public were now excluded.

Once Sheward had ascended the gallows, it took only moments for the final preparations to be completed. A crash as the trapdoor fell open, accompanied by the hoisting of a black flag over the gaol gate, signalled to the now silent crowd that retribution had finally been exacted from William Sheward.

Certainly ranking as one of the most gruesome killings of the nineteenth century, the Sheward case has several unusual aspects. Sheward's confessing to a crime that had taken place eighteen years earlier, a lapse of time that would almost certainly have ensured that Martha Sheward's disappearance would have remained a mystery, was the first extraordinary feature. Since such ineffectual efforts had been made by the police and other authorities to establish the identity of the human remains found in 1851, his confession seems even more remarkable. If the remains could not be positively identified in 1851, it is inconceivable that they could in 1868.

Sheward's second confession, made while he was awaiting execution but not revealed publicly until after his death, removed any doubt as to his guilt. The suggestion that his wife had left him to seek out the man called Worseldine was revealed for what it had really been: a spurious and desperate attempt to extricate himself from the fearful situation in which he had placed himself.

The real motive for Martha Sheward's death was never determined. Escalating financial problems leading to increasing acrimony between the couple; the knowledge of her husband's philandering, made harder for Martha to bear because of the disparity in their ages, and culminating in a final showdown, or maybe a sudden, impetuous act committed in the heat of the moment? If such was the case, it may explain the overwhelming remorse felt by Sheward during the years that followed.

Once it became known that Sheward was to be put on trial for the murder of his wife, the question was whether, if found guilty, as seemed likely, he should suffer the ultimate penalty. Some maintained that after such a lapse of time, and taking into account the years of suffering the anguish of remorse that had so afflicted him physically and mentally, it would be inhumane to execute him now. Others took the view that his crime had been so evil, perpetrated as it had been with such savagery and followed by the pitiless dissection and disposal of his wife's body, that only his own death could atone for it.

The latter argument prevailed; in an age not generally noted for its magnaminity towards those who unlawfully slew their fellow men or women, the arguments advanced in favour of a reprieve were denounced and failed to persuade Mr Bruce, the home secretary, to save the condemned man. For Sheward the argument was academic: he had calmly resigned himself to the fate awaiting him, and as he was carried out on that April morning in 1869, small, vulnerable and infirm, he may well have looked upon his imminent death as his final act of purification.*

* Exactly twenty years to the day before William Sheward's execution, James Blomfield Rush had stepped out onto the scaffold outside Norwich Castle where he was executed for the murder of Isaac Jermy and his son.

– 4 –
Market Town Murder
1862

'The deceased was in full uniform with his greatcoat on. He had no belt or cutlass on, and he had no staff or handcuffs about him ....' The speaker was Daniel Keeble Taylor, a police sergeant testifying at the inquest into the death of a colleague, Ebenezer Tye, who had died during the early hours of Tuesday 25 November 1862.

The 24-year-old, slightly built PC Tye had been in the force for only sixteen months, the last seven of which he had spent at the small Suffolk market town of Halesworth, but he was well known in the town, where he had established a reputation as an affable, conscientious but above all fearless young officer. Regard for him was enhanced after he was seriously beaten by two men whom he had interrupted while robbing a barn, an intervention for which he was subsequently rewarded at the quarter sessions.

In November 1862 the inhabitants of Halesworth were preoccupied with local events, George Fuller's Christmas meat sale of 'horses, beast, sheep and pigs etc', due to take place on Wednesday 10 December at his premises adjoining the Angel Inn, focused housewives' attention on the forthcoming Yuletide festivities, while other folk speculated as to who would buy the 'substantial, stone-built cottage' with low rooms, including a washhouse, which was soon to be auctioned. Currently rented at £7.3.0d per annum, the property had adjacent to it a pump of spring water to which the tenants enjoyed a right of way – a valuable selling-point.

The evening of Monday 24 November 1862 started normally for PC Tye. He was scheduled for night duty, so a little before ten o'clock he went to the police station, where he met Sergeant Taylor and Constable William Lucas from Westhall who was also to patrol Halesworth that night. The three men had a short discussion during which Tye was told by Taylor to watch John Ducker's house in Clarke's yard off Chediston Street in the hope of seeing him return from some illegal nocturnal expedition. It was agreed that Tye should patrol the town during the night and then keep observation from 5 a.m. until breakfast time on Tuesday morning. Lucas meanwhile would continue patrolling.

John Ducker was a familiar figure in Halesworth, in his blue smock and drabbett trousers, and wearing either a 'wide-awake' hat or a glengarry cap atop his thick black hair. Local people were used to seeing his stocky, powerful figure hobbling around the highways and byways of the town. As a younger man he had been a well-known wrestler, but now he worked as a hay-trusser at the stackyard of maltster and corn-merchant Thompson George.

The town's policemen regarded the 63-year-old countryman less benevolently than did his neighbours. They suspected that his nocturnal excursions – he had several times been spotted returning home in the small hours – indicated that he had some questionable means of supplementing his paltry wages. Ebenezer Tye was certain that Ducker was a miscreant.

The night passed uneventfully. Sergeant Taylor and Lucas both saw Tye, Taylor suggesting to him when they met that he don a pair of galoshes before commencing his watch on Ducker's house, to deaden the sound of his footsteps. Lucas twice spoke briefly to his colleague, the second time at quarter-past four, five minutes before he went off duty.

At about twenty minutes to six on the Tuesday morning, soon after John Winter, a labourer on his way to work, had bid the time of day to Constable Tye, the policeman became aware of Ducker's approach. He heard his uneven-sounding footsteps and then saw his shadow as he entered Clarke's yard, apparently on the way home. In the dawn light the policeman noticed that he was carrying what appeared to be a truss of hay, so he followed him into the yard and challenged him. After they had spoken for several minutes, apparently Ducker handed Tye the hay and then walked on down the yard, the policeman following. Suddenly Ducker broke away and ran across a stream at the bottom of Clarke's yard onto rough ground opposite. Tye, throwing the hay to one side, pursued him and caught up with his quarry on the far side of the stream. A heated argument ensued which soon developed into a fight between the two men.

Tye, although young and fit, was physically disadvantaged against the older but stronger man. Back and forth they struggled, splashing into the stream, punching, kicking and gouging, the origin of their conflict forgotten as they fought desperately for mastery over each other. Tye succeeded in landing two heavy punches to Ducker's face and struck the older man on the head with his staff, opening up a wicked-looking gash on his scalp. His infuriated opponent retaliated by half-strangling the policeman with his leather stock. Breaking away, gasping for breath, Tye paused to recover. It was Ducker's opportunity: summoning up his last reserves of strength, he launched himself at the younger man and landed a final, crushing blow to his forehead. Whether this was delivered by his fist, a handy piece of wood or even by the policeman's own staff was never determined and matters not. Whatever the means used, the blow knocked the younger man unconscious. With two audible groans he collapsed to the rubble-strewn ground.

Grunting and gasping for breath, Ducker dragged Tye's body to the stream, into which he heaved it with one last effort, tossing the policeman's top hat in after him. The stream, polluted with the effluent of a dozen nearby privies, was barely sufficient to cover Tye's upturned face; nonetheless, within seconds of his immersion the final measure of air bubbled from his lungs.

It was several hours before Ebenezer Tye was missed. Had he not been detailed to keep observation on Ducker's house, he would have gone off duty between 4 and 5 a.m. on Tuesday morning, returning to work about noon the same day. He failed to arrive, and when William Lucas arrived back at the station at 2 p.m., he immediately joined in the full-scale search that by then was in progress.

It seems not to have occurred to anyone that John Ducker might have been able to provide a clue as to Tye's whereabouts, least of all that the hay-trusser might have been involved in his disappearance – that is, until Sergeant Taylor returned to the police station just before six o'clock. After checking on the situation he went with Lucas to pay Ducker a visit. They found him at home, sitting in an armchair eating his supper. Both policemen immediately noticed his two black eyes, prompting Taylor to leave his colleague in the house while he went to fetch Superintendent Jeremiah Gobbett.

During Taylor's absence, in response to Lucas's questioning Ducker denied any knowledge of Tye's disappearance, stating that he had not got out of bed until seven o'clock that morning. When Sergeant Taylor and Superintendent Gobbett returned, the former asked Ducker to account for the black eyes, an injury to his face and a head wound under blood-matted hair. Ducker's replies were unconvincing: he explained that the injuries to his eyes had resulted from a piece of wood he had been chopping the previous Friday flying up and hitting him in the face, and that the wound to his head had been caused by a comb.

When Lucas asked to see his clothes, Ducker showed him a suit and said that, apart from what he was wearing, this was the only clothing he possessed. As he rose from his armchair, however, the policeman caught sight of an old pair of trousers under the cushion.

'Ducker, what do this mean? Ain't these yours?' he asked.

'Yes, they are an old pair,' the other admitted.

Although still damp after an apparent attempt at washing them, the trousers stank and traces of mud and weeds remained on them. This find persuaded Taylor upon his return to delay no longer; he told Ducker that he was taking him to the police station, where he would be detained while the search for Tye continued.

It was a busy evening for Sergeant Daniel Taylor. After depositing Ducker at the station, he returned with Superintendent Gobbett to Clarke's yard, where together they entered Ducker's other property, opposite the house where he lived. This he used as a store for lumber and other bits and pieces. There, concealed in a cupboard, Taylor discovered a truss of hay which the two policemen carried to the station before joining the search for their missing colleague. A sample of the hay was later to be produced in court.

For several hours policemen and townsfolk alike had been looking for Tye. Alleys, yards, fields and ditches had been scoured without there being found any trace of the missing constable. Lucas and Taylor concentrated their efforts in and around Clarke's yard, and it was Lucas who just before ten o'clock that evening saw the outstretched fingers of Tye's left hand breaking the surface of the stream as if reaching for the willows draped across the water. The policeman lay on his back just beneath the surface about forty yards downstream from where he had fought his last battle.

Sergeant Taylor and others lifted the policeman's body out of the water. Apart from his top hat, which was floating a few yards away, Tye was still fully dressed in uniform. As Taylor later deposed, '...his clothes were saturated with mud, water and weeds ... and the smell of the mud was very offensive ....'

Taylor accompanied Tye's body when it was removed to the Corn Hall in Halesworth for later examination and post-mortem by Dr Frederick Haward, a local surgeon who also examined Ducker's injuries. Immediately afterwards the policeman returned to the station. Tye had been found, and Taylor had spoken to Ducker, the man for whom Tye had been watching earlier that day. Ducker's face showed obvious signs of recent injury, and Taylor gave little credence to his explanation as to the cause of those injuries. As far as Police Sergeant Daniel Taylor was concerned, the circumstantial evidence already pointed unerringly to Ducker as the person responsible for his colleague's death. There would be time enough later to seek out corroborative evidence.

Late on Tuesday evening Taylor sat facing his truculent prisoner across a table at the police station and formally charged him with the wilful murder of Police Constable Ebenezer Tye. Ducker denied any knowledge of the policeman's death.

The events surrounding the death of Tye and the subsequent developments had a predictable effect on Halesworth's 2,500 inhabitants. From about noon on Tuesday, when he had been discovered as missing, speculation and rumour had proliferated as to the policeman's whereabouts and possible fate. Men young and old had joined in the search for him, while groups of their womenfolk gossiped about the situation and what they thought might have happened.

A few people wandered down Chediston Street and into Clarke's yard, an area that most of them generally avoided. With its dilapidated one-up/one-down houses, many of which were unoccupied and boarded up, and the stream at the bottom carrying sewage and effluent away from the town, it had little appeal.

When news came that Tye's body had been found, excitement mounted and many people remained out of doors Tuesday night, anxious not to miss any further drama. After the body had been removed to the Corn Hall, police activity died down, but Thomas Mills, a searcher raking through the mud and debris at the bottom of the stream, retrieved Tye's handcuffs from the spot where his body had lain. Next morning Police Constable Henry Cattermull, searching the rough ground bordering the far side of the stream, recovered Tye's staff a few yards from where he had been found.

Soon after arriving at the police station on the Wednesday, Sergeant Taylor went again to Ducker's address. This time, while carrying out a more thorough search than had been possible the previous evening, he found a pair of stocking legs concealed under the bed upstairs, together with a coat and a pair of boots in the room below. The boots and men's stockings were soaking wet, and all three items bore traces of mud and weeds.

The inquest into Police Constable Ebenezer Tye's death opened at the Angel Hotel promptly at 5 p.m. that day. After the jury had been sworn, the coroner, Mr B.L. Gross, told those in court: 'I regret to say that there can be very little doubt that a frightful crime has been committed in this neighbourhood .... That some person or persons unknown have deprived this officer of his life whilst in the execution of his duty, there can be no doubt ....' After thus pre-empting the jury's verdict, Mr Gross went on to explain the law as it stood in 1862: '... all peace officers, all police officers, and all ministers of justice are protected, and if killed under circumstances which, were they only private individuals, would make the crime that of manslaughter, the killing of these persons even though it be involuntary, *amounts to the crime of wilful murder ....*'

When the coroner had finished speaking, the jury went to an adjacent room to view Tye's body. Scarcely had they returned to their seats than the door of the room opened and John Ducker entered, escorted by two policemen. Burly, ruddy-faced and with large, strong hands, he gazed round the room through his swollen and blackened eyes, which, together with the barely concealed head wound, bore testimony to recently sustained violence.

Ducker listened as Sergeant Taylor outlined the circumstances surrounding PC Tye's disappearance. He described the steps he had taken upon learning on Tuesday evening that the policeman was missing, and of the subsequent recovery of his body, concluding by telling of his later visits to Ducker's address. Asked by Mr Gross if he had any questions to ask Taylor, Ducker's reply was brief and succinct: 'No, Your Honour, I haint got nothing to say. I am innocent.'

The only other witness to be heard before the proceedings were adjourned until the following morning was Harriet Tooke, a neighbour of Ducker's in Clarke's yard. After she had told the inquest that she knew both Tye and Ducker, the widowed Mrs Tooke went on: 'I heard the town clock strike six, and that is how I speak to the time. I knew Tye's voice very well, and I heard him talking to Ducker .... The voices were very loud, but I could not distinguish what they said. I swear positively that the voices were those of the deceased and Ducker .... I saw Ducker on Monday afternoon and he had no marks or scars about his face then ....'

At 10 a.m. on Thursday the inquest reconvened at the Corn Hall instead of at the Angel Hotel, the former having more room to accommodate the large number of spectators it was expected would attend the hearing. Ducker arrived from the police station looking pale after his overnight stay.

Police Sergeant Taylor, recalled to the makeshift witness-box, told the inquest of having examined Tye's soaked and muddied clothing, and of his finds when the day before he had searched Ducker's room: 'The mud, weeds, and dirt on the stockings are of the same description as those found on the clothes of the deceased. The weed is what is called duck-weed. There was the same offensive smell as upon the clothes of the deceased ....' Taylor illustrated his rudimentary forensic evidence with three samples of the duck-weed for the jury to examine.

William Lucas, the constable who had also been on duty on Monday night, was the next to testify. He described first going to Ducker's address on Tuesday evening and retrieving the trousers from under the armchair cushion, and then later finding Tye's body in the stream. Lucas said that, when found, '... the body was stiff and swollen and when first taken from the water a great deal of blood came from the mouth and nose. The right eye was much swollen and very red. The hands and face were covered with mud .... I could distinguish the features but the mud was smeared all over.'

The police contribution to the hearing ended with PC Henry Cattermull's telling of the finding of Tye's handcuffs and staff.

Smelling-salts were produced by some of the ladies present when Dr Haward told of his post-mortem findings and of Ducker's injuries. The post-mortem examination of PC Tye had been more revealing after Haward's preliminary examination had shown little external injury.

'There was a contusion on the forehead over the left eyebrow ...,' he began; '... on dissecting the scalp the veins were found much congested, as also those of the neck. On examining the skull cap the veins and sinuses were filled with dark venous blood, otherwise the brain appeared healthy. I examined the internal surface of the skull, especially that part under the place where the blows had been received, but could discover no fracture. On examining the chest the lungs were congested .... The stomach contained a small portion of food with mud and water. From my examination I am of opinion that the deceased died *from asphyxia, caused by immersion in the water. The contusion on the forehead was sufficient to have caused insensibility.*'

In reply to the coroner, Dr Haward said that the blow to the forehead had been inflicted while Tye was alive and that it was possible, although unlikely, that it had been delivered by a fist.

Haward referred to the 'few notes' he said he had made when telling of Ducker's injuries: 'I examined his face, and found both eyelids much swollen, and of a dark, livid colour. The nose was scratched in several places, and there was a wound on the left cheek. On examining the scalp, I found the hair matted together on the left parietal bone. On removing the hair from this, I discovered a scalp wound one and a half inches in length, extending down to the periosteum ....'

The doctor dismissed Ducker's explanation as to how the injuries had arisen, and in reply to a juryman's question said that, 'The injuries, in my opinion, were all received at one time in some recent, severe struggle.'

After Mr Seaman Garrard, a surgeon who had assisted at Tye's post-mortem, had confirmed Haward's findings, there seemed little doubt as to what had taken place between Tye and Ducker during their early morning confrontation two days previously.

There followed a succession of witnesses all of whom were neighbours of Ducker. It was a unique situation for most of them: for unsophisticated, mainly illiterate countryfolk, to be thrust unexpectedly into the limelight before their friends and neighbours was an unnerving experience, one that nearly all of them were to undergo twice more, before the town's magistrates and at the assizes in Ipswich. For those not required to give evidence, the hearings provided an entertaining diversion from the routine of their daily lives.

Spectators craned forward, anxious not to miss a word, as Elizabeth Sawyer, the widowed mother of a 14-year-old daughter, told Mr Gross that she lived in Clarke's yard, four doors away from Ducker's house. She had risen early on the morning of Tye's death and had '... heard a scuffle at the top of the yard, it was about six ... after the noise of the scuffle had ceased, I heard a man coming down the yard. I cannot say whose footsteps they were, but I have heard this man walk [indicating Ducker], and I thought it was him ....' Mrs Sawyer added that she had in fact heard the footsteps of two people, one of whom '... walked heavier than the other'. Soon afterwards, she '... heard a shriek as if they were struggling in the direction of the bottom of the yard, and I heard a man's voice ....'

'Can you swear whose voice it was?' asked Mr Gross.

'No, sir, not at all ...,' the witness replied. Despite this, her evidence hammered another circumstantial nail into Ducker's coffin.

Fanny Sawyer, well scrubbed and wearing a clean pinafore, followed her mother into the witness box. Although not knowing how old she was or understanding the significance of taking the oath, Fanny nevertheless told the inquest hearing that on Tuesday morning, when calling on Ducker with some cooked bullock's feet, she had seen him cleaning a spot of blood from his waistcoat, and he had told her that his eye had been blackened when he had been cutting hay. In reply to a doubting juror, Fanny said, 'I am quite sure it was blood I saw upon his waistcoat ....' She then identified a waistcoat when it was shown to her in court.

Ducker became agitated as Hannah Tooke described the clothes she had seen him wearing on Tuesday morning, and then in the afternoon after he had apparently changed. His discomfiture increased when she also told the hearing: 'I am able to speak so positively to the prisoner because I saw him come home three mornings last week, Thursday, Friday and Saturday. I had often seen him go out early in the morning, before daybreak.' At the end of this damning testimony Ducker complained to the coroner, 'She will swear to anything ....'

Worse was to follow. After lunch Harriet Warne, who lived with her father in Clarke's yard and who worked at the stackyard with Ducker, told the inquest that, at work on Monday afternoon, 'He had on a pair of drabbett trousers and a drabbett waistcoat. He had no coat on.'

'Had he any bruises or marks about his face on Monday?' asked Mr Gross.

'No, sir,' Harriet replied.

'What clothes had he on on Tuesday?' the coroner enquired.

'He was dressed the same as he is now,' was the reply.

'Did you notice anything particular about his face?'

'He had a black eye and other marks about his face on Tuesday morning ....' Harriet ended by identifying clothes, including a pair of drabbett trousers, as those Ducker had been wearing.

One of the last witnesses to testify was Charles Todd, a painter who lived in Rectory Lane less than a hundred yards from where PC Tye's body was found. He said that at about six o'clock on Tuesday morning, as he was about to get up, he had heard 'two groans'.

'Was it quite close to the house?' asked Mr Gross.

'It appeared to sound close, but I cannot tell how near it was,' Todd replied.

Before reading over the testimony and summing up, the coroner asked Ducker if he wished to make a statement under oath. Ducker gave it a few moments' thought before telling him, 'I leave it to the gentlemen.'

After pointing out that murder is seldom witnessed, Mr Gross went on to tell the jury that an accumulation of circumstantial evidence could nevertheless have much the same impact as direct evidence: '... if the general tenor of the evidence points out to you that the prisoner Ducker, on the morning of the 25th inst was present in company somewhere or other with the deceased, and it is clear to you he was afterwards in the osier [willow] ground with the unfortunate deceased, and that a struggle ensued between them, and that a blow was struck by the prisoner, which struck the unfortunate man into the water, that evidence alone would be sufficient to justify you in finding a verdict of wilful murder, if you are persuaded that the prisoner Ducker entered into the conflict knowing the deceased to be a policeman in his uniform ....'

This direction left the jury little choice. After a short retirement they returned to announce to the crowded room a verdict of 'wilful murder against John Ducker'. The accused, looking ahead grim-faced, then listened as the coroner committed him to stand trial at the next assizes. Watched by a large crowd, Ducker was escorted back to the police station. The next day he was to make his first appearance before a specially convened bench of magistrates as a preliminary to his being committed for trial.

Meanwhile in his Halesworth police station cell Ducker contemplated a bleak future. The case against him was formidable and his principal hope lay in the absence of direct evidence.

Later on the Wednesday evening Dr Haward was summoned to the police station. Anticipating either a prisoner or policeman in need of examination and treatment, he was surprised to find Captain Hatton, the chief constable, and Mr Read, the prosecuting solicitor, awaiting him. Read said that Ducker wanted to speak to Haward about the case and had agreed that the solicitor should be present.

'The prisoner spoke to me,' Haward later testified. 'He said he wished to speak the truth to me for it could do no harm. He said, "It was old Ben Warne." He asked me, "Had I seen the policeman?" and he said, "I'll be damned if I have not done for him. I mean the sweep. He married the girl Chilvers who gave evidence today".'

This clumsy attempt by Ducker at accusing one of his neighbours of killing Tye does not appear to have been given much credence by the authorities, although Ben Warne's grandson and his wife, Stephen and Emily Warne, were later arrested on suspicion of having been accessories after the fact of Tye's murder. The case against the couple was later dropped.

The legal proceedings continued on Friday 28 November

1862, when at midday four magistrates, Messrs A.R. Johnson, J.W. Brooke and T. Rant and the Reverend W.C. Edgell as chairman, filed into the courtroom set up in the Angel Hotel. Ducker, who had spent another night in the police station, was brought into court handcuffed to PC Lucas. He listened without apparent emotion as the charge was formally read out – 'That he feloniously and wilfully, and of his malice aforethought, did kill and murder one Ebenezer Tye, on 25th November, at Halesworth.'

During the two days of the committal proceedings the evidence heard was largely a repeat of that given at the inquest.

Sergeant Taylor told the court that, apart from the truss of hay found in Ducker's storage house, he had found other pieces of hay in his living-accommodation, examples that matched some obtained from the stackyard where he worked.

'Pray ain't you ashamed of yourself? Where wor you to see me? You said you never opened the window. How could you see me in the dark? You could not see; I should be ashamed to say so.' This outburst by Ducker was directed at Hannah Tooke after she had again told of having looked out of her window on Tuesday morning, after having seen him on other mornings returning home laden with wood. She then identified the coat she said he had been wearing.

The Sawyers, mother and daughter, and Drs Haward and Garrard testified without interruption or challenge by Ducker. Not so Harriet Warne. During her examination by the prosecuting solicitor, Mr Read, she identified the waistcoat she said Ducker had been wearing on the Tuesday. This was too much for the prisoner.

'Had not I this same waistcoat on on Monday?' he asked her.

'No,' she replied.

'I had my best slop on and you could not see it …,' he insisted.

When Harriet told the court that, '…Ducker generally calls me up when I go with him [to work] but he did not do that [Tuesday] morning,' the man in the dock disagreed: 'I called you, and your mother said she would send you,' he told her.

'If you did call, I didn't hear you,' the witness replied.

After Harriet Warne had marked her cross on the copperplate-written deposition, the hearing was adjourned until the following Wednesday. Ducker stepped from the dock to be replaced by Stephen and Emily Warne. Captain Hatton stated that a recently washed shirt belonging to Ducker had been found in their house on the morning of Tye's death, whereupon the couple were remanded in custody until the following Wednesday.

As the courtroom emptied and the crowd in the hotel courtyard dispersed, many people hurried to the railway station in the hope of seeing Ducker arrive to board the train for Ipswich. They were disappointed, as he was to remain at Halesworth police station until the resumed hearing. Meanwhile preparations were being made for the funeral of Police Constable Tye the following afternoon.

It was a melancholy affair attended by Tye's service colleagues and watched by silent townsfolk. Tye's father collapsed as his son was lowered into the ground, and was helped from the cemetery as the mourners dispersed.

Judging from his appearance, John Ducker's physical condition had deteriorated during the few days separating the court hearings. When he reappeared before the magistrates on Wednesday 3 December, he looked thinner, his former jauntiness had disappeared and his face was pale and haggard, despite the fading black eyes.

The courtroom was again packed; those unable to gain entry thronged the corridors and courtyard of the Angel Hotel, keen to learn even at second hand what was going on within. Two additional magistrates, the Reverend H. Owen and Mr. H.A.S. Bence, were sitting; Mr Read again prosecuted, but despite the efforts of Ducker's family to obtain the services of a solicitor, he was still unrepresented.

As at the first hearing, much of the evidence was a repeat of that given at the inquest, but this time it was frequently interrupted by questions from the bench and by Ducker's arguing with a witness.

The proceedings opened dramatically, with Superintendent Gobbett entering the witness-box to tell the court that early on the previous Sunday morning Ducker, after asking to see him, had requested him to write a letter on his behalf to his daughter. He had afterwards alleged to Gobbett that on the evening before Tye died, Ben Warne, the sweep, had borrowed his old clothes, returning only the waistcoat the next morning after he had gone to work.

Ducker had again spoken to Gobbett later on Sunday morning, this time to tell him that on the Monday afternoon he had seen a man in Clarke's yard with 'a long dark coat on', carrying a truss of hay which he had thrown down upon seeing Ducker. Ducker told the policeman that he had decided at the time to '... take this into my old house and keep it until I heard of an owner for it'. It seemed that with these unlikely stories Ducker had been preparing the ground for his defence.

Police Sergeant Taylor entered the witness-box for a third time to say that two days before the resumed hearing he had again been dragging the stream and had there found an old battered glengarry, similar to one he had previously seen the prisoner wearing. Hannah Tooke was recalled and to Ducker's disgust confirmed that she too had often seen him wearing such a cap, including early on the morning Tye died. Ducker disputed this, saying that he had left the cap at work on Monday and had retrieved it later the next morning.

'It is no use to ask her anything. If you speak to her fair, she will swear to anything,' he ended dismissively. This remark amused the spectators, some of whom even clapped, indicating perhaps some measure of agreement with the prisoner's sentiments.

Harriet Warne said that she had seen Ducker wearing the glengarry at work on the Monday, but the following day he was wearing a wide-awake hat, one she said she had never seen him wearing previously at work.

Asked by the clerk if he had any questions to put to the witness, Ducker replied resignedly, 'No, it is no use; she will say anything.'

The Warne family were to figure prominently in the prosecution case. Harriet's grandfather, old Ben Warne, followed her into the witness-box. He said he had gone into his son Stephen's house in Clarke's yard at eight o'clock on the Tuesday morning and had there found Ducker examining his eye in a looking-glass; this caused further merriment among the spectators.

'Jack, you have got a rum one,' he had remarked to Ducker, who he said had replied, 'Yes, it is, I have had a scurry along with the policeman.'

At this Ducker erupted: 'No, no!' he shouted at the witness, who remained unperturbed: 'You did, John. I stand here, between God and man, and I o'nt swear to lie for none on ye. You said, "It was a rum one".'

Stephen's brother, Ben Warne the younger, entered the courtroom dressed in his sooty working clothes. 'I am a chimney sweep, and live in Clarke's yard,' he stated before emphatically denying ever having borrowed any clothes from Ducker, so repudiating the statement the latter had made to Superintendent Gobbett.

There followed a minor sensation as Stephen and Emily Warne were brought into court to hear Captain Hatton say that, as he had no evidence to offer against them, they should be discharged and examined as prosecution witnesses. This was agreed to by the magistrates, whereupon a much-relieved

Stephen Warne immediately prepared to testify. Both he and his wife said that Ducker had called at their home on the Tuesday with a shirt which he asked to be washed.

Ducker was not having this: 'Didn't your wife ask me for my shirt – didn't she come and ax me and said, "Ar'n't you going to have your shirt washed this week, because you hadn't one last week?" ' he demanded.

Stephen Warne replied with equal force. 'That is a lie. I have told the truth, and I will tell the truth.'

'It ain't the truth,' Ducker persisted.

Warne went on to tell the court that on the day before Tye's death Ducker had confided in him and his wife that he proposed stealing some wood from a local brickyard. When he had warned him that he would probably be caught in the attempt, Ducker had said that he '... would not be stopped by one policeman – if there were only one, he would go "life for life".'

'He said he would go "life for life", were those the words he used?' asked the Reverend Owen from the bench.

'Yes, sir,' replied Warne.

Emily Warne largely corroborated her husband's statements, although she was more specific about Ducker's reply when her husband had cautioned him against stealing the wood. According to Emily, Ducker had said, 'If Mr Tye or any other policeman come after me, I have got something in my old house that will satisfy him.' When asked by the Reverend Owen, she was unable to clarify what Ducker had meant by 'satisfy him'.

Emily Warne's evidence ended with an acerbic exchange with the man in the dock.

'Didn't you come here to speak the truth?' he asked her.

'Yes,' she replied.

'Well, didn't you come and ax would I have a shirt washed?' Ducker went on.

'You liar, you. I never said such a word.'

'You did.'

Emily was beside herself with anger; 'You wicked old story-teller you – why don't you hold your tongue?'

'What did your husband say to me when I came on Sunday night?' asked Ducker.

'My husband never spoke to you.'

'Didn't he say, "There's plenty of wood at Mr Smith's brickyard?" '

'No, you old villain – you liar – how could you say so?'

To the disappointment of the spectators, who were hugely enjoying the exchanges, the Reverend Owen intervened at this point to tell Mrs Warne that she must answer questions put to her in 'a proper way'. Soon afterwards the prosecution case ended.

Those who hurried again from the court to the railway station, hoping to catch a last glimpse of Ducker, were this time rewarded by seeing him arrive handcuffed to his escort in time to catch the 4.25 p.m. train to Ipswich; there he was to await his trial in the town gaol.

A public meeting in Halesworth in mid-December 1862 typified the attitude and concern of the Victorian middle classes to crime. The recent events in Halesworth had focused local attention on the town's inadequate police resources; it emerged during the debate that two years before police manpower in the Halesworth area had been redistributed, leaving only a superintendent and a lone constable to serve 2,500 people. At the end of the meeting a resolution moved by Archdeacon Hankinson, 'That in the opinion of this meeting an increase in the permanent staff of the police force stationed in this town is absolutely necessary for the efficient protection of the person and property of the inhabitants', was passed and later communicated to the county's magistrates and the chief constable.

It is doubtful whether additional police resources, had they been available, would have helped PC Tye. He was a brave but impetuous young man who had tended to act without thought of the possible consequences to himself.

The day before John Ducker's trial opened at the Suffolk Lent Assizes sitting at Bury St Edmunds, Lord Chief Justice Erle, who was to preside, sentenced two women shoplifters to six months imprisonment with hard labour for stealing two cambric pocket handkerchiefs. If news of this filtered through to Ducker before he also stood before Lord Erle on the morning of Thursday 26 March 1863, it could have done little to inspire confidence in the outcome of his own trial. Nonetheless there was a noticeable improvement in his appearance since his committal: gone were the bruises and other injuries, and his face had regained some of its colour. He gazed enquiringly about the crowded courtroom, occasionally nodding at and giving a fleeting smile of recognition to one or two of his former neighbours. A small number of these had journeyed to Bury to witness the trial.

The counsel for the prosecution, Mr Bulwer, stood up to make his opening address at 9.25 a.m. Assisting him was his junior, Mr Smith, while Ducker's defence relied upon the advocatory skill of Mr Phear. The Crown was to call seventeen witnesses, eleven of whom were known to the accused. He had formally pleaded 'not guilty' to the charge and now sat in the dock, looking relaxed.

Mr Bulwer detailed the circumstances of the case and outlined to the jury the evidence he proposed to call. His was a lucid exposition, couched in plain language; from telling of when Tye had last been seen alive until the moment he called his first witness, the prosecuting advocate drew a vivid mental picture of the sequence of events culminating in the policeman's death: '... the case on the part of the prosecution was simply this,' he concluded, 'that the policeman early in the morning saw the prisoner in the act of taking this hay, and followed him, and endeavoured to apprehend him ... seeing him [Ducker] disappear at the bottom of the yard, Tye ... went after him. That Ducker made his escape over the brook ... followed by the policeman. That Ducker made a violent resistance, and in that resistance the policeman met his death ....'

Police Sergeant Daniel Taylor replied to a question put to him in cross-examination by Mr Phear: 'It was between six and seven when I went with Lucas to Ducker's house .... I don't think it was half-past seven when I returned with Gobbett. The prisoner was seated in the chair before the fire both times. I said when I saw the two black eyes, "Ducker, how did you get them?" ....'

Taylor's evidence had largely been a repeat of that given at the inquest and committal hearing. The policeman exuded an air of dependability, and so far he had not been shaken during cross-examination.

In reply to another question from Mr Phear, Taylor told him: 'Stephen Warne and his wife were arrested in the middle of the night on Tuesday; taken out of their beds .... They were detained at the station that night, but not kept there afterwards. Warne and his wife were taken away the next day in the afternoon ....'

'On what charge were they taken?' asked the defence advocate.

'As accessories after the fact.'

'What fact?'

'The murder.'

'What murder?'

'The murder of Ebenezer Tye ....'

'I ask you whether they were before the justices on the Friday?' said Mr Phear.

'No, I don't think they were; they were remanded to the adjourned inquiry. They were before the magistrates on December 3rd and were discharged ...,' Taylor replied.

Mr Phear was to allude again to the statements made to the

police by Stephen and Emily Warne, hinting that the couple might have been coerced into turning Queen's Evidence on the promise that the charge against them would be dropped.

PCs Lucas and Cattermull repeated their earlier evidence. Both had been involved in the search for Tye and had been present when his body had been found. Furthermore, Lucas had been suspicious when questioning Ducker earlier, more so when he found the damp and muddy trousers under his armchair cushion.

Ducker glowered at Hannah Tooke when she stated that early on Tuesday morning she had seen him: 'He was going towards Chediston Street. He had on drabbett trousers, fustian coat and a Scotch cap .... After about ten minutes, I heard some scuffling and talking very loud .... The voices I heard with the scuffle were those of Ebenezer Tye and Ducker ....'

Under cross-examination Hannah admitted not having mentioned the Scotch cap until the second day of the committal hearing.

'Did you tell Harriet Warne to swear to the cap to make your story come true?' asked Mr Phear.

'No,' Hannah replied.

'Did you not go to the second meeting of the justices for the purpose of swearing about the cap?' Mr Phear next enquired.

'Yes,' she admitted.

'Did not Harriet Warne go for the same purpose?'

'Yes,'

'Well, then, did you not, before that, tell Harriet Warne to swear to the cap, because it would make your story come true?' Mr Phear repeated.

'No, I did not,' insisted Hannah.

'Did not Hannah Tooke say to you, "You must swear to the cap because it will make my story come right?" ' Mr Phear was now questioning Harriet Warne about the Scotch cap.

'Yes,' she replied.

Ducker looked round the court in satisfaction at her answer.

Mr Bulwer was on his feet. 'Was that not after you had given your evidence before the magistrates about the cap?' he put to Harriet.

'Yes, but she did not know that,' the witness replied.

'Will you tell us how it happened?' Mr Bulwer pressed.

'It was outside the court. Some people were standing about. She did not know I had been swearing to the cap. She said, "Do you swear to that there cap, and make my tale come right?" I had sworn to it then.'

'What answer did you make?'

'I said nothing.'

Counsel between them had confused the issue and cast doubt on the veracity of both Hannah Tooke and Harriet Warne; which of them was lying? The answer may not have been critical to the outcome, but it could raise doubt in the jury's mind as to the reliability of the evidence, and that had to be in Ducker's favour.

Elizabeth Sawyer and Charles Todd both said that they had heard sounds of anguish soon after six o'clock on the Tuesday morning: 'I heard a man shriek as if in distress ...,' said the former, while Todd '... distinctly heard two groans ....' It was further confirmation that something very unpleasant had taken place not far from Clarke's yard.

Superintendent Gobbett was another witness who repeated the evidence he had given previously respecting Ducker's allegation that Ben Warne, the sweep, was the guilty party. This, together with the prisoner's statement to Haward, contradicted his later assertion that he had killed Tye in self-defence. If such had been the case, why try to cast blame elsewhere?

Ben Warne, the sweep, emphatically denied Ducker's allegations and was not cross-examined. His father, Ben the elder, was confused under cross-examination, and there was laughter among the public at his discomfiture. After administering a mild rebuke, Lord Erle himself gave up trying to make sense of the old man's replies.

Not so Stephen and Emily Warne; both stood up well to Mr Phear's questioning after repeating what they had told the magistrates. Stephen requoted Ducker's remark that, if he met a policeman, '... he would go life for life with him.' Asked in cross-examination, 'In that conversation at your house on the Sunday, was Tye's name mentioned?', Stephen Warne replied, 'No. Ducker said he would not be stopped by one policeman: he would go life for life with him.' Warne went on to tell the court that the case against him and his wife had been discharged *after* they had given their evidence at the lower court. This was untrue; whether deliberately so mattered not to Mr Phear, who was continuing to suggest that the couple had testified after the police had promised not to pursue enquiries into their alleged involvement. Ducker's advocate further tried to discredit Stephen Warne by extracting an admission from him that he had served three prison terms, albeit for minor offences.

Mr Phear scored a minor success a few minutes later when cross-examining Emily Warne about her and her husband's conversation with Ducker.

'Will you swear that Tye's name was mentioned?' he asked her.

'Yes. I'll take my oath on it,' Emily replied.

'Then if he said anything about Tye, your husband must have heard it?' Mr Phear continued.

'Of course he did,' Emily confirmed.

'Was anything said about "life for life"?'

'No, he did not tell me so; he said that he had got something in his old house that would satisfy him.'

'If he said anything about "life for life", must you not have heard it?'

Emily was no match for Mr Phear's circumlocution: 'Oh no, my head might have been turned another way,' she replied lamely.

It was astute questioning by Ducker's counsel, but Lord Erle put it in perspective when, during his summing-up, he pointed out that people such as the Warnes '... did not impress the exact words said at any time upon their minds, and a verbal difference between the account given by the two witnesses of the same conversation might reasonably be expected ....'

The final prosecution witness, Frederick Haward, after starting to detail his gruesome post-mortem findings, was interrupted by the lord chief justice, who told him, 'I don't know that we want the anatomical details if you will give the effect of your examination.'

Haward took the hint and thereafter omitted from his testimony the more lurid details. He told briefly of the examination he had carried out on Tye, and also of Ducker's injuries, reaffirming the conclusions he had reached previously. The defence tried to establish that, after Tye had fallen to the ground as a result of the non-fatal blow, his heavy and restrictive uniform would have made it difficult for him to regain his feet.

'I certainly think it might ...,' agreed Dr Haward, although when asked by Mr Bulwer during re-examination, 'Assuming him [Tye] to have been sensible to the last, was there anything in the stock or the neck to prevent him rising from the horizontal position?', he replied somewhat ambiguously, 'I certainly think there would not be anything sufficient to prevent him from getting up.'

Mr Phear obtained a useful admission from Haward regarding Ducker's injuries, one that he would later rely upon during his closing speech.

'Were any of the wounds on the prisoner the result of violent blows?' he asked.

'Yes, the wound on the head was from a very violent blow.'

'With a policeman's staff, do you think?' ventured Mr Phear.

'I should think so,' agreed Haward.

Soon afterward the prosecution case ended.

'A life had been lost, and the question was whether another life should be taken to pay the penalty.' It was just after four o'clock in the afternoon when Mr Phear opened his final plea to the jury. Forbidden by law to testify on his own behalf, Ducker listened attentively to the man charged with saving him from the gallows. The defence advocate continued by decrying the prosecution case, 'circumstance upon circumstance', as he referred to it. He went on to explore every avenue. The witness Elizabeth Sawyer's testimony '... was in itself nothing but conclusions from circumstances ...'. Hannah Tooke's evidence '... had grown considerably since her first examination ...'. He spoke scathingly of her having told Harriet Warne to swear to the Scotch cap '... to make her own tale come true ...'.

The Warne family was Mr Phear's next target. After speaking derisively of old Ben Warne, saying that he had '... fenced with him in the witness-box till everybody in the court must have been weary ...', he moved on to Stephen Warne and his wife, who, he said, '... were taken into custody and cross-questioned by the policeman, and at last, to escape from custody they told the story in which they so much contradicted each other ...', which, counsel maintained, '... was not worthy of any credence ...'.

This was not the defending advocate's only disparaging reference to the police. He had earlier told the jury, '... that it was to be a policeman's death that was to be accounted for .... It would be in a certain sense highly dishonourable to them as a body if they could not avenge their comrade's fall, and it could easily be believed that the police would be in such a case induced to show an activity which perhaps they would hardly show in other cases ....' Again, when referring to the testimony of PC Lucas, Mr Phear said that he '... thought the jury would agree with him in particular that the witness Lucas, especially in his cross-examination, showed a zeal on behalf of the prosecution, which ought not to have been exhibited ...'.

After censoring the witnesses' evidence, Mr Phear questioned the legal propriety of the Crown's case. Speaking of the hay, which it seemed had been the cause of Tye's stopping Ducker originally, he submitted that, as there was no evidence of the hay's having been lost, equally there could be no evidence of the prisoner's having stolen it. It followed, said Mr Phear, that Tye had no power to arrest Ducker and that any attempt to do so was an assault that the accused had been entitled to resist.

Mr Phear asked the jury that, knowing '... the prisoner at the bar was an unarmed man, that he was an old man, that he was a lame man, was he the person to attack the armed man, the young man, the strong man, the policeman?' He suggested that the reverse was the case, that, for reasons he omitted to mention, Tye had carried out an unprovoked attack on Ducker, who had struck him in self-defence, partially stunning him and knocking him into the water. If the jury came to the conclusion that Ducker had used excessive force, at worst he would be guilty only of manslaughter, submitted Mr Phear. It was a competent speech during which Ducker's counsel made some interesting submissions and introduced a number of speculative theories. It remained to be seen what the lord chief justice would make of it in his summing-up.

After interpreting the law relating to the murder of law officers, Lord Erle referred to the identification evidence of Hannah Tooke and Harriet Warne. Earlier in the day both women had undergone an unpleasant experience in the witness-box, so undoubtedly they were relieved when the judge told the court that he thought '... it clear from the evidence of Hannah Tooke, who was a neighbour of the prisoner's, and acquainted with his dress, that he passed up the yard at twenty minutes before six. She also knew Tye, and she swore that she heard an altercation and scuffling at the top of the court shortly after ... *he could not say that he saw anything in the demeanour of that witness to lead him to doubt the truth of what she was saying.* The same with the girl Harriet Warne ... *he must confess that he could not see anything to lead him to suppose that she tried to swear to anything which was not true when she spoke of the clothes he usually wore* ...' (author's italics).

As these words were uttered, Ducker slowly shook his head in disbelief. Worse was to follow. After agreeing with Mr Phear's submission that Tye would had to have had '... fair reason to believe that a felony had been, or was in the course of being committed' before arresting Ducker, His Lordship continued: 'There was no reasonable ground to suppose that he [Tye] took any steps to apprehend the prisoner till he saw occasion ...' – thus demolishing in a few words another bastion of the defence case.

Even the testimony of Stephen and Emily Warne, arguably the weakest link in the chain of prosecution evidence, was not discounted by the judge. After saying that Ducker's words on the Sunday '... appeared to him to have considerable bearing upon that part of the case ...', he added a cautionary note: '... the jury would also weigh the fact that the evidence was given at a time when the witnesses were in custody of the police; and it would be for them to say whether that story was fabricated by Warne to gain his freedom ...'.

Lord Erle saved his most devastating comment until near the end of his discourse: 'It appeared that the evidence was strong that the death was caused by the prisoner being in the water with Tye and using violence ....' Those words surely ended any hope Ducker might have had of being acquitted of murdering PC Tye.

After listening to the lord chief justice for three-quarters of an hour, the jury were absent for about the same length of time considering their verdict before returning to announce that they found the prisoner, John Ducker, guilty of murder. Ducker remained silent and stood white-faced and tight-lipped as Lord Erle formally sentenced him to death. He stepped down from the dock as the crowd spilled out into the street after the ten-hour trial. Many of them surged round the horse-drawn prison van hoping to catch sight of the condemned man as he was taken back to Ipswich gaol.

Nineteen days were to elapse following his conviction before John Ducker paid the supreme penalty. He was not devoid of hope during this time, as there was a sizeable number of people, including three of the jurors, who, although agreeing with the verdict, considered that the sentence should be commuted. A petition urging a reprieve was submitted by Ducker's supporters to the secretary of state, accompanied by a letter written by his solicitor Mr Salmon. The letter referred to the doubtful evidence given by some of the less reputable witnesses and more pertinently submitted that the crime had been unpremeditated and that it had not been proved that Ducker was, or had been, engaged upon a felonious enterprise.

Four days before the execution, all hope of a reprieve was finally dispelled in a reply received by Mr Salmon from the Home Office:

> ... after a careful consideration of the evidence, and of the observations of the Lord Chief Justice on the case, and on the arguments pressed by Mr Phear and yourself, Sir George Grey can see no reason to doubt the correctness of the verdict; and he regrets that he does not feel justified in advising that the law should not take its course.
>
> I am Sir, your obedient servant
> H. Waddington

With hope now gone, preparations went ahead for the execution. Accommodation was arranged in Ipswich for the deputy sheriff, Mr Crabtree of Halesworth, and the acting deputy sheriff, Mr Sparke of Bury St Edmunds, while construction of the scaffold proceeded on the lodge roof of the County Hall.

Ducker stayed composed while awaiting the end. He was said to have eaten and slept well, and like others in a similar situation he found solace in religion. Apart from the prison chaplain, the Reverend J. Daniel, he was ministered to by the Reverend Bolton from Ipswich and by Archdeacon Hankinson, who journeyed from Halesworth to visit him.

It was perhaps as a result of these ministrations that on the eve of his execution Ducker confessed to killing Tye, although still insisting that his death had been unintentional. In a final abjuration he also absolved Ben Warne, the sweep, from involvement in the crime: 'I am sorry for what I have said to set that about him …. I could not go out of this world with this false charge against him …. I admit the justice of my sentence' – so the Reverend Daniel reported Ducker as having told him.

Shortly before eight o'clock the next morning, John Ducker, dressed as he had been at his trial, with the addition of an old felt hat, was helped up the narrow staircase to the lodge roof. Seconds later, in front of 4,000 people who had been assembling in Orchard Street for over three hours, executioner Calcroft launched the 63-year-old man into eternity.

The murder of PC Tye gradually faded from peoples' memories. He is now remembered as being one of the two Suffolk police officers to have been slain in the line of duty (the other being PC James McFudden, shot at Gisleham near Lowestoft in 1844). Apart from his crime, John Ducker goes down in history as the last person to have been publicly executed in Suffolk.

The crime was almost universally condemned, as by the 1860s police officers were becoming accepted and were more highly regarded than hitherto. Nevertheless some people considered that the situation which had culminated in the death of PC Tye should never have arisen, and that the policeman had contributed to his own violent end by precipitously arresting Ducker. A letter published in the *Ipswich Journal* four days after the execution said that, '… this sad event should be a warning to Constables and others against excess of zeal in discharge of their duty … we may lament the consequences which ensued from an attempt which was (in this case) unnecessary!

Over the years an increasing number of policemen countrywide have seen fit to disregard the advice and sentiments expressed in the letter.

– 5 –
Baby Death at Girton
1908

To most people Girton, Cambridge, is synonymous with the women's college which forms part of the university. Less well known is the village of Girton which lies a couple of miles north-west of the city.

In 1908 Girton was a hamlet of a few dozen souls, among whom was Jesse Kidman, a former farm labourer, now paralysed, who lived in a three-bedroomed cottage with his wife Harriet and their seven children. Poverty was no stranger to the Kidmans: since Jesse had become immobile, his wife had assumed the role of main bread-winner, working locally as a housemaid for a Miss Fanny Whybrow. Her wages were supplemented by those of her 14-year-old son Harry, a van boy employed by Girton laundry, and his older brother George, who was a milkman.

In February 1908 a family crisis arose. Alice, a married daughter, was deserted by her husband Frank, who took with him their son, leaving his wife with their two daughters, Alice Kathleen, who was seven months, and three-year-old Harriet Victoria. Frank East went home to his parents, while Alice and the two babies descended on her family, thereby adding three more to the already overcrowded and under-financed household. Frank had promised to pay his wife 12 shillings a week to help support her and the girls, but after his contributing only 13 shillings over two weeks, the payments ceased.

For 24-year-old Alice East the year dragged by. There could scarcely have been a greater contrast than between her life, spent toiling as a laundress while trying to care for her two young children, and that of the undergraduates only half a mile away in the long, red-brick building on Huntingdon Road. At the end of each week she handed her wages to her mother as her contribution towards the family budget, knowing that even with this money it was a struggle for the family to maintain even the minimum subsistence level. She was aware that her presence, together with her two daughters, exacerbated the situation, evidenced by the increasing tension within the family. Quarrels among the older members, together with the squabbling children, encouraged Alice in the belief that resentment was directed especially towards her and her two little girls.

Thursday 19 November 1908 started no differently from any other day in the Kidman household. After rising, Harriet and her elder sons lifted her husband out of bed and, after dressing him, carried him downstairs to a chair by the window; there he would remain until his wife returned in the evening. Meanwhile a squabble had broken out between Harriet's granddaughter, 4-year-old Harriet East, and her own youngest child. After a brief scrimmage accompanied by a few sharp words between Alice East and her mother, the bickering fizzled out. After the children had separated, Alice was heard to remark, 'I wish I could follow my children to the grave' – a comment that her mother was later to recall.

Alice East had been more than usually depressed recently, after hearing from Frank that he intended sending their son back to live with her and her family. Although her mother and older brothers tried to reassure her that they would cope, Alice knew that even one extra mouth to feed would add considerably to the family's burden. Mrs Kidman was worried by the concern of her daughter. Alice's husband had first deserted her for six months soon after they were married, and after regularly ill-treating her he had since left on several occasions. Each time she had returned to her family feeling an increased sense of failure and in an agony of recrimination over her continuing dependence on her kinsfolk. Furthermore, Mrs Kidman, aware of the mental instability in her husband's family (Jesse had spent time in an asylum, while others had died within asylum walls), was deeply concerned lest Alice had inherited this trait.

After the younger children had eventually departed for the little village schoolhouse, Harriet and her older boys, apart from George who was on his milk round, set off for work. Alice, pleading that she felt unwell and would not be going to work that day, stayed at home with her father and daughters.

It was luck that prevented the tragedy that occurred later that morning from being greater. Fourteen-year-old Harry Kidman had rushed off to work without the sandwiches and the slice of cake his mother had prepared for his midday break. He remembered them later, and soon after ten o'clock, as they were passing his home in the laundry van, he asked the driver, John

Naylor, to stop and wait a few moments while he called in to collect his food.

Harry was the second Kidman brother to call back that morning; his older brother George, the milkman, had preceded him a few minutes earlier. After exchanging a brief word with his sister and seeing her two children in the kitchen, George had left. Everything had appeared normal.

Not so when his younger brother arrived soon afterwards. Alice by now was standing inside the back door leading into the garden; of her children there was no sign. In response to Harry's greeting she replied, 'I have made an end of the children, and I am going myself.' She started to run down the garden path towards the cesspool at the bottom. Harry immediately chased after his sister, soon catching up with her and grabbing her by the wrist; at the same time he shouted to John Naylor for assistance. Naylor ran up and restrained the struggling woman while Harry had a quick glance into the cesspool. There to his horror he saw his niece Alice Kathleen floating on her back in the water. Without further hesitation the boy raced to Miss Whybrow's house to fetch his mother.

By this time the commotion had attracted others to the garden, including George, who had still been within earshot. He ran back to the house where Naylor, who was still holding on to Alice, gasped out to him what had happened. Leaving Alice temporarily in the care of neighbours, both young men ran to the cesspool, arriving in time to rescue Harriet East.

Another at the scene was Seymour Smith, a farm foreman. He dashed to the cesspool, where he saw baby Alice Kathleen floating face downwards on the surface. Lifting her out, he carried her along the garden and lay her down beside her sister outside the back door.

Harriet Kidman, out of breath after running from Fanny Whybrow's house, arrived with Fanny close behind. Both women hastened to where the two little girls were lying. Alice Kathleen was dead, but her sister was alive, so Fanny carried her indoors to wash off the dirt and effluent that clung to her. Harriet Kidman meanwhile turned to John Naylor, who was again holding her daughter, and persuaded him to release her so that she could go indoors. She then asked one of the neighbours to fetch Dr Lock from Huntingdon Road. By the time Lock arrived, at 11.15 a.m., the local policeman, Constable Arthur North, was on the scene, and the excitement in the Kidmans' garden had died down.

Alice East soon admitted to both Fanny Whybrow and PC North what she had done. In reply to Fanny's question, 'Why?', she replied, 'I thought they were a lot of trouble, and if I got rid of them they would be out of the way', while in answer to a like query from the policeman she told him, 'I can never do anything right here.'

North did not stay long but cycled to the county police station to report what had happened. Soon afterwards a Police Constable Evans went to Girton; there he saw Alice Kathleen's body lying on a table in the front room of the Kidmans' house, with her sobbing mother sitting nearby. The policeman told Mrs East that he would have to detain her pending the arrival of the deputy chief constable, and then wrote down a statement she dictated in which she described the events that had led to her despairing act.

Forty minutes later, at 12.30 p.m. PC Evans was still with Mrs East when the deputy chief constable arrived and announced to her, 'I am Superintendent Webb, and I shall arrest you on a charge of murdering your child, Alice Kathleen, by drowning it in a cesspool at Girton today.'

The unhappy woman, scarcely aware of what was happening, made no reply to the charge and did not object to accompanying PC Evans to the police station. That evening she appeared before Professor Courtney Kenny at the Shire Hall on the murder charge. After listening to the formal evidence of arrest given by Superintendent Webb, Professor Kenny remanded Alice to appear before the Cambridgeshire divisional bench two days later.

On Friday morning, while Alice languished in gaol, Dr Lock carried out a post-mortem examination on her baby. This confirmed that death had been caused by suffocation due to drowning. Meanwhile the police were making ready a room in the village school, warning witnesses and completing preparations for the inquest to be held that evening.

A feature of many nineteenth- and early twentieth-century murder cases was the promptness with which the judicial proceedings were instituted. Nowadays months may elapse before an accused person is brought to trial; in former days, after an arrest had been made, the inquest and preliminary lower court hearings leading to the committal for trial were often completed within a few weeks.

The Girton case was no exception. On Friday evening, less than thirty-six hours after baby Alice Kathleen had died, an inquest into her death was opened at the village school house before Mr A.J. Lyon, the county coroner. News of the case had not extended much beyond the village, so only a few of the Kidmans' neighbours were present.

The first to testify was Alice's mother. After giving evidence of identification, Harriet Kidman described the scene that had greeted her in her garden the previous morning after she had run back from Fanny Whybrow's: 'She [Alice Kathleen] was lying in the garden with the other little girl, Harriet Victoria, who was lying on her face, breathing. Alice Kathleen was dead.'

'What was their condition? Were they dirty?' asked Mr Lyon.

'Yes, sir,' replied Harriet.

'Did they appear as though they had been in the cesspool?'

'Yes, sir.'

Fourteen-year-old Harry Kidman told how he had restrained his sister and his van-driver mate John Naylor described how, with the help of Harry's older brother George, he had rescued Harriet Victoria from the cesspool.

PC Arthur North, the local constable, said he had gone into the front room of the Kidmans' cottage and there seen Alice East crying.

'Did you say anything to her?' asked the coroner.

'Yes, sir. I asked her why she had drowned her child.'

'What did she say?' continued Mr Lyon.

' "Because I can never do anything right here," ' the policeman replied. This answer was similar to that which had been given by Alice to Fanny Whybrow, and left little doubt as to her motive.

Fanny Whybrow had long had reservations about Alice's mental state. Asked by the coroner for her opinion as to Alice's intellect, Fanny told him, 'I should not consider her quite right. I frequently told her mother that' – a view shared by others, judging from the nods of affirmation and the muttered words of agreement among the villagers present.

The last witness was Dr Lock, who said that, having been called at about 11.15 on Thursday morning, he had examined the body of Alice Kathleen East but had found no external marks of violence. On the morning of the inquest Lock had carried out his post-mortem examination and had found '... the lungs and stomach choked up with debris and dirty water. Otherwise the child was perfectly healthy and well kept and nourished. The cause of death was suffocation from drowning, and the water and debris was such as would be found in the cesspool.'

Summing up, Mr Lyon displayed to the jury the compassion he felt for Alice: '... It was a very sad affair,' he said. 'There was no doubt in his mind, and he did not expect there would be in theirs, that the mind of Alice East was quite unhinged, but that was not the question that concerned them that day. All they had to do that day was to find in what manner the child came to its death. If they found as he expected they would, a verdict of wilful murder against the woman, when the time came for her to be tried at the Assizes, the people who represented her would be able to set up a plea of insanity ....'

The jury had no doubt; after a short retirement the foreman, Mr T.H.M. Searle, conscious that all eyes were on him, cleared his throat and read carefully from a piece of paper: 'The child met her death by suffocation from drowning, by being placed in the cesspool by its mother.' Mr Lyon thanked him and then announced that Alice East would be committed for trial at the next assizes.

The following morning, Saturday 21 November, Mrs East made her first appearance before the full complement of magistrates. A tiny figure, she was dwarfed by the wardress who stood with her in the dock. After listening to the charge being read out by the magistrates' clerk, she was overcome with emotion and sobbed uncontrollably as Superintendent Webb gave evidence of arrest. The bench, including the chairman, Colonel H.W. Hurrell, Alderman W.P. Spalding, mayor of Cambridge, and Colonel Caldwell, master of Corpus Christi College, anxious not to prolong her ordeal at the preliminary hearing, then remanded the accused woman back into custody until the following Saturday.

The magistrates were unable to extend the same consideration to Alice at the remand hearing a week later. By then news of the tragedy had spread, and from early morning a crowd had begun to gather outside the Shire Hall in Cambridge hoping to gain admittance to the hearing, or at least catch a glimpse of Alice as she arrived. Colonel Hurrell again presided as chairman and, together with his colleagues and others in court, watched in silence as Mrs East with her wardress escort stepped into the dock. As before she was sobbing bitterly into her small, flower-patterned handkerchief.

The prosecution was in the hands of Mr D.H. Prynne from the office of the director of public prosecutions, and as he stood up to open the case it seemed inconceivable that his words could lead eventually to the execution of the diminutive, unhappy figure in the dock. Mr Prynne described the situation prevailing at Jesse Kidman's home on the morning of Thursday 19 November 1908. As he told of events leading up to the death of Alice Kathleen East, the stress and reality of living impoverished in a small, overcrowded house were for the first time revealed to many of those crowded into the public seats.

'There were in that family already eight or nine, and it was hardly necessary to say what a burden on the family were those three extra mouths to feed ...,' said Mr Prynne. The prospect of having yet another child join the household, if Frank East carried out his threat to send his son to live with Alice, '... depressed her very much, and she had expressed her regret to her people ...,' the prosecutor continued.

Coming to the fateful morning, Mr Prynne told of Harry Kidman's unexpected arrival home, where he was told by his sister, 'Harry, I have made an end of the children, and am going myself', before she had run off down the garden towards the cesspool, her young brother in pursuit. 'The very prompt action of this small boy had undoubtedly saved one of those small children, and it had probably saved the prisoner's life as well ...,' said Mr Prynne.

Dr Lyonel John Lock was the first witness called. Before telling of his post-mortem findings, he told the court of Alice East's distracted response when he had spoken to her after his arrival on the Thursday morning.

'What's up, Mrs East?' he had asked.

'I have drowned my two children in a hole at the bottom of the garden. I thought that was the best way out of the trouble .... My husband's left me these nine months, and my brothers are complaining of having to keep the family of four of us, and they are quite right too, for how can they do it on their small earnings, and I thought it the best way out of the trouble.'

This was the reason that Alice maintained throughout had prompted her deed. Not for her a motive of greed, jealousy or revenge but the final, despairing act of a woman who believed that by ending her own life and that of her daughters she would make easier the lives of those of her family remaining. If such a concept exists, her action could be regarded as a selfless murder.

Alice's brothers George and Harry told of their unforgettable experiences that morning. Both had helped save lives – George that of Harriet East, whom he had assisted in rescuing from the cesspool, Harry that of his older sister. The court listened in admiration as the under-sized 14-year-old described how he had clung to his struggling sister near the cesspool, shouting at her, 'You ain't going, Alice.'

After John Naylor, the laundry-van driver, and the farm foreman Seymour Smith had given evidence of their contribution to the morning's events, it was the turn of Harriet Kidman. Dressed in her Sunday best, the hard-working, rosy-cheeked countrywoman gazed compassionately across at her weeping daughter before telling the magistrates of life at home since Alice had returned to live there with her two little girls.

'Now I want to know: have you at any time while your daughter has been living with you, heard her threaten these children?' Mr Prynne addressed his question slowly and clearly at the witness, who replied without hesitation, 'No, sir.'

'Has she been apparently from what you have seen, a kind mother to them?'

'Yes, sir.'

The next three questions and their replies caused a stir in the court.

'Have you ever had occasion to say anything to her about beating the children?' asked Mr Prynne.

'Well, sir,' replied Harriet carefully, 'I have told her at times not to do it too much.'

'Did she used to hit the children?' pressed Mr Prynne.

'Yes, sir, sometimes,' Mrs Kidman admitted.

'Was that only when she was in a temper?'

'Yes, sir.'

The prosecutor did not pursue the matter; he perhaps realized that Harriet Kidman, a God-fearing woman, conscious that she was testifying on oath, was being scrupulously honest about family situations that were not uncommon and which had been symptomatic rather than the cause of the events that had ensued.

The answers to Mr Prynne's final questions probably reflected more accurately the explanation for Alice's behaviour on Thursday 19 November.

'I think, Mrs Kidman, that there were nine of your family without the prisoner and her children?'

'Yes, sir.'

'Living in a cottage with three bedrooms, I think?'

'Yes, sir.'

Harriet Kidman had borne up stoically in the witness-box, but a sudden renewed outburst of sobbing from the dock proved too much, and she collapsed in a faint. As officials carried her from the courtroom, the tangible feeling of sympathy that was already extended to Alice East embraced also her mother.

Harriet's employer, Fanny Jane Whybrow, expressed doubts as to the soundness of Alice East's mind.

'You have known the prisoner for some time?' enquired Mr Prynne.

'Oh, yes,' replied Miss Whybrow.

'And fairly frequently had conversations with her?' continued the prosecutor.

'Yes. I did not think she was quite *compos*, and had frequently told her mother so' – a response that echoed the thoughts in many people's minds.

The last two witnesses were Police Constable Evans and the deputy chief constable, Superintendent Webb. Evans told the court of the situation upon his arrival at the Kidmans' house on the Thursday morning, and of his subsequent interview with Alice East, who he said was 'rather excited'. In the statement she had dictated, Alice had told him of the marital troubles that had led to her and her daughters returning to live with her parents, and the problems this had caused. 'I did it to drown my troubles,' she had told Evans.

Finally Superintendent Webb stepped into the witness-box and, after telling of his arrest of the prisoner on a charge of murdering her child, was asked by Mr Prynne, 'When you were at the house of Mr Kidman's, were you shown the cesspool in the garden?'

'I was.'

'About how far would it be from the house?'

'It is thirty yards from the back door,' Webb replied.

'Was the cesspool about five feet seven inches in depth?'

'Yes, sir. I measured it,' said Webb.

'How much water was there in it?' next asked Mr Prynne.

'Two feet eight inches, the drainage from a farm adjoining.'

'Did you see by the side of the cesspool a large door?'

'Yes, a large heavy door which was used as a cover.'

'What was the diameter of the opening?'

'Twenty-two inches.'

The prosecutor moved to a different line of questioning. 'Have you known this prisoner's family long?' he asked.

'Yes, I have known them for nine years,' replied the superintendent.

'Do you know of your own knowledge that the prisoner's father was in the asylum?'

'Yes, he was in eighteen months,' the policeman confirmed.

'And you have also ascertained that other members of the family have been in the asylum?'

'The father's sister died in an asylum. One other member of the family has died in an asylum, and I know others have been insane,' Webb agreed.

This ended the prosecution case; it remained only for the chairman of the magistrates formally to commit Alice for trial at the next county assizes, just under seven weeks away.

Among Alice's visitors was Mr Barnard, the barrister who was to defend her. He had decided that, in view of her family's history of mental instability, he would dwell particularly on her state of mind and would appeal also to the jury's emotions to elicit maximum sympathy for his client.

The Girton murder was listed for hearing on the first day of the Cambridgeshire winter assizes, which opened in the Shire Hall, Cambridge, on Thursday 14 January 1908. It was preceded by two other cases, those of a bicycle thief and a housebreaker, who were sentenced respectively to three years penal servitude and nine months hard labour. The public seats were crammed with spectators, Cambridge citizens sitting alongside the prisoner's friends and neighbours from Girton.

Presiding over the trial was the Honourable John Compton Lawrence; a vastly experienced judge, he had been on the bench for eighteen years and was noted not only for his shrewdness but for his dry sense of humour. Alongside him sat the high sheriff, Mr J.A. Fielden, Mr J. Percy Maule, the under-sheriff, and the judge's chaplain. When Mr Beaumont Morice, who with Mr W.R. Briggs appeared for the prosecution, stood up to make his opening speech, it was to introduce evidence that was largely a repeat of that given at the committal hearing.

During cross-examination Mr Barnard had little difficulty in eliciting from witnesses confirmation of the emotional and family turmoil to which his client had been subjected.

'Is your father capable of work?' he asked Alice's brother George Kidman.

'No, sir,' he replied.

'Having these two children and your sister was a considerable strain on the family?' Mr Barnard continued.

'Yes, sir, it was,' George concurred.

'Did you know your sister was unhappy at being a drag on the family?'

'Yes, sir.'

Similarly when Harriet Kidman gave evidence: after stating that her daughter had been a kind mother, she agreed that Alice had been troubled at having to rely on her parents for her subsistence. Under cross-examination Harriet confirmed that her husband had spent some time in Fulbourne asylum and that her sister-in-law had died in a similar institution. The prisoner had also confided in Dr Lock and PC Evans that it was her husband's desertion and her feelings of guilt at her dependence upon her family that had precipitated her action.

When it was the turn of the defence, Dr Gray, the prison medical officer, told the jury that he had seen Alice soon after she had first arrived at the prison. She was '... quite quiet and calm and was in no ways depressed. She did not appear to realize the seriousness of her position,' he said. Indeed, although Alice had been distressed at the magistrates' court, this appeared to have been a belated reaction of guilt rather than an awareness of her own perilous situation. She remained composed during her trial, but observers felt that, even with her life in the balance, she did not fully appreciate the implications of the proceedings going on around her.

The jury listened as Mr Barnard made an impassioned plea on her behalf: '... many women had stood in the dock through the cruelty or neglect of man,' he said, 'but one had never heard a sadder story unfolded than the one that he had made before them that day.'

Whether or not as the result of Mr Barnard's rhetoric, the jury appeared to have little doubt. After retiring briefly, they returned with a verdict that Alice East was guilty but not responsible for her act according to law at the time the act was committed. As Sir John Lawrence ordered that Alice East be kept in custody as a criminal lunatic until His Majesty's pleasure should be known, few there were who disagreed with either verdict or sentence for a crime that under different circumstances would have attracted nationwide opprobrium. Both were just and appropriate according to the penal and social climate prevailing in 1908.

For Mrs East, woefully inadequate and totally ill-prepared to cope with her husband's ill-treatment and desertion, it had been a logical step for her to return to the haven of her parents' home. Her arrival with her children added to the Kidmans' already heavy burden; her awareness of this in all likelihood prompted Alice to end her own life and that of her two little girls. Ironically due largely to the efforts of her brothers her attempt only partly succeeded. Alice was later to follow the path of others in her family to an asylum where she would ponder on the perverse fate that had ordained that not only should she be deprived of her husband and children, but also of the family to whom she had turned for salvation.

– 6 –
No Fury Like a Man Scorned
1913

Tuesday 10 July 1913 opened unexceptionally at Lowestoft police court. There were only four cases on the list that day. Ernest William Tooke, a baker, applied for £1.10s costs against his aptly named employee William Bunn, for having left his employment without notice. Tooke's application was followed by one for a separation order against 45-year-old Louis Thain, described as an artist, by his wife Fanny Chadd Thain, who was three years younger than her husband. This promised to be a lengthier hearing than usual as there were nine witnesses to be heard. Finally two labourers were to appear charged with having used obscene language at Suffolk Plain in Lowestoft.

The marriage of the Thains, on 20 March 1905, had been an ill-conceived union between two disparate individuals. The couple had first met in late 1904 when the well-to-do widow, Fanny, had become attracted to the impoverished Louis Thain. Upon learning that she was of independent means (although she would lose a third of her private income upon remarriage), lived in her own house and possessed a collection of valuable jewellery, Thain decided that marrying her was an attractive proposition, one that would enhance his social and financial standing. To encourage her to accept his proposal of marriage, he passed himself off as a wealthy fish-merchant and told her that he would compensate her for her depleted income by contributing a regular weekly sum towards the housekeeping expenses.

After their marriage in Lowestoft registry office, Thain initially paid his wife the money he had promised, but his benevolence lasted only four months. In July the payments ceased; thereafter it was he who was to rely upon his wife's generosity.

For the next 3½ years there were apparently only occasional skirmishes between the couple: providing Fanny Thain was prepared to support her husband and subsidise his drinking, he stayed reasonably content. For her part she had married hastily and had belatedly realized that her husband much preferred bar-room conviviality to working for a living and supporting a wife, albeit one who was able financially to cushion the effects of his indolence and drinking.

The situation deteriorated in October 1908. After Thain had promised her that he would help with its management, his wife financed the leasing of a modest hotel at Hillington, near Kings Lynn. Thain soon discovered that the long hours and hard work required to ensure the success of such an enterprise were not to his liking, and took to riding and driving about the Norfolk countryside, leaving his wife to run the hotel. For nearly two years she struggled to make it a success, but the establishment lost money, and the effort demanded took its toll, resulting in her having to enter hospital for nine weeks in the summer of 1910.

Upon leaving hospital she was appalled to find that during her absence the entire stock of hotel bed-linen had disappeared. The effect on her of this latest disaster can be imagined, but she appears not to have taken any steps to recover the missing linen, perhaps suspecting her husband's involvement in its disappearance and loyally not wishing to implicate him. Nevertheless, the event precipitated the closure of the hotel, with a loss to herself of £300.

In October 1910 the couple moved back into rented accommodation at 12 Cleveland Road, Lowestoft. Although the tenancy was in Louis Thain's name, he immediately reverted to his familiar habits, leaving his wife to pay the rent and rates. It may have been a sense of inadequacy, or perhaps resentment at being financially dependent upon Fanny and thus obligated towards her, but for whatever reason from the day of their return to Lowestoft Thain's behaviour worsened. During the ensuing months he regularly arrived home at night drunk to berate and assault his wife. He frequently dragged her out of bed during the early hours of the morning to subject her to verbal and physical abuse. On one occasion he hurled a piece of wood at her, fortunately missing his target.

After her enduring over two years of such treatment, matters came to a head in January 1913 when Mrs Thain took in an ailing, musically inclined gentleman boarder. From the time of Frederick William Davis's arrival, Thain objected to his presence. His animosity towards the travelling salesman manifested itself in various ways, from subtly insinuating that Davis and Mrs Thain were having a clandestine affaire, to bellowing his objections and hammering on the floor of his room, as downstairs Davis attempted to play the piano. The first time this happened Davis had the temerity to complain to Mrs Thain. She in turn spoke to her husband, who became incensed and threatened them both with violence.

On Easter Sunday another furious confrontation took place when Thain asked for money to enable him to spend the day with some friends on the Broads. When his wife refused, Thain took hold of a dinner knife and threatened to kill her, then threw a vase which hit Fanny, causing her to fall and injure herself. That night she moved out of the matrimonial bedroom, never to return.

Although the severing of connubial relations provided some relief when Louis Thain returned home at night drunk, it did not help his wife at other times. The violence, abuse and humiliation peaked in the summer of 1913. So frightened was Fanny on one occasion that she took an unloaded revolver that had belonged to her late husband and threatened Louis that she would 'do for herself and him'. Terrified, he fled into an empty room, locked himself in, broke a window and shouted to passers-by that his wife intended to murder him.

For the boarder Frederick Davis it was all too much; as a result of regularly being under physical intimidation from Thain, his nerves were in a parlous state. Between going about his daily business and trying to relax at the piano, he had been subjected to threats and abuse and had witnessed the frequent maltreatment of Mrs Thain. As he testified later, 'I thought the man was insane ....' When he left his lodgings, in June, Davis was unaware that he had certainly not seen the last of Louis Thain.

Since the arrival of the Thains at 12 Cleveland Road, local officers had frequently been called to disturbances at the address. The day following Davis's departure they returned. It was Louis Thain who this time instigated their intervention when in the morning he called at the police station to report the incident concerning the revolver. He later told his wife where he had been, whereupon she lost no time in going to the station, where she poured out again her account of the treatment regularly meted out to her by her husband.

Events hereafter verged on the farcical. That evening Police Sergeant Borley went to 12 Cleveland Road, where Mrs Thain and two friends, a Mrs Bewley and her daughter Ethel, were having tea. Soon after Borley's arrival Thain returned home from a drinking session, carrying with him a bottle of beer. Almost immediately an argument broke out between him and the women, after Mrs Thain had asked Ethel to pull down the window blind. Thain immediately released it, whereupon his wife relowered it. This infuriated her husband who, ignoring Sergeant Borley, who had been watching the proceedings with interest, hurled the bottle of beer into the street. This prompted the policeman's intervention, and he succeeded in quietening Thain and persuading him reluctantly to leave the house.

Soon after departing, Louis Thain – for the second time that day – met Superintendent Page. Page was purposely in the vicinity of Cleveland Road – evidence of the concern the local police felt over the warring couple. He agreed to return home with Thain. Soon after their arrival the latter provoked another argument with his wife and her friends. This one culminated in his throwing a second bottle of beer, this time at his wife, who was struck a glancing blow on the cheek, fortunately without causing serious harm. Again Thain was unwillingly prevailed upon to leave the premises, this time to seek a bed elsewhere. Meanwhile Mrs Bewley and Ethel agreed to remain overnight with Mrs Thain.

Three days later she left Cleveland Road to stay with the Bewleys in Denmark Road. The move coincided with an incident that probably did more to alienate her from her husband than had his former unacceptable behaviour. A few days before, she had lent Louis a diamond ring; her mortification upon discovering a pawn ticket for the ring was matched by the humilation she felt at having to pay £6.8s. to redeem it.

Fanny determined then to rid herself of her incorrigible spouse. A few days after moving to Denmark Road her resolve was stiffened when she discovered that another ring was missing. She immediately informed the police, and Sergeant Borley succeeded in retrieving it from Thain before he had disposed of it.

The following day Mrs Thain visited the offices of Watson & Everitt (solicitors), to institute proceedings for a judicial separation, on the grounds of her husband's persistent cruelty. During the next 2½ weeks, Thain continually pestered his wife at her temporary address. He would arrive unannounced by day or night to prowl around the house in Denmark Road, rattling the windows and trying to force his way in. The three women lived in a constant state of apprehension, and it came as a profound relief when the day of the hearing, Thursday 3 July, arrived. To their chagrin the case was not dealt with immediately but was adjourned for a week to enable witnesses to attend.

Negotiations had meanwhile been going on between the

respective lawyers to try to reach a mutually satisfactory settlement. Fanny Thain did not desire a payment order to be made against her husband; she merely wished to be rid of him. Upon this understanding Thain signed an agreement prepared by his solicitors. However, a day or two before the adjourned hearing they sent the documents to Watson & Everitt and informed them that they were no longer prepared to represent Thain, who, it seemed, was acting as perversely as ever.

In Lowestoft there was nothing to indicate that Thursday 10 July 1913 was anything other than a normal day. The harbour was alive with activity while nearby trams rattled over the swing bridge bringing workers and shoppers into the town.

'All stand please.' Promptly at ten o'clock on that Thursday morning the usher in Lowestoft police court called upon those present to rise as F.T. Dewey Esq., mayor and chairman of the borough bench, led in the other magistrates. Of Louis Thain there was no sign; this was of no immediate consequence, as there were several preliminary matters to be attended to, and Mrs Thain's application was not expected to be heard for another hour.

Accompanied by Mrs Bewley and her daughter, Fanny Thain had arrived at court a few minutes before ten o'clock, as had Superintendent Page, Sergeant Borley and half a dozen other witnesses. Most of these were Cleveland Road neighbours of the Thains, but among them was their former boarder, Frederick Davis.

Louis Thain was roaming about Lowestoft, fortifying himself at local public houses for what he knew lay ahead. For him it had been a busy morning. After rising early he had left his lodgings at 35 Old Nelson Street and prevailed upon an acquaintance to drive him in his motor car along the coast to Great Yarmouth. There he had gone to the post office and, calling himself William Machin, with an address at 'Offendene', Christchurch Road, Norwich, had at 8.35 a.m. obtained a gun licence. Before leaving the post office he sent a telegram to his wife, purportedly from her brother George, asking her to meet him at 10 a.m. at Lowestoft railway station. Finally, before leaving Yarmouth, Thain visited a gunsmith and, producing the false gun licence, bought a revolver and some ammunition.

Mrs Thain had received the telegram before leaving for court; then, on learning that her case was not to be heard immediately, she hurried to the railway station. She was perhaps fortunate in that the train from Yarmouth had arrived punctually and her husband, having decided not to wait, had disappeared into the town.

At 11 a.m., with Mr Tooke and Mr Bunn departing happily together, their differences amicably resolved, the usher called again for Louis Thain. There was still no answer, so after some discussion between the magistrates, the court clerk and Mrs Thain's solicitor, Mr Nelson Wyles, it was decided to proceed with the application in the defendant's absence.

Mr Wyles recalled some of the incidents that had taken place during the Thains' turbulent marriage before calling upon his client to enlarge upon her life with Louis Thain. Those present in court listened as she described simply and undramatically the unkindness to which she had been subjected. As she ended, the clerk of the court asked, 'Was it solely in consequence of Thain's treatment that caused you to leave Cleveland Road?'

'Yes, I was afraid. I was all alone.'

'Were you afraid at that time that he was going to do you harm?'

'Yes,' Fanny replied quietly.

Superintendent John Page was the next to enter the witness-box. He told of Louis Thain's visiting him in June and reporting the incident with the revolver, and of the developments that evening. When speaking of the bottle of beer thrown by Thain which had struck his wife on her cheek, Page said that he thought it was 'the most cowardly action he had seen'.

At that moment Thain, nattily dressed in a light-coloured suit and straw hat, arrived at court. Pushing past the court usher, he paused as the magistrates' clerk asked him why he had not been present when the case had been called. He had been in Yarmouth trying to get extra witnesses, he explained, adding that he was sorry. This prompted a sharp retort from the clerk, who told him that it was not sorrow that was wanted but an explanation.

Thain resentfully sat down to listen to Mrs Bewley tell first of the episode with the window blind and then corroborate Superintendent Page's evidence. She continued by describing Thain's visits and behaviour since his wife had been staying at her address. While Mrs Bewley was testifying, Thain was reproved several times for interrupting, but perversely he declined to ask any questions when she had finished.

Sergeant Borley was the last witness to give evidence in support of Mrs Thain. Having been more closely involved in the various Cleveland Road incidents, Borley was able to enlarge on Page's testimony. He spoke of events he had witnessed, and told of recovering Mrs Thain's diamond ring from her husband, who, the policeman said, after having admitted taking it, maintained that his intention had been to return it. Finally Borley described the damage Thain was alleged to have caused at the Bewleys' home in Denmark Road.

A succession of witnesses were then called by Thain to rebut the earlier testimony. Not all of them lived up to his expectations. While most of them agreed that to the best of their knowledge the couple had been happily married, one witness confined herself to speaking well of Mrs Thain, while Mrs Ellen Young complained that, having known them only as neighbours, she was annoyed with Louis Thain for having brought her to court as a witness. George Sheppard, Mrs Thain's brother-in-law, expressed mystification as to why he also had been called; after pointing out that Mrs Thain had never complained to him of cruel treatment, he turned to Thain as he left the witness-box and told him, 'You ought to have more work to do' – a remark that caused a ripple of laughter in the court.

Alice Rose, a former servant of Mrs Thain, surprised everybody by saying that her mistress had been a secret whisky-drinker, a theme continued by Thain when he followed her into the witness-box. He said that his wife's drinking had been the source of their marital problems. He alluded also to an alleged intrigue between his wife and Frederick Davis but then denied the suggestion under cross-examination. Louis Thain made a poor showing in the witness-box; his assertion that he had frequently slept on the kitchen floor to keep out of the way of his wife was received with scepticism by the bench. 'Surely there was a more comfortable place in the house?' he was asked. When Nelson Wyles cross-examined him, he admitted that he was not a teetotaller but denied ever having been the worse for drink, a statement that brought forth an audible gasp of disbelief from his wife.

'Have you done any work prior to October [1912]?' asked Mr Wyles.

Thain bristled at the question. 'What has that to do with you?' he demanded. 'I'm not going to fill your mouth, or fill your ears.' Ordered by the magistrates' clerk to answer the question properly, he muttered that he had worked in the market and had paid his wife £60 in the year.

In view of Thain's allegations regarding his wife's drinking and association with Frederick Davis, Mr Wyles offered to call the former boarder and a public house landlord to refute the suggestions. The magistrates, however, decided that this was unnecessary.

After the bench had retired to make their decision, those in court barely had time to sit down before being summoned to their feet again as the magistrates returned. Mr Dewing announced that they had decided to grant Mrs Thain's application and award costs of £2.3.0d against her husband.

While Fanny Thain and her friends broke into relieved smiles and conversation, and Nelson Wyles publicly thanked Superintendent Page for the protection that had been afforded his client, Thain slipped out of the courtroom, a strange expression on his face.

Thain's departure did not go unnoticed. Frederick Davis, who had long thought him mad, had seen the look on his face as he left the building, and felt distinctly uneasy. So as not to alarm Mrs Thain or the Bewley women, he did not mention his apprehension to them but decided to accompany them back to Denmark Road.

After thanking Mr Wyles and the two policemen, the quartet left the court building and walked along Clapham Road in the direction of Tonning Street. Thain had meanwhile hurried along London Road into Denmark Road, from which a passageway connected with Tonning Street. It was at the Tonning Street end of Junction Passage that Thain loitered. Soon afterwards, seeing his wife and her companions enter the street, he stepped back further into the passage.

What happened next took everyone by surprise. As they entered Junction Passage, Mrs Thain and the others were confronted by her husband, who shouted, 'Ah, now I've got you all together.' With pounding hearts the small party attempted to pass the wildly excited man, but they were transfixed as he produced a revolver. Before any of them could move, he pointed the gun at Mrs Bewley and fired. Either his aim was erratic or his hand was unsteady, for the bullet missed its target and hit instead Ethel Bewley, who fell to the ground with a wound to the back of her head. Shouting to Mrs Thain to run, Davis simultaneously propelled her along the passage towards Denmark Road. His effort was to no avail: Thain caught up with them and fired again. His wife screamed and fell down as the bullet struck her in the face, miraculously without killing her. Thinking now only of self-preservation, Davis fled along the alleyway, with Thain in pursuit and still firing.

At 2 Junction Passage, Arthur Myhill, a 48-year-old fisherman, and his wife Elizabeth were finishing their dinner when three or four loud reports outside their front door caused them to hurry out to investigate. At a glance the couple took in the woman, blood on her face, lying against their fence, and a man running down the passage towards Denmark Road. Without hesitating, Myhill sprinted after the fleeing man, leaving his wife to help the injured woman indoors.

By now other people were emerging from nearby shops and houses, and passers-by, drawn by the commotion, were hastening towards the scene. Henry Pemberton, a greengrocer, had come out of his shop in time to witness the entire sequence of events. After the women had been shot, Pemberton had shouted for someone to fetch a doctor before setting out after Arthur Myhill in his pursuit of Thain. In Denmark Road, Pemberton later told the coroner, 'I saw Myhill catch hold of Thain's shoulder, and a slight scuffle took place between them. I saw Thain raise his arm and shoot at Myhill. Myhill ran a few yards and fell to the pavement bleeding. I then stopped running ....' Myhill was mortally wounded and lay dying on the pavement in a pool of blood.

The drama was approaching its climax. After shooting Myhill, Louis Thain, staring wildly round spotted a police constable a short distance away. Pemberton again: 'I saw Thain put the revolver to his head and fire, and he fell down in the gutter ....'

Police Constable Rowe, whom Thain had seen, ran up to where the two injured men lay bleeding; he was joined by Dr Augustus Marshall, who had been nearby. Myhill died seconds later but Thain was alive, so a passing cab was stopped and, accompanied by Dr Marshall, he was rushed to the town's hospital. A few minutes afterwards the police ambulance arrived at the scene and took PC Rowe, together with Arthur Myhill's body, to the mortuary.

Back in Junction Passage there was still plenty of activity. While some people soothed a distraught Mrs Bewley, others were tending her injured daughter. In No.2 Elizabeth Myhill was still looking after Mrs Thain, as yet unaware that their husbands had been in fatal confrontation.

Although Fanny Thain and Ethel Bewley had been gravely injured, both were to survive. Not so Louis Thain; after his arrival at the hospital he was hurried to the operating theatre where Drs Bell and Fardon worked feverishly to save him. Their joint efforts were unavailing; the self-inflicted injury was too gross, and Thain died at half-past three that afternoon.

No time was lost in opening an inquest into the deaths. That evening in the court building where earlier in the day one of the deceased had appeared, the coroner, Mr L.H. Vulliamy, opened the inquiry. Only evidence of identification by Superintendent Page and Myhill's widow was given at the initial hearing. Elizabeth Myhill was still in a state of shock following the afternoon's events, which for her had culminated in attending the mortuary to identify the body of the man with whom a couple of hours earlier she had been having dinner.

Two days after the shooting a melancholy ceremony took place in Lowestoft cemetery. With only the undertaker, the pall-bearers and the Reverend C.W.M. Cadman, a curate from nearby St Margaret's Church, in attendance, the body of Louis Thain was interred. The time of his burial was deliberately kept secret to prevent the attendance of what the local paper referred to as a 'large crowd of morbid people'.

The inquest which reconvened on Monday 14 July aroused considerable interest in the town. The courtroom was full of local people anxious to hear at first hand details of the tragic circumstances surrounding the deaths of two of their neighbours. Again absent were Mrs Thain and Ethel Bewley, both of whom were still in hospital.

Superintendent Page was the first witness. As he was recalling the events which had taken place in the magistrates' court on the previous Thursday morning, he was asked by the coroner, 'As to Thain's apparent mental condition – did he appear at the magisterial proceedings?'

'Yes' replied Page, 'he came into court an hour and a half late.'

'How did he strike you then as to his mental condition?'

'He was in a very excited state.'

'He was not drunk?' enquired the coroner.

'No: but I should say knowing him that he had had drink.'

The question of Thain's mental state was taken up by one of the jurors, who interrupted to ask, 'Can the superintendent say from what he saw of him at the police court and before, as to whether he was sane or insane?'

Page told him: 'Ever since the proceedings commenced he has been in an agitated state, and waxed himself up to such a degree that you could hardly consider him responsible .... There is no doubt he was agitated by the proceedings that his wife had taken.'

Before stepping down, Page revealed that two of Thain's brothers had also committed suicide.

Dressed in deep mourning, Arthur Myhill's widow excited the pity of all present as she relived the nightmarish happenings of the previous Thursday afternoon. After telling of the police ambulance's arriving to take Mrs Thain to hospital, she ended bleakly, 'I then enquired for my husband and was informed that he was dead.'

After Mrs Myhill had been assisted to a seat at the back of the court, Frederick Davis went into the witness-box, no doubt regretting that he had ever gone to live with the Thains. He told of the terrifying events that had occurred after he and his companions had left the police court, including his own narrow escape from injury when a shot passed through his coat.

'You say that Thain was aiming at Mrs Bewley when he struck Miss Bewley?' the coroner asked.

'That is my belief,' Davis replied.

'And in hitting Miss Bewley it was accidental?'

'I think so.'

Mr Vulliamy knowingly commented, 'Mrs Bewley had given evidence against Thain, and Miss Bewley did not,' thus pointing to the reason for the older woman's being targeted.

'That is so,' Davis agreed.

The coroner then produced a letter written by Thain in June, soon after Davis had left 12 Cleveland Road, in which he covertly threatened his former lodger or any of his friends with violence should they return to the address. The letter went on to suggest that Davis had caused trouble while staying with the Thains, a point Mr Vulliamy picked on – 'He seemed to have formed some idea that there was something reprehensible – that there was something between you and Mrs Thain,' he said to the witness.

'Evidently,' replied Davis, 'but there was no ground for it. I always treated his wife as a lady and she treated me as a gentleman.'

There the matter was allowed to rest.

After Henry Pemberton and Police Constable Rowe had told the inquest of the shootings and their immediate aftermath, it was the turn of the medical witnesses. Dr W.L. Bell, who had operated on Thain, was asked the cause of his death.

'A bullet wound on the right side of the head,' he replied.

'Did the bullet enter the brain?' asked the coroner.

'Yes.'

'And his case was quite hopeless?'

'Yes,' Bell confirmed.

Dr Marshall, who had tended Arthur Myhill at the scene and had later examined his body at the mortuary, said, 'He was shot into the lungs, which caused suffocation from extensive bleeding. There was a point of entry of the bullet, but no signs of exit.'

'Was he dead when you arrived?' the coroner asked.

'He gave two gasps when I got to him, and he was not really dead, although practically so,' the witness replied.

Before summing up, Mr Vulliamy produced another letter addressed to him and written by Thain prior to the police court hearing. After making some undisclosed allegations, Thain had given instructions as to the disposal of his property in the event of his death. The coroner said that from the fact that the letter had been addressed to Vulliamy and must have been written before the police court hearing, one could infer that Thain had intended to kill himself *before* the court proceedings. There was also mention of his wife's predeceasing him, from which the jury might further conclude, said Mr Vulliamy, that Thain might also have intended to shoot her.

In his summing-up the coroner pointed out that the testimony of Henry Pemberton left little doubt that Thain had deliberately shot Myhill; on the evidence, therefore, he thought a verdict of 'Wilful murder' against Louis Thain should be returned. He dwelt rather longer on Thain's own demise, although again the manner of his death was indisputable. The coroner confined himself principally to comments relating to Thain's mental state before and at the time he shot himself. He suggested that the deceased might have been contemplating suicide for some weeks, and certainly there was evidence pointing to the likelihood that he had decided to kill himself before he ever appeared in the police court.

Superintendent Page's reference to Thain's brothers having committed suicide might influence the jury when considering his mental condition, said Mr Vulliamy, adding that his mental state and his judgement had possibly been affected by his excessive alcohol-consumption. The summing-up ended with the coroner's reminding the jury that the law presumes a man to be of sound mind unless it be proved otherwise, and that in this case there was sufficient evidence to justify a verdict of *felo de se* – feloniously killing himself whilst of sound mind. The jury evidently agreed, for it took them only five minutes to decide that Thain had murdered Arthur Myhill and had then killed himself while being of sound mind.

The verdict was predictable, as there was no doubt as to how either man had met his death. The only relevant matter to be determined was Thain's state of mind when he had killed himself. Whether anyone can strictly be considered rational when committing such an act is debatable. The jury, however, confined within the parameter of the law and guided by Mr Vulliamy, had little option but to find that Thain had been in possession of his senses at the time. The question was, and remains, largely academic.

The day after the inquest, in pouring rain, the body of Arthur Myhill was laid to rest in Lowestoft cemetery, not far from where Louis Thain had been interred a few days earlier. The cortège wended its way past silent onlookers, and at the graveside mourners peered down through the rain splashing onto the pine lid of the coffin to read on a brass plate the simple inscription,

ARTHUR GEORGE MYHILL
Died July 10th 1913
Aged 47 years

Mr S.C. Rowe, a missionary at the Sailors' and Fishermen's Bethel, referred to the fact that Myhill had courageously met his death in trying to prevent further harm being caused to others. It was a fitting tribute to a brave but otherwise ordinary man.

– 7 –
A Family Dies in Cambridge
1913

Two letters, one addressed to Mr H. Saunders French, HM
coroner for Cambridge borough, the other to Mr Louis von
Glehn MA of King's College, heralded a tragedy in the
university town born of retribution and nurtured by despair and
the occult.

Both letters had been written by Albert Paule Schule, a teacher
of languages in Cambridge, and were delivered on the morning
of Saturday 5 April 1913. Their author's background was never
clearly established. He had been born in Hungary, and his real
name was believed to be Szeky; he had spent many years living
in Germany, but his claim to have been discharged from the
German Army at the end of the Franco-Prussian War (1871),
with the rank of captain (a title which henceforth he used), is
inconsistent with his stated age of fifty-six. It is believed that at
the time of his death he was nearer sixty-five.

By 1912 Captain Schule, his 34-year-old wife and their
children, Natalie, who was nine, and 6-year-old Albert, had
been living in Cambridge for over four years. They led a quiet
life and kept much to themselves; their one friend and
confidant, who had helped them out financially since their
arrival in the city, was Louis von Glehn.

Albert Schule had a deep-rooted belief in the occult. To a
lesser extent his wife shared his convictions – whether from her
own fundamental belief or in deference to her husband is not
known. Both, however, regularly consulted mediums and
fortune-tellers, crystal-gazed and were guided in their daily lives
by what they read in their horoscopes.

It was in the summer of 1912 that the cycle of events that was
to end in tragedy began. In June Mrs Schule discovered that she
was expecting her third child. Her announcement came at a bad
time for her husband, whose fortunes were at a low ebb. His
number of pupils had declined to such an extent that he was

finding it increasingly difficult to pay the substantial rent of the large house he and his family occupied. The expected infant would increase his financial burden, so the couple decided to move into smaller, less expensive accommodation. Three months later the family moved from Panton Street to a house in Regent Street, Cambridge. Here Schule continued giving language tuition, and although their prosperity did not markedly increase, he and his wife at least found it easier to manage.

Dr Graham, a medical practitioner in whom Albert Schule had confidence, was monitoring Mrs Schule's pregnancy. Graham, familiar as he was with the unconventional beliefs and philosophy of the Schules, was nonetheless concerned at Mrs Schule's conviction, following consultation with a fortune-teller, that she would die in childbirth and leave her husband to bring up their children unaided. Schule likewise was worried by his wife's feelings, but he refused to be reassured by the doctors, preferring, like her, to rely instead upon more esoteric opinion.

Towards the end of October 1912 Dr Graham arranged for Mrs Schule to visit Nurse Elizabeth Edwards, the midwife who was to attend her during her confinement. The nurse was nonplussed when during her visit Mrs Schule expressed the wish that her baby arrive before the end of the year, as 1913 was to be unlucky.

'A few days later I had an uncanny interview with Captain Schule,' said Nurse Edwards some time afterwards. 'I was taken into the drawing-room and introduced to him. I felt I did not like him. He came downstairs to see me off and was going on about chloroform ....'

Christmas 1912 was a sombre affair in the Schule household, overshadowed as it was by Captain and Mrs Schule's presentiment about the forthcoming birth, now only a few weeks away. Despite Dr Graham's repeated assurances, Schule was especially anxious, and his worries transmitted themselves to his family.

Dr Graham was due to attend a funeral on the morning of Wednesday 19 February 1913. Before then he visited Mrs Schule, who had gone into labour. After checking on her condition, he telephoned a colleague, Dr Searle, and asked him to deputize for him during his absence. Dr Searle agreed and went immediately to the house in Regent Street. He was greeted by Captain Schule, who told him that the crystal ball and his wife's horoscope both predicted that neither she nor the baby would survive. The doctor soon came to the conclusion that Schule was mad, and happily passed responsibility back to Graham when the latter returned from the funeral.

Searle's relief was to be short-lived. The following day Dr

Graham (perhaps not surprisingly) felt unwell and at 10 p.m. telephoned Searle again. After explaining the situation, he asked him to return to 82 Regent Street and see Mrs Schule through her confinement. Reluctantly Searle agreed.

His misgivings were soon confirmed: he found Mrs Schule exhausted and her physical condition deteriorating, while her husband's mental state seemed also to have worsened. When Schule said that his wife was dying, Dr Searle and Nurse Edwards, who was also in attendance, had to prevent him forcing his way into the bedroom. This incensed Schule, who threatened them both. The commotion had been heard by Mrs Schule, who, despite her condition, warned Searle and Nurse Edwards that, if provoked, her husband was capable of shooting them. In this volatile situation Searle decided that the assistance of another doctor was essential, so he dispatched a maid with a message for Dr Campbell, who arrived at midnight.

The two men conferred, and after being apprised of the situation, Campbell agreed that the condition of Mrs Schule was such that only a Caesarean section could save her life. The decision having been reached, immediate preparations were made for the operation. Mrs Schule unhesitatingly agreed to its being performed under anaesthetic. Not so Captain Schule. Searle and Campbell both tried to discuss their proposed action with the irrational husband, who, while accepting that surgery was imperative if his wife's life was to be saved, was strongly opposed to her being anaesthetized by chloroform, saying that it would destroy her astral body and her brain.

In the early days of the twentieth century chloroform was the most commonly used anaesthetic for producing deep unconsciousness. Although it was effective, its after-effects were unpleasant, and in 1913 there was no recognized antidote once it had been administered.

Dr Searle was experienced in anaesthetics and despite Schule's opposition he eventually succeeded in rendering Mrs Schule unconscious, while persuading her husband not to interfere. The two doctors and the nurse then applied their collective skills to saving the life of mother and child. For almost two hours they toiled, aware that elsewhere in the house Captain Schule was brooding over their activity.

Their efforts were only partially successful. At 2 a.m. on Friday 21 February Dr Searle had the unhappy task of telling Captain Schule that, although they believed his wife would survive, he and his colleagues had been unable to save the baby. Schule's reaction was less agitated than the doctor had anticipated.

Drs Searle and Campbell remained with their patient until 3 a.m., by which time she had awoken from the anaesthetic and was resting in bed. Alas, for Mrs Schule this situation was not to last.

After instructing Nurse Edwards that the patient should be kept warm and left quiet, the doctors departed. The nurse had tidied up the bedroom when Captain Schule suddenly burst in, ranting to the startled woman that his wife had been poisoned by the chloroform. She tried to pacify and reassure him, telling the deluded man that his wife needed complete peace and quiet if she was to recover. Schule's response was to stamp dementedly on the floor of the bedroom before rushing downstairs.

Minutes later he returned with a glass of water. His wife, by now awake, sipped a little. Schule then produced a tiny case. Nurse Edwards said later that, after rubbing some of the contents of the case onto his wife's face, he '... put something slily into her mouth, which she resented ... it may have been a little capsule or something of that sort'. Not content with having administered something unprescribed to his wife, Schule then removed some of the bedclothes and opened the windows, saying that the room was too hot. Nurse Edwards, now beside herself with anxiety for her patient's well-being, managed to prevent him from completely uncovering his wife.

By now Mrs Schule, fully aware of her husband's frenzied activity, was nearing the end of her long ordeal. About twenty minutes after Schule had given her something to swallow, she gave a final short gasp and died.

Doctor Searle was both shocked and surprised when, less than two hours after leaving Mrs Schule, apparently with a good chance of recovering, he was telephoned by Nurse Edwards with the news that their patient had died. With the thought at the back of his mind that Captain Schule might decide to shoot him, it was with some trepidation that Searle returned to 82 Regent Street. Although he stopped short of such drastic action, Schule's attitude was intimidating and threatening. He left Searle in no doubt that in his view the chloroform administered to his wife had contributed directly to her death. The doctor was now even more convinced that Captain Schule was insane.

For some inexplicable reason, Nurse Edwards refrained from telling Searle what had taken place since he and Dr Campbell had left the house earlier. Being thus unaware that Schule had administered something to his wife, and ignorant also of his removal of some of the bedclothes and opening the windows, Searle issued a certificate stating that the cause of Mrs Schule's

death was an obstructed labour and exhaustion. As far as
Captain Albert Schule was concerned, this document served to
cover up the fact that his wife had been murdered.

For Schule, his wife's death bore out his belief in the occult.
Despite reassurances by those who had scoffed at his faith in the
predictions of clairvoyants and mystics, his wife had died. Not
that this made her death easier to bear: for weeks afterwards
Schule was grief-stricken. With his sadness went the realization
that, as an elderly man with two children, his future was bleak.
He was able to afford only a maid to carry out routine household
tasks, so that his problem of earning a living while ensuring that
Natalie and young Albert were adequately cared for was
formidable.

As he had so often in the past, he turned to Louis von Glehn.
His friend tried his best to haul Schule from the clouds of
despair which threatened to envelope him. The two men
discussed the situation, with von Glehn offering advice and
suggestions as to how Schule could cope with, and overcome,
his difficulties. For Louis von Glehn it was a depressing
experience. 'Of course he was broken down. He cried very
easily; almost every time I parted from him he had tears in his
eyes …,' he said later.

Schule agreed eventually to move with his children into
lodgings, but it would seem that this decision was made only to
placate his friend. Unbeknown to von Glehn, Captain Schule
was already contemplating a more drastic means of solving his
problems. On 3 March he commenced writing the letters that
would not be completed until the following month before being
delivered to von Glehn and the coroner. In the meantime he
meditated further on his proposed action.

Von Glehn continued to visit Schule in an effort to cheer him
up, but Schule preferred to consult mediums and fortune-tellers
and to rely upon their counselling rather than on the more
homespun advice of his friend.

Louis von Glehn read with increasing dread the letter that
arrived on the morning of Saturday 5 April 1913. It was from
Albert Schule, and in the first sentence the letter made clear the
writer's intention. Hastily dressing, von Glehn rushed off to
Schule's house.

Not far away Mr Saunders French, the borough coroner, had
read Schule's letter with equal alarm and consternation. In view
of its contents, Saunders French telephoned Police Constable
Joseph Potts, the coroner's officer. After telling him briefly of the
letter, he instructed Potts to go immediately to 82 Regent Street
to find out what, if anything, had happened. The policeman's

arrival at the address a few minutes before ten o'clock coincided with that of von Glehn. After briefly conferring, the two men set about gaining entry to the house. Getting no reply to their knocking, they forced open the back gate; the rear door of the premises they found to be unlocked.

Potts and von Glehn entered the house and carried out a rapid but fruitless search of the ground floor. Upstairs a bedroom door was unlocked, and upon entering the room they came upon an awful scene. On a bed lay the bodies of Captain Schule and his two children. In his right hand Schule was gripping a revolver, while his other was being tightly grasped by his son; next to them lay Natalie. Each had a small bullet wound in the temple. Remaining only long enough to verify that Schule and the children were dead and to remove the partly loaded gun from the man's hand, PC Potts and von Glehn retreated, ashen-faced, from the room. Downstairs the policeman telephoned the coroner to inform him of what had happened, and then the police station, asking that the chief constable and police surgeon be notified and requested to attend immediately.

'FATHER'S TERRIBLE CRIME. SHOOTS HIS TWO CHILDREN. AND COMMITS SUICIDE. POVERTY AND SPIRITUALISM': Thus did *the Cambridge Chronicle and University Journal* of Friday 11 April 1913 announce to its readers news of what had taken place six days earlier.

The inquest into the deaths opened at the police station two days after the bodies were found. The jury's first grim task was to attend the scene and view the mortal remains of the victims which lay undisturbed. After the shaken jurymen had departed, preparations were at once set in hand for the funerals the next morning.

Before witnesses were called, the coroner, Mr Saunders French, read extracts from the letter he himself had received the previous Saturday. At the adjourned hearing the letter was to be read out in full in the presence of Drs Searle and Campbell and Nurse Edwards, who would then have the opportunity to refute the allegations it contained. Meanwhile the extracts reflected the tortured emotions of Captain Schule and showed up the distorted logic that had directed his actions. After the coroner had finished reading, a few moments elapsed as the jury digested his words before Louis von Glehn began to testify.

The friend of the dead man, who had tried to understand him and who had offered his advice and support to the end, gave brief details of Schule's background and then told the coroner, 'After his wife's death Captain Schule was absolutely broken down .... I have seen him and his children constantly since then, and I have been doing all I could to give him a little more courage ....'

'Can you tell the jury what he means by taking his children away to a higher life ...?' asked Mr Saunders French.

'He had a strong belief of a spiritual existence and of the development of the soul above the development of the body and intellect. He had some belief that the soul had an independent existence, and that there were occasions when it would be better to get rid of one's body for the sake of the development of one's soul,' von Glehn explained.

He went on to say that Schule had applied the same philosophy in respect of his children and had come to the conclusion that, '... the fight for life would be too much for them as it was for him .... Of course he always had occult reasons, more or less, for everything he did ... he told me after his wife's death that the reason why she ought not to have had chloroform was that the astral body was insufficiently connected with her physical body ....'

One of the other significant factors influencing Schule's actions was also referred to by von Glehn: 'He saw perfectly well that they could not go on living as they then were, an old man with those two children ....'

Despite Captain Schule's strange beliefs, neither von Glehn nor Dr Graham had considered him to be mad: 'I saw Dr Graham and talked with him, and asked him whether one could by any stretch of phraseology call his attitude madness, and he said, "Quite impossible",' von Glehn told the inquest.

The witness agreed with the chief constable that Schule had been in financial trouble, while admitting his liking for the Schules: 'He was a very fine person, and I had a very high esteem for both him and her.'

After Louis von Glehn had finished, his place was taken by PC Joseph Potts, the coroner's officer. Potts told of finding the bodies and of later recovering two notes left by Schule, one referring to the letter he had sent to Louis von Glehn, the other forbidding '... any medical man to interfere with my or my children's body ...' – his final swipe at the doctors.

The last witness on the Monday afternoon was Dr H.B. Roderick, the police surgeon who had been summoned to Schule's house. The court was hushed as he told of the scene he had found upon entering the bedroom: 'The body of the father was lying on the left side of the bed facing the two children, who were lying on their backs with their heads inclining towards their father.'

As Roderick continued, the horror and poignancy of the scene he was describing overcame some of those in court, who wept openly.

'The father's left hand was gripping the little boy's hand, and the little girl's right hand was resting on the little boy. The father and the little boy appeared in the act of kissing. The bodies were warm .... There were wounds in the left temple of the two children and in the right temple of the man. He must have leaned over and fired at close range at the two children and turned the weapon to himself. Death must have been instantaneous.'

After listening to Dr Roderick's graphic description of the scene, the coroner decided to pass to a less emotive aspect of the inquiry. Referring to allegations Captain Schule had made in his letters to Louis von Glehn and himself, Mr Saunders French invited 'any of the doctors' and Nurse Edwards to give evidence if they wished.

Nurse Edwards was insistent: 'I demand that my name should be cleared ...,' she said, while Dr Campbell – after pointing out that, 'I was present for three hours at the time. I think we should give a statement' – suggested that Dr Searle, who was unavoidably absent, should also have an opportunity to speak. The coroner agreed, and late on Monday afternoon the proceedings were adjourned until Friday.

The next morning there took place the funerals of Captain Schule and his children. It was a quiet, unpublicized ceremony, and only a few small groups of people watched as two hearses containing Captain Schule's coffin and those of his children, left their home for Mill Road cemetery. There Louis von Glehn led other mourners as the plain elm coffins were lowered into the ground. For von Glehn it was the end of a sad, five-year-long episode of his life.

When the inquest reconvened on Friday 11 April, Drs Searle and Campbell were present and represented by Mr Hempson, a London solicitor retained by two medical defence organizations. When it became known that Nurse Edwards had only the support of Miss Wilson, the county inspector of midwives, Mr Hempson agreed to act for her also. The official presence was completed by Inspector McCullock of the National Society for the Prevention of Cruelty to Children and the chief constable, Mr C.E. Holland.

The coroner, after making his introductory comments, at Mr Hempson's request agreed to read out in full the letter from Captain Schule which had been quoted only in part at the previous hearing. The letter comprised accusations against the medical team who had tended his wife and self-justification for

Schule's subsequent actions: '... it is my unshaken conviction [that my wife] could have been saved and with us still if an expert anaesthetist had the operation of her performed. But there has been by far too little experience, energy and forethought, and too much carelessness and neglect ... my wife got killed under a horrorful torture, lasting five-and-a-half hours.'

Mr Saunders French continued: 'After this ghastly end my broken children do not fear for theirselves ... they are longing with every fibre of their bleeding hearts to get re-united with their murdered mama .... As far as I am concerned I now claim to have the same right to do with my children and myself exactly what doctors did with my wife ....'

Schule, while saying in his letter how much he respected the medical profession, criticized its autonomy. He claimed to have experienced anaesthesia by chloroform and to have considerable knowledge of its properties and effect. Indeed, as the coroner read on, this proved to be the case. For a layman, Captain Schule's knowledge of the science of anaesthetics was above average. In one vital respect, however, that knowledge was deficient: awareness of the criteria by which a particular anaesthetic, e.g. chloroform, nitrous oxide, ether or another, was selected for a specific operation. Schule was convinced that it was the use of an inappropriate anaesthetic that had resulted in his wife's death.

He criticized in particular Dr Searle, to whom he referred throughout as 'Dr H': 'I charge Dr H with having used this most dangerous of all anaesthetics [chloroform] and that for the tremendous time of four-and-a-half hours,' he wrote. 'Dr H promised that he would not use chloroform at all but a much milder and safer one, namely nitrous oxide. To this my poor wife agreed, and she believed him also when he said that the operation would be an easy matter, not dangerous at all for both mother and child.'

Dr Searle, listening intently to Mr Saunders French, then heard him read out Schule's allegation that, 'He [Searle], afterwards attempted to hush up his frivolous criminal action with saying that his other anaesthetic had failed.'

The diatribe continued with a denunciation of the way in which the anaesthetic had been administered – the 'open method', sprinkled on a towel placed over the patient's face, rather than by inhaler.

Schule did not confine his disapprobation to Dr Searle. Dr Campbell and Nurse Edwards also came in for censure. He said that after Campbell had arrived to assist Searle, '... both men then worked leisurely again two-and-a-half hours, so their victim had to be in that horrible condition for four-and-a-half hours .... I shudder now if I remember that awful long time, seemingly lasting many years.'

Mr Saunders French here paused to give time for his audience to assimilate what had been read out, before continuing. According to Schule, Nurse Edwards had '... all the time pressed me to fetch another nurse, she wanted to go home and have her sleep ....' He went on to ask why, in contravention of Dr Campbell's instructions, '... she performed the most stupid and most dangerous action imaginable directly after such an operation? She used my absence and gave an injection ....'

Schule's criticisms and allegations were almost through. In summarizing, he wrote, 'Thoughtlessness and carelessness before, during, and after the operation have been the most prominent characteristics .... The true cause of death was: The most careless misuse of chloroform and suffocation – the consequence of the criminal action of the midwife.'

As final justification for his own deeds he concluded: 'If my statement would become the medium to put a stop to the present cruel and gruesome killing, if it induces doctors to think and learn to treat the most valuable gift of God more carefully, it would be a blessing to suffering mankind and our lives would be not sacrificed in vain.'

They were strong words. Unfortunately, although the whole tenor of his letter illustrated Captain Schule's obsession with what he considered to be the shortcomings and criminal ineptitude of the medical profession, he could not be challenged. Had he been alive, he would undoubtedly have been subjected to the most rigorous and searching cross-examination by those determined to contest and refute his allegations.

After Mr Saunders French had finished reading the letter, he adjourned proceedings for a few minutes to allow time for a short consultation between Mr Hempson and those whom he represented.

When the inquiry resumed, Nurse Elizabeth Edwards, the midwife, stepped into the witness-box. She described the sequence of events from the time of her initially attending Mrs Schule. After telling of their early appointments and of her unpleasant introduction to Captain Schule, the nurse told the inquiry of developments as the time of the birth drew near.

'Dr Searle called in Dr Campbell, and Mrs Schule was put under chloroform, as an operation was necessary. At two o'clock in the morning a dead child was born ....' She went on to tell of Captain Schule's interference with her post-natal treatment of Mrs Schule: 'He came in the room and shouted something about Mrs Schule having been poisoned by chloroform ....'

The witness said that, despite her having tried to quieten and reassure him, Schule '... rushed down to fetch something; he said he would fetch some antidote for chloroform'. Upon his return his wife appeared to swallow something he gave her.

'A certain amount of force was used to administer what he did administer?' asked Mr Hempson.

'Yes, it appeared to me so,' replied the nurse.

'Did the patient's resistance prevent him?'

'She had not power enough to resist him.'

'What was the effect, if any, on the patient?' the solicitor asked.

'She changed; I cannot tell you how long it would be; it may have been twenty minutes and she was gone,' was the reply.

After Nurse Edwards had referred to Schule's pulling off the bedclothes and opening the bedroom windows, Mr Hempson asked a last question: 'So far as your care and attention of your patient are concerned have you anything with which to reproach yourself?'

'No, thank God I have not,' she replied feelingly.

Dr Searle's response to Mr Hempson's questioning was uncompromising. After giving a short history of the case prior to his involvement, he was asked about his first encounter with Captain Schule.

'What was his demeanour toward you; was it rational or otherwise?'

'Otherwise.'

'Did you form any conclusion?' Mr Hempson asked.

'I thought he was insane,' Searle replied.

'Did he make any reference to his wife and prospective child?'

'Yes, he said they would both die. He said he had seen it in the crystal and also in her horoscope.'

Searle then told the court of Schule's persistent interference while he was attempting to minister to his wife: 'He insisted on being present. He said his wife was a dying woman and he must be there.'

'Embarrassing to the patient and to anyone attending her,' remarked Mr Hempson.

'Yes, it would have a very bad effect on the patient,' Searle agreed. 'I formed the opinion that she was frightened of him ....'

'Did he threaten you?' asked Mr Hempson.

'Yes.'

After telling of the decision to operate and the subsequent still-birth of the baby, Dr Searle was asked his opinion as to the use of nitrous oxide to anaesthetize the patient, the alternative suggested by Schule, in preference to chloroform.

'Chloroform was the only anaesthetic,' the doctor replied. He went on: 'It was impossible to use nitrous oxide, because anaesthesia would only last a few minutes.'

'The subject of the anaesthetic was discussed with Captain Schule?' asked Mr Hempson.

'Yes.'

'He was very much opposed to it?'

'Yes.'

'Supposing you had attempted the operation without an anaesthetic, could it have been done?'

'No, she could not have stood it,' replied Searle emphatically.

Turning to the post-natal situation, Mr Hempson asked, 'Had the patient recovered from the effects of the anaesthetic when you left?'

'Yes.'

'What was Mrs Schule's condition when you left?'

'She was fairly comfortable ... I thought she would pull through, if she had quiet and warmth,' Searle told the lawyer.

'Would Captain Schule's entrance into the room, the opening of the windows, and the removal of the bedclothes, and his violence ... affect her?'

'They would accelerate her death.'

Here Mr Hempson paused before asking the witness, 'Is there anything, Dr Searle, in connection with the treatment of this case which leads you to reproach yourself with having done anything which ought not to have been done, or omitted to have done anything which ought to have been done?'

Turning to the coroner, Searle replied, 'No, I have never worked so hard.'

Hempson continued: 'You have had considerable experience of the administration of anaesthetics?'

'Yes' Searle told him.

'Was there anything in connection with the case that would have justified you, in your opinion, in withholding your certificate at the time?'

'No.'

This reply by the doctor introduced a puzzling element into the case. Why did Nurse Edwards wait until 29 March, five weeks after Mrs Schule had died, before telling Searle of the 'antidote' administered to the patient by Schule shortly before her death? The nurse was not recalled to explain the delay, and the question remained unresolved. Had Dr Searle known soon after Mrs Schule's death that her husband had earlier administered something to her, there would have been a post-mortem. It is speculative, but nonetheless conceivable, that the findings of such an examination could have radically changed the course of later events. Instead the matter was not pursued at the inquest, and questioning of Dr Searle was confined to asking him about an antidote for chloroform.

'Do you know any antidote to chloroform?' – the question was put by the coroner.

'There is no recognized antidote,' Searle replied.

'Do you know of anything which would throw light on what would be used as an antidote with the result that followed?' was Mr Saunders French's next question.

'Any poison might cause death. I don't know any antidote for chloroform,' repeated the doctor, hinting now at a dark possibility.

Dr Searle's opinion was endorsed by Dr Campbell, who was the next witness. After corroborating his colleague's version of events surrounding Mrs Schule's confinement, Campbell told Mr Hempson, 'I concur with what Dr Searle has said, particularly in regard to the anaesthetic.'

'I should like to get from you whether nitrous oxide would be fitting and proper for the purpose?' said Mr Hempson.

'It would not be the slightest use. The effect would be too short,' Campbell told him.

Hempson repeated his usual question: 'Did you by your united efforts do everything you could to save the child and preserve the life of the mother?' he asked.

'Yes,' the doctor replied.

'You had nothing with which to reproach yourself in connection with the case?'

'Nothing whatever.'

With only a passing reference to the substance Schule had given his wife, Mr Hempson enquired of the witness, 'Speaking of what occurred subsequently, would what Nurse Edwards has said happened, *quite apart from the capsule* [author's italics], been prejudicial to the chance of recovery, or even of her life? The throwing up of the window, and throwing off the bedclothes?'

'It would be most detrimental to her recovery,' stated Campbell.

It was Campbell's reply to Hempson's final question that confirmed the belief that, whatever Schule had administered to his wife, it had not been an antidote for chloroform.

'You have heard what the nurse stated as to Captain Schule procuring some antidote for chloroform? Do you know what could be used to be of any effect?'

'None is within my knowledge,' said Campbell unequivocally.

Before Mr Saunders French summed up, Mr Hempson created a minor sensation by producing a letter, dated 25 March 1913, from Captain Schule to Nurse Edwards. Mr Hempson told the inquest jury that he could refer to the letter only in general terms, as, 'It contains some of the most awful threats that can be put on paper, and I wonder that they did not burn through the paper.' However, after Nurse Edwards had insisted that it would clear her, the solicitor agreed to read the letter out in full. The contents could have been drawn from a Victorian melodrama script:

> Dare to come again under my eyes [Schule had written], and you will not only be surprised by my unseemly behaviour, but I shall treat you as you deserve as the murderess of my wife! If it were possible for my murdered wife she would kill you for having brought ruin upon her children, and me, you stupid, careless monster you! .... The money for your bloody deed I shall pay when it suits me, for it is the price of blood! .... I shall be ready and only too glad to get your criminal deed publicly known. A.P. Schule.

It seemed that in part the letter was Schule's response to requests from Nurse Edwards for the fee owing to her for attending Mrs Schule's confinement. Since her death, Schule had been gossiping about the alleged mistreatment of his wife by the medical team in attendance; the nurse felt that reading the letter in open court would show up Schule's instability and absolve her from any suggestion of blame for his wife's death.

The nurse appeared to have judged correctly. Mr Saunders French did not mention the letter in his summing-up: '... he had formed his own conclusions that the nurse and medical gentlemen who attended the wife did all that could possibly be done to see that the woman was properly delivered. She was given every attention and he thought the jury would agree that there was nothing else which could have been done for her.' Someone in court, agreeing with the coroner's remarks, endorsed them with an enthusiastic 'Hear, hear!'

This begs again the question of why, upon Dr Searle's return to the house, Nurse Elizabeth Edwards did not inform him of what had occurred during his absence. Was she afraid of being criticized or blamed for what had taken place? If so her fears were surely groundless; both Doctors Searle and Campbell, after having witnessed Captain Schule's aberrant behaviour, regarded him as mentally deranged. Searle is unlikely therefore to have doubted Nurse Edwards' account of what had happened, if she had chosen to tell him. This she failed to do, and with her omission went also the opportunity of discovering from what precisely Mrs Schule had died.

The jury, after having listened to the testimony for two hours, took only a few minutes to decide that Schule, while temporarily insane, had murdered his two children and then committed suicide. The jury foreman added a short rider that gave far greater satisfaction to those who had tended Mrs Schule than did the verdict: 'We think the doctors and the nurse have quite vindicated themselves against the allegations made in the deceased's letters.'

So ended a strange, terrible case with its overtones of mysticism and the occult. There is little doubt that the mysterious beliefs and practices of Captain Schule contributed largely to the death of himself and his family. However, it was the combination of circumstances that provided Schule's final motivation. Growing financial problems; his wife's pregnancy and the loss of the baby; her death, followed by the realization that he was too old to bring up young children, were fused together by his irrational obsessions and behaviour. Facing them separately, he might have coped; together they proved overwhelming and led to his ending his own life and that of his children in the hope and belief that by so doing they would all be reunited with his wife in another, better world.

– 8 –
Carnage in Hills Avenue
1932

A milkman's working life is normally not one of high drama and sudden death. Autonomy, daily contact with a generally friendly public, and the sense of freedom inherent in an outdoor job compensate for early mornings, inclement weather and the occasional difficulties surrounding the collection of their dues.

On Saturday 28 May 1932 this routine was dramatically interrupted for Joseph Allington, a roundsman with Stetchworth Dairies in Cambridge. It was nearly one o'clock, and Allington was returning to the dairy when, upon entering Hills Avenue, not far from where Addenbrooke's Hospital now stands, two frantically waving young women ran out in front of him, calling upon him to stop and accompany them. Leaving his horse and float, Allington joined them, and together they entered the front door of 'Meads End', a large detached house standing nearby. Confronting them was a nightmarish scene: a man lying face downwards and a woman on her back on the hall floor, pools of blood still spreading from beneath their heads.

Allington and the terrified women stepped past the couple and entered the kitchen. There they were met by an even grimmer sight. On the floor in another pool of blood lay a girl of about twelve or thirteen, while two little boys, each in his pram, although just alive had both been shot in the head. The scene proved too harrowing for one of the women with Allington. Half sobbing, half screaming, she ran to a neighbouring house, where she blurted out to the occupant a description of the scene she had just witnessed.

Meanwhile the milkman acted with commendable resource. Using the hall telephone, he first called the police and then, in the vain hope that something could be done to save the two babies, he telephoned Dr Albert McMaster, who lived in nearby Hills Road, and asked him to come immediately to the house. It was a futile gesture. Although McMaster soon arrived at 'Meads

End', one infant died five minutes later and his brother survived for only another forty minutes. The carnage in Hills Avenue was complete.

During the last week in May, Jack Hulbert was starring in the film *Sunshine Susie* at the Capitol Cinema in Cambridge. Sixty miles away the Reverend Harold Davidson, rector of the small parish of Stiffkey in north Norfolk, was standing accused in the consistory court in Norwich of having indulged himself with a number of 'Sunshine Susies' in London's Shepherds Bush district, indiscretions that were to result in his being defrocked later in the year.

To his friends and neighbours in Cambridge, Herbert Tebbutt seemed a wealthy, successful and popular – albeit quick-tempered – man. With a reputation as a local philanthropist, the 47-year-old former captain of Cambridgeshire county cricket team had inherited £20,000 upon the death of his father and had received even more when the family brewery had been sold in 1928. Since then he had adopted a more leisurely, self-indulgent lifestyle, playing golf, game-shooting (he was inseparable from his three gundogs) and socializing in the Cherry Hinton Constitutional Club, of which he was vice-chairman.

Helen Margaret Williams was an American by birth, although the good-looking, 38-year-old Californian had until 1928 been living in Liverpool. In that year she had left her husband and moved to Cambridge with her 8-year-old daughter Betty, leaving a 13-year-old son with her mother in Liverpool. In Cambridge she obtained a post as a hotel manageress, and shortly afterwards she met Herbert Tebbutt. They were soon attracted towards each other, and within a few weeks Tebbutt bought a house outside the city in which Mrs Williams and her daughter were installed. The relationship flourished. Tebbutt made no secret of the affaire, commuting frequently between 'Meads End' and the house in which Mrs Williams awaited him.

His wife, Alice, whom he had married in 1913, was angry and bitter over her husband's infidelity. At first she tried to recapture his affection, but she abandoned the attempt at the end of 1929, after Helen Williams had given birth to a baby son of whom her husband admitted paternity. In December of that year Mrs Tebbutt filed for divorce on the grounds of Herbert's adultery with Mrs Williams.

The divorce was an acrimonious affair. Although Tebbutt did not contest it, the question of maintenance was a continuing source of friction between him and Alice. Litigation went on for several months until eventually the court ordered Tebbutt to pay his ex-wife £300 a year. Amounting to a third of his annual income, this in itself was bad enough, but far worse was an additional order that he deposit securities of £3,000-£4,000 with two trustees, so that in the event of his death Alice would still be provided for. Another problem surrounded his efforts to regain possession of 'Meads End' and its contents. Mrs Tebbutt was reluctant to give up either, and for almost a year she remained in the house, until the concessions she gained from her ex-husband persuaded her to move out.

With 'Meads End' empty, Tebbutt was anxious for Helen Williams, her daughter Betty and their baby son Michael to move there, so that he could sell the other property, thus increasing his capital whilst reducing his outgoings. Again things were not to be straightforward: it was now Mrs Williams' turn to be contrary. She had become as attached to 'Little St Bernard's', as the house at Shelford was called, as Alice Tebbutt had been to 'Meads End', and she was equally averse to leaving her home. However, on the premise that he who pays the piper calls the tune, Tebbutt soon prevailed upon her to move with the children to 'Meads End'.

Throughout this eventful period between 1928 and 1930, when Herbert Tebbutt had been involved in the unpleasant divorce proceedings and maintenance litigation, he had found solace with Mrs Williams. It was not surprising therefore that during the summer of 1930 she announced that she was expecting a baby; another son was born at the end of the year.

What of her legal husband? Little is known of Mr Williams apart from the fact that he was a one-time railway porter who later worked for the Royal Air Force. It seems that he was either ignorant of his wife's behaviour and whereabouts or insufficiently concerned to sue for divorce, so they stayed married until the end.

Following the birth of their second child, Anthony Richard (Dick), Tebbutt and Mrs Williams seemed to have settled into a reasonably contented and happy lifestyle. By all accounts he was devoted to her and their children, and they were all frequently seen enjoying outings together in the family car. Nevertheless, he was quick to anger, and both their maid and their neighbours were used to hearing the couple quarrelling, the rows usually subsiding as quickly as they had arisen.

Tebbutt's irascibility was not diminished by his resentment at the maintenance payments he had been ordered to make to his ex-wife; it almost boiled over when he contemplated the securities he was required to deposit. It was apparently during 1931 that his interest in firearms extended to small hand-guns, and he acquired the disturbing habit of keeping a loaded revolver not only in a chest of drawers but occasionally under his pillow.

As the old year merged into the new, to their friends and neighbours all seemed well with the Tebbutts. While he played golf, went shooting during the game season and socialized with his friends at the Cherry Hinton Constitutional Club, his 'wife' appeared content to manage the domestic routine and enjoy the family outings for which Herbert always found time. When, early in 1932, Helen again found herself to be pregnant, their happiness looked to be complete.

Such was not, in fact, the case. By now Tebbutt was drinking heavily at home, as well as at the club; he had fallen well behind with the maintenance payments and was sharply aware that his ex-wife would not tolerate such a situation. Sooner or later he would be embattled again with her lawyers. Although he was outwardly delighted, the expected arrival of another baby exacerbated his financial problems; already he was drawing upon his capital. Finally his recent interest in hand-guns frightened Mrs Williams and was an additional source of discord between them.

In mid-April 1932 the family engaged a nurse to look after the children during the latter stages of Helen's pregnancy. They already had a maid: Florence Southgate had been with them for several years and had witnessed the vicissitudes of their life together. The arrival of Phyllis Henderson was a further burden on Herbert Tebbutt's overstretched resources.

The following month Tebbutt and Mrs Williams decided that a family holiday was needed, and they settled on a bungalow at Gorleston. While for Tebbutt it would provide an opportunity to relax and reassess his situation, for Helen Williams it meant a welcome break before she again became preoccupied with family and domestic affairs.

During the ten days preceding Saturday 28 May 1932, there occurred several incidents which by themselves did not have any great import but which collectively may have significantly influenced Tebbutt's mental state that day.

Since Alice Tebbutt had commenced divorce proceedings, her husband had made a succession of wills, often adding codicils before discarding the documents, only to repeat the procedure later. These wills were, it would seem, all drawn up with the object of ensuring that Alice would not benefit from his estate upon his death. Tebbutt was obsessed with the thought that his ex-wife would have a greater claim to his estate than would his co-habitee and their children.

The most recent will had been drawn up by his solicitor, Albert Alexander, in January 1932 – Alexander was also one of the executors. In his will Tebbutt had amply provided for Mrs Williams and the children, but on Wednesday 15 May he added a codicil making even more specific provisions for the children should their mother predecease them. This was witnessed not by his solicitor but by Mr Martin, steward of the Cherry Hinton Constitutional Club.

A week later a Miss Olga Dudley was due to arrive at 'Meads End'. Miss Dudley had been engaged by Mrs Williams as a temporary children's nurse, as Phyllis Henderson was due to go into hospital. Phyllis was to introduce her to her duties while she accustomed herself to her surroundings. However, Olga did not arrive as expected, and mystery surrounds her non-appearance. It emerged later that for some unknown reason Tebbutt sent Olga a telegram cancelling the arrangement; at the same time he told Mrs Williams and Phyllis Henderson that he had received a telegram from Olga Dudley stating that she was ill and would delay her arrival until Thursday. When she failed to arrive, Mrs Williams, who was both annoyed and mystified, discussed the matter with Tebbutt, who repeated his earlier story.

On the morning of the family's departure for Gorleston, Olga's mother twice telephoned 'Meads End'. The first time she spoke to Tebbutt, but nothing is known of what was said; the second call, at about 10.30 a.m., was answered by Mrs Williams. Phyllis Henderson heard her mistress enquire several times after Olga's health and gathered from the ensuing conversation that Mrs Dudley knew nothing of any illness, saying her daughter had merely received a telegram cancelling the arrangement. Mrs Williams confirmed that it was she who had engaged Olga, and therefore she would expect her as arranged, bringing with her confirmation of the telegram she had supposedly received.

By now Helen Williams was even more annoyed and per-plexed. After telling Phyllis that Olga Dudley had apparently received a telegram of cancellation, she later telephoned the general post office to try to resolve the matter. What transpired during this call was never disclosed, and the mystery surrounding the telegrams remains.

Two other events that may have influenced developments occurred at the weekend. As Tebbutt had still not deposited with his own solicitor the securities ordered by the court, on the Friday or the Saturday a writ of attachment for his arrest was applied for by Alice Tebbutt's lawyers. Although his solicitor said later that Tebbutt would not have known before Monday whether or not such a writ had been issued, he would have been aware that such action was likely – hardly conducive to his peace of mind. Finally, before leaving on holiday one of his beloved dogs, a 14-year-old retriever, was put down. This conceivably tipped the balance of Tebbutt's overwrought mind on that late spring morning.

Saturday 28 May 1932 was wet and miserable. Most of the local cricket matches were rained off, including that between Sawston Paper Mills and the YMCA, a team for which Herbert Tebbutt had occasionally played in the past. The weather did not dampen the spirits of those at 'Meads End'. Phyllis Henderson and the maid Florence Southgate were up before eight preparing breakfast for the family and doing last-minute packing. Soon after nine o'clock, much earlier than usual, Tebbutt and Mrs Williams came down for breakfast, a meal which passed without incident. Soon afterwards came the first telephone call from Olga Dudley's mother. Florence answered it and handed the receiver to Tebbutt, who, out of Helen Williams' earshot, had a brief conversation with Mrs Dudley.

Later Tebbutt drove into the city to pay some bills. Mr Bennett, a veterinary surgeon, arrived before he left and took away his dog. Florence Southgate later said that, although Tebbutt did not seem too greatly distressed, '… if anybody spoke about having the dog destroyed tears came into his eyes, and he could not speak for a few minutes'. Certainly the incident did not deter him from calling into the Cherry Hinton Constitutional Club on his way home. There he chatted happily to those present, who formed the impression that he was looking forward immensely to his holiday.

Tebbutt arrived back at 'Meads End' about noon, by which time preparations for the family's departure were almost complete. The arrangement was that Tebbutt would first drive Phyllis Henderson and Florence Southgate to the railway station, where they would catch the train for Gorleston. He would then return home to pick up the others, and they would all travel by car to the coast.

During Tebbutt's absence, Mrs Dudley had made her second telephone call, the one answered by Mrs Williams. Although Florence Southgate later denied that her mistress had suspected Tebbutt of having sent a telegram to Olga Dudley, after her conversation with the girl's mother Helen Williams was undoubtedly very puzzled by what had occurred, and when Tebbutt arrived home she asked if he could explain.

Again one has to rely upon the testimony of the two servants as to what transpired between Herbert Tebbutt and Helen Williams during that last hour. Both women maintained that the atmosphere remained calm and that no harsh words were exchanged. Asked by the coroner, 'Can you tell the court if there was any unusual trouble between Mr Tebbutt and Mrs Williams?' Phyllis Henderson replied simply, 'No,' while Florence Southgate told the inquest jury, 'Mr Tebbutt did not express any annoyance or give any explanation.'

Although Tebbutt appeared not to show any sign of emotion, it seems likely nonetheless that it was this conversation with Mrs Williams about Olga Dudley, the telegrams and the telephone calls that underlay his subsequent actions. The final incident that upset his mental equilibrium was a third telephone call, this time made by Mrs Williams as Phyllis Henderson and Florence Southgate left the house to wait for the others in the car.

'Can you say where she was telephoning?' the coroner later asked Phyllis.

'I think to the general post office,' she told him.

'She wanted to know about the telegrams?'

'Yes.'

'Would Mr Tebbutt know she was doing that?'

'Yes,' Phyllis replied.

It was a few minutes later, when she was in the car, that Florence Southgate heard 'three shots and then a scream'.

'We got out of the car and went in the back door. Betty was lying on the floor, her head in a pool of blood. Dick was in the perambulator, Michael was in another perambulator, their heads down. They were bleeding from the nose and mouth .... We saw Mr Tebbutt lying face downwards in the hall and Mrs Tebbutt on her back at the foot of the stairs.' Thus did Phyllis Henderson graphically describe at the inquest the scene at 'Meads End' as she and the maid entered the house.

The inquiry into the deaths opened at the Guildhall in Cambridge on Tuesday 31 May 1932, before the city coroner, Mr G.A. Wootten. One of the first to arrive at the hearing was Alice Tebbutt, and she sat weeping silently as she listened to the proceedings.

Phyllis spoke of events at the house on Saturday morning prior to the shooting. After saying that Tebbutt had been 'quite normal' first thing, she went on to tell the jury about the proposed holiday in Gorleston, her temporary replacement and the confusion surrounding the telegrams and telephone calls.

'Did you know Mr Tebbutt had sent a telegram to her [Olga Dudley]?' the coroner asked.

'I don't know ...,' Phyllis replied.

'Did you also understand that he received a reply stating that she was ill?' continued Mr Wootten.

'Yes.'

'And that she would come the following day?'

'Yes.'

'Was there any misunderstanding about the engagement of her?' the coroner enquired.

'Yes, I think so,' Phyllis told him.

'Did that affect Mrs Tebbutt [Williams] at all?'

'She was rather annoyed about it ....'

The young nurse went on to recall the telephone conversation that had taken place between Mrs Williams and Mrs Dudley. Yes, Mrs Williams was surprised, and yes, she was suspicious; she later telephoned the post office regarding the telegram that Tebbutt had apparently sent to Olga. Phyllis said that despite this there had not been any undue friction between Tebbutt and Mrs Williams on the Saturday morning.

She ended by telling of what happened after she and Florence Southgate had gone to wait in the car: '... we heard three bangs. We did not think they were shots at the time. Miss Southgate said, "Listen". We listened for a few minutes and heard three or four more bangs ... we heard a baby crying ....' Miss Southgate '... burst in the back door. She immediately came back and said, "They have been shot. They are on the floor." ' Finally the witness agreed with Mr W.B. Frampton, counsel acting for the executors and relations, that Tebbutt and Mrs Williams (or Mr and Mrs Tebbutt as she knew them) were leading an apparently normal married life and that he was devoted to the children.

After largely corroborating Phyllis Henderson's testimony and then tearfully describing how she had found the bodies, Florence Southgate filled in some of the background of life at 'Meads End'. She agreed that Tebbutt's hasty temper had led to occasional quarrels between himself and Mrs Williams, mainly over money and the maintenance he had to pay his ex-wife. She recalled that on one occasion Mrs Williams had confided in her that Tebbutt had threatened to shoot himself rather than pay his ex-wife any money. On the same theme, the maid told of finding a revolver under Tebbutt's pillow, and of her mistress's concern over his possession of small hand-guns.

'Mr Tebbutt was not a teetotaller?' Mr Wootten put to Florence.

'No,' she agreed.

'Do you think he would drink more than was good for him?'

Florence was unsure how to answer this question: 'Well, I don't know,' she replied.

'Can you say how much of your own knowledge he would drink?' asked Mr Wootten.

'I used to take two or three empty bottles out a week,' she told him.

'Bottles of what?'

'Whisky.'

'He was a good master and she was a good mistress while I was there, and that is all that I have to say.' Florence's spirited outburst was in response to the coroner's enquiry as to whether she was aware of Tebbutt's marital status.

The coroner persisted: 'Do you think he was married to this woman?' he asked.

'I do not know …. I never called her Mrs Williams, and most people who knew her called her Mrs Tebbutt.' Florence went on: 'I used to love being there …. Mr Tebbutt in particular was devoted to the children. Apart from the ordinary little tiffs there was no trouble at all between them. Mr Tebbutt himself had made all the arrangements for going to Gorleston and he was keen on it. He was dressed and ready to go.'

'Whatever it was that made him do the dreadful thing, it took place all of a sudden?' suggested Mr Frampton.

'Yes,' whispered Florence.

The evidence of Dr McMaster presupposed the inquest jury's verdict. After he had described the scene that had greeted him at the house in Hills Avenue, and had stated the clinical cause of the deaths, he was asked by Mr Wootten, '… what opinion did you form as to how he [Tebbutt] met his death?'

'He had shot himself.'

'He had committed suicide,' pedantically corrected the coroner.

'Yes,' replied McMaster.

'Do you think it probable and consistent with what you saw – you say you found him with a revolver in his hand – that he had shot these other four people?'

'One would be able to draw that conclusion ….'

'You formed the opinion that he had shot these people?'

'Yes.'

There were two other witnesses before Mr Wootten summed up. Inspector Percy Sharthan, with other officers of the Cambridge borough police force, had gone to 'Meads End' in response to Joseph Allington's telephone call. After recovering seven empty shells and a .22-calibre pistol containing two live rounds and an empty cartridge case, Sharthan had come to the conclusion that Mrs Williams had been the first victim, shot while speaking on the telephone. The first round had missed, the second had killed her. Herbert Tebbutt had then entered the kitchen and killed the three children before returning to the hall, where he had shot himself in the right temple.

The police had acted quickly and efficiently, interviewing and taking statements from those closely involved and others who might have been able to throw some light on the tragedy, but despite the most diligent enquiries they had failed to discover the motive for the shootings.

Tebbutt's solicitor was the last person to testify. Albert Alexander told of the protracted and acrimonious divorce proceedings between his client and Alice Tebbutt. The solicitor said he had heard Tebbutt state that he would rather shoot himself than deposit the money that would ensure his ex-wife's financial security.

'Was there a substantial sum of money due to his wife in respect of alimony?' Mr Wootten asked.

'Yes, about £250,' replied Alexander.

'Practically a year's income,' remarked the coroner.

'I forget the amount of the permanent order, but it was antedated some time back,' the solicitor informed him.

After he had mentioned that Tebbutt was inclined to be quick-tempered, the coroner asked the witness, 'When papers in regard to the divorce proceedings were taken to the house and served upon him, did he make any objection?'

The solicitor replied obliquely, 'Once he came up to London with me when the proceedings were on for the recovery of the house, and he was rather quick-tempered when he had to give evidence, but it was soon over and forgotten.' He agreed with Mr Frampton that Tebbutt's resentment was due to his belief that under the deed his wife would be better off than if she was living with him, concluding, 'It amazes me that he should have done this, and I can think of no other reason than that something suddenly unhinged his mind.'

The coroner seemed to agree; when addressing the jury, he told them that, 'It might be said that he [Tebbutt] was suddenly seized by a brainstorm and lost control of his temper, but that was no excuse whatever for crime, and the jury would have no hesitation in coming to the conclusion that he feloniously shot himself and murdered those unfortunate people.' Almost as an afterthought Mr Wootten added, 'They might mercifully say that he did it during temporary insanity.'

Having listened to the evidence, the jury agreed with the coroner and returned a verdict that Herbert Tebbutt had 'feloniously, wilfully and with malice aforethought' murdered Helen Margaret Williams, Elizabeth Rosemary Williams,

Michael Charles Hazeltine Tebbutt Williams and Anthony Richard Hazeltine Tebbutt, and then committed suicide during temporary insanity.

No one came up with an acceptable explanation as to why Herbert Tebbutt had slaughtered the woman and children to whom he had apparently been devoted. The acrimonious divorce proceedings and maintenance negotiations; a diminution of his capital; heavy drinking, any one of these factors could have precipitated the events that took place on 28 May 1932. Whatever the reason or reasons, it seems that the telephone call made by Helen Williams that Saturday morning to try and resolve some of the matters that were puzzling her, was the act that finally triggered off the carnage that followed.

– 9 –
A Soldier's Death in Essex
1944

On Thursday 22 June 1944, as Allied armies fought their way inland from the Normandy beaches on which they had landed sixteen days earlier, Private 147367722 Henry Arthur Jones of the Somerset Light Infantry killed another soldier. Unfortunately his victim was dressed not in a field-grey uniform but in one of khaki, and the incident occurred not on the battlefield but in an isolated spot in the Essex countryside.

Captain Samuel Herbert Grundy was a 57-year-old regular Army officer attached to the 18th Battalion of the Essex Home Guard, which had its headquarters at Bull Farm near the village of Abberton, south of Colchester. With the invasion threat that earlier in the war had loomed over the east coast of England now gone, the likelihood of Grundy, at his age, seeing action was remote. The Home Guard was becoming increasingly redundant, and if, as seemed possible, the force was disbanded before the end of the war, Grundy would in all probability see out the conflict in some other administrative backwater. On the evening of 22 June he set out from Bull Farm for a spot of rabbit-shooting in the surrounding fields. It was an outing from which he was not to return.

Private Henry Arthur Jones had been a soldier for less than three months, the 22-year-old Westcountryman having enlisted in the Somerset Light Infantry on 6 April 1944. Jones had been eligible for his call-up in 1942, but in July that year, a month after his eighteenth birthday, he had joined the Merchant Navy. However, naval life was not to his liking and after five months he had absented himself from his ship. The following month a shopbreaking offence led to his appearing in March 1943 at Somerset quarter sessions, where he was sentenced to Borstal training for a period not exceeding three years. He was released after only ten months, and three months later joined the Army.

Like thousands of other soldiers, Private Jones was posted to the garrison town of Colchester. To a young man not long free of the stringent Borstal regime, the rigours and discipline of military life soon began to be irksome. Despite the camaraderie that existed within his barrack room, Jones dismissed any scruples he may have had, and on the evening of 22 June, during his room-mates' absence on a training exercise, he broke open another soldier's locker and stole from it 15 shillings.

Aware of the anger and retribution that would inevitably follow from both his erstwhile friends and those in higher authority, and fearful of the confrontation that would soon take place, Private Jones decided to take permanent leave of the Army.

Knowing that in uniform he would be unlikely to get far from Colchester without being challenged by either the military or civil police, he broke into a building in which he knew he would find weapons and ammunition. Half an hour later, armed now with a sten gun, two loaded magazines and a pocketful of loose ammunition, Jones left the camp by an isolated path and made his way across the fields and marshes in the general direction of the sea. At the first opportunity the young deserter planned to hold up and rob a civilian of his clothes, which he would then put on to make himself less conspicuous.

Not far away, Captain Samuel Grundy was out with his shotgun looking for rabbits. He first caught sight of Private Jones when he was still some distance away. The officer was surprised and puzzled to see a lone soldier in an area generally not frequented by troops, whether training or otherwise. Keeping out of sight, he moved closer and was concerned to see that the other man was carrying a sten gun. Grundy decided to challenge him, demand an explanation for his presence and ask why he was armed.

Jones was taken aback by the unexpected arrival of Grundy; although the newcomer was not wearing a cap or jacket, the soldier recognized from the pips on his shirt epaulettes that he was an officer. With his opening question, 'What are you doing with that gun?', Grundy effectively sealed his own fate. Jones's unconvincing reply – that he was on an exercise and that the rest of his platoon were nearby – certainly did not satisfy his questioner. Now thoroughly suspicious, Captain Grundy demanded that Jones hand over the weapon. The soldier refused and, stepping back a couple of paces, cocked the gun. He was surprised when the older man moved quickly forward and grabbed the weapon in an attempt to wrest it from him. Realizing that, whatever else happened, he was already in deep trouble should this persistent officer succeed in detaining and identifying him, and determined to prevent this happening, Jones fought to hold on to the sten gun.

For several seconds the two men struggled, grunting and panting, the difference in rank forgotten in their determination to overcome each other. Suddenly there was a shot. Both men paused before Grundy broke away from his young opponent, threw aside his shotgun and ran across the field. Jones fired another shot in the direction of Grundy's retreating back before setting off in pursuit. For over a quarter of a mile the two of them ran and stumbled across the fields, Jones gradually overhauling the less athletic officer. When he eventually caught up with him, an even more violent struggle ensued, with Grundy by now seemingly aware that he was fighting for his life. Again he managed to break loose, to stagger frightened and exhausted a couple of hundred yards before coming up against a hedge laced with barbed wire. Jones had meanwhile tried again to shoot at the fleeing man, but the sten gun jammed and he had stopped to change the magazine. Now, as he caught up with his quarry, cowering against the hedge like a cornered fox, Jones decided that he was going to contend the matter no longer.

It seemed as though Grundy had a presentiment of his pending fate as with a final despairing effort he launched himself once more at his assailant. For a few moments they stayed locked together before the effort proved too much for the older man, who fell back on the grass, chest heaving. Mercifully his spectacles had fallen off during that final struggle, so possibly he had difficulty in focusing on Jones as he raised the sten gun and pointed it at him. As the soldier squeezed the trigger, a burst of six 9-mm rounds thudded into the body of the helpless man. Captain Samuel Grundy's body arched and, after a final twitch or two, lay still.

Private Henry Jones stared down at the body. He had never intended this to happen. He picked up the dead man's army pay book that had fallen from his pocket as they had fought. 'Captain Samuel Herbert Grundy,' he read. 'Well, Captain Grundy, I didn't intend this to happen, but your curiosity killed you.' Jones walked slowly away from the scene, the memory of the dead officer's blood spreading from beneath his body, his dentures and spectacles lying on the ground nearby, imprinted upon his mind.

All ideas of desertion had gone. Jones had no thought now but to surrender himself and face the consequences. Throwing away the pay book and then hurling the sten gun, a magazine of ammunition and several loose rounds into a stream, he hurried off towards Colchester.

Edgar Lilley regarded the young soldier standing on his doorstep. He seemed nervous and upset, and his request that Lilley telephone the police suggested that he had something serious to impart to the authorities. After he had been admitted, the soldier refused to enlighten Lilley as to why he wanted the police contacted, but repeated his request. Lilley hesitated no longer but had no sooner got through to Colchester police station than the receiver was peremptorily snatched from him by the soldier, who blurted out to the person at the other end of the line, 'Can you please send a police car? It's a case of killing' – and then, 'My name is Private Jones.' After handing the receiver back to Lilley, Jones collapsed into an armchair and shakily lit a cigarette while the other man gave the address to the police.

Detective Constable Hart was on duty that evening in the police station when Private Jones's telephone call was received. As soon as the message was passed to him, he summoned a uniformed constable, and together they drove to Edgar Lilley's address on the southern outskirts of the town.

After brief introductions, the policemen listened to the soldier's account of what had taken place earlier in the evening. His story did not take long to recount, and ended by his telling the others, '... this happened about three hours ago. I will take you there.' Detective Hart then drove the three of them to the village of Abberton, from which they set off to walk across the fields. They passed the spot where Jones had discarded his victim's pay book, and the stream into which he had thrown the sten gun and ammunition, items that were all recovered the next morning. Further on, the soldier stopped and pointed to the place where Captain Grundy would be found. Advancing a few yards the policemen discovered the officer lying where Jones had indicated.

After a brief examination to verify that Grundy was dead, and a quick scan of the ground in the immediate vicinity, Hart left his uniformed colleague to the unenviable task of keeping watch over the scene until other officers arrived, while he and Jones retraced their steps to Abberton. There the soldier was detained in the local police station.

The man who would thenceforth take over the inquiry was Detective Superintendent 'Tot' Totterdell, the head of Essex

CID.* Later that night, in company with other police officers, including Detective Inspector Draper, Totterdell set out to visit the scene of the latest killing, rendezvousing with the pathologist on the way. It was the early hours of the morning before the party arrived, to be met by a relieved uniformed constable who emerged from the darkness to greet them.

Nothing much could be done during the rest of the night, but at daybreak police activity commenced. While uniformed and plain-clothes officers combed both the field in which Grundy had been found and others surrounding it, Totterdell and his senior colleagues stood by while the pathologist made a preliminary examination of the body, and a police photographer took pictures of the scene before the dead man was taken away. They then transferred their attention to the ground around where the body and Grundy's pay book had been found, and to the stream from which the sten gun and ammunition were recovered. A picture corroborating Private Jones's statement soon emerged. The trampled-down grass, divots of turf and broken hedgerow, together with the dead man's scattered belongings and the sten gun, bore ample witness to the mortal conflict that had taken place.

During the morning one of the policemen searching a quarter of a mile away found Grundy's loaded twelve-bore shotgun, while another discovered the empty sten-gun magazine discarded by Jones after the weapon had malfunctioned. The accumulative evidence and the suspect's brief statement clearly showed the sequence of events. When later Jones's fingerprint was found on the shotgun barrel, it provided the final thread in the pattern of evidence.

By early afternoon Totterdell had finished at the scene, so he returned with Detective Inspector Draper to Abberton police station, where he oversaw the charging of Private Jones with Captain Grundy's murder. Afterwards the accused man elected to make a second, more detailed statement.

Jones made his first appearance before the Colchester magistrates the following morning. After evidence of arrest had been given he was remanded in custody for a week. The police meanwhile continued to gather evidence: statements were taken from the few witnesses able to make a useful contribution, a firearms expert confirmed that a 9-mm bullet removed from Captain Grundy's body was of a type used in a sten gun (the

---

* Six months earlier Totterdell had been involved in the trial of Private Eric Brown of the Suffolk Regiment, who had killed his father. See *Murder in East Anglia* by Robert Church (Robert Hale, 1987).

murder weapon was identified as having been a War
Department issue from Colchester) and a post-mortem was
carried out.

The examination revealed that six rounds had entered
Captain Grundy's upper body. One that had penetrated from
the back of his right armpit had passed through his chest and
neck before emerging on the left side. During its travel it had
critically injured his vocal organs and had fatally clipped his
jugular vein. By the time Private Jones was committed for trial at
Essex assizes, the prosecution case was complete and damning.

The trial opened at Chelmsford on Wednesday 8 November
1944. Mr Justice Singleton and the court listened as the Crown
presented a formidable case against the youthful-looking soldier
sitting impassively in the dock.

Company Sergeant-Major J.H. Blount of the 18th Battalion,
Essex Home Guard, had been the last known person to see
Captain Grundy alive before he had met his killer. Blount told
the court that the deceased had left Bull Farm at about 7.15 on
the evening of 22 June, dressed in his army shirt and battledress
trousers, with the intention of doing some rabbit-shooting.

Fifteen minutes later another witness had heard shots from
the field in which Captain Grundy had died, followed by the
sound of groaning. After Edgar Lilley had told of his unexpected
visitor later the same evening, it was the turn of the professional
witnesses.

The jury listened to the pathologist's testimony, which
indicated that the unfortunate Army officer had been
deliberately shot as he lay helpless on the ground. The police
evidence confirmed the cold-blooded nature of the shooting. In
the statement he had made to Superintendent Totterdell, Jones's
motive was made clear: 'After the first struggle with the officer
when I fired at him I knew I would be in trouble anyway and in
temper I fired again.'

When it came to the defence, Jones insisted from the
witness-box that he had fired 'in temper', although his
admission under cross-examination that he had shot Grundy as
he had run away because he was 'angry' and had fired, 'four or
five shots' at close range as his victim lay on the ground scarcely
helped his case.

Mr Linton Thorp, his vastly experienced counsel, faced a
daunting task. There was no disputing that his client had shot
Captain Samuel Grundy in what appeared to have been the
most calculating manner. Despite the poor showing of the
accused in the witness-box, and his damaging admissions under
cross-examination, Mr Thorp decided nevertheless to try to

convince the jury that, contrary to the prosecution's contention that it had been a cold-blooded shooting committed to facilitate Jones's escape, Grundy had in fact been shot in the heat of the moment, when his attacker had temporarily lost control of himself. If the jury accepted this submission, a verdict of manslaughter was conceivable. Mr Thorp further suggested that Grundy might have contributed to his own demise by attempting to disarm Jones of a sensitive and unpredictable weapon.

It was an accomplished defence eloquently advanced; nevertheless, after hearing Mr Justice Singleton's objective summing-up, Mr Thorp was probably surprised, albeit inwardly elated, when the jury, after retiring for only twenty minutes, returned to the courtroom to announce a verdict of manslaughter.

In sentencing Henry Jones to fifteen years penal servitude, the judge commented: 'I cannot imagine a worse case of manslaughter' – a sentiment with which few people would disagree. That Private Henry Arthur Jones was fortunate to escape the gallows is indisputable.

It was later revealed that in 1938 Jones had spent three weeks in a mental home near Taunton following a violent episode at his sister's home. This was one of a number of relatively minor brushes the young man had had with the police before he had joined the Army, and appeared to be symptomatic of his delinquent tendencies, rather than an indication of any inherent mental instability.

As an ironic postscript, on 11 November 1944, three days after Jones had appeared at Essex assizes, the Home Guard was finally disbanded. With its demise went the 18th Battalion's headquarters at Bull Farm from which the middle-aged Army officer had set out on his ill-fated rabbit-shooting foray.

– 10 –
American Death at Sculthorpe
1958

Filed in the office of the Judge Advocate General (Military Justice Division), Department of the Air Force, Bolling Air Force Base, Washington DC is the 539-page record of a trial unique in British jurisprudence. In December 1958 a master sergeant in the United States Air Force was tried by a US general court martial for the murder of his wife and for committing adultery with a married British woman – also a criminal offence under US military law.

It had all started over two years before in July 1956, when Marcus M. Marymont, a 35-year-old veteran of the Second World War and the Korean conflict, called into a pub in the riverside town of Maidenhead in Berkshire. Marymont was the senior non-commissioned officer in the intelligence unit at the USAF base at Sculthorpe, near Fakenham in Norfolk, and his duties frequently took him to Air Force headquarters at Bushy Park on the south-west outskirts of London. From there it was less than twenty miles into Maidenhead, with its pubs and clubs a popular rendezvous for American servicemen and their families. On this particular summer day, a few days before the Suez Canal crisis erupted, there took place an encounter that was to lead from marital infidelity to murder.

Cynthia Taylor was a dark-haired, attractive shop manageress of twenty-two. She had been married less than a year when she met Marcus Marymont, but she and her husband had already separated and she was now living in Maidenhead. The attraction between the British woman and the mature, good-looking American airman was mutual and immediate, and from that first meeting a pattern of deception commenced. Although Mrs Taylor did not attempt to disguise the fact that she was married, Marymont told her that he was divorced and that his wife and three children were living in the United States.

The relationship flourished. Not only did Marymont visit

Cynthia Taylor at least once a month, but they also wrote to each other regularly. Sixty-nine of her letters to him were subsequently discovered in his desk drawer at Sculthorpe.

In the months subsequent to their meeting the couple became increasingly involved. Marymont was to remark later of his feelings at this time, 'I would say I was in love with Mrs Taylor.' Whether or not that was an accurate reflection of his feelings for a woman thirteen years his junior, it would seem that she certainly hoped that their relationship would become permanent, for she agreed to marry him after she had obtained her divorce.

What of Marymont's wife during this time? Mary Helen Marymont, forty-one years old and the mother of 12-year-old twins and a 7-year-old boy, was described by one of her American woman friends at Sculthorpe as, '... a very pleasant, sweet, helpful, naïve sort of individual ... a very nice home-loving type .... She thought only of her children and her husband.'

Certainly there was nothing to indicate otherwise. Admittedly the marital relationship had cooled following the couple's return to the United States from the Far East in 1954, but after Marymont's posting to Britain in January 1956 matters improved. Initially the family lived in a flat in King's Lynn, but later the same year, by which time Marymont had met Cynthia Taylor, they moved to a house at the Sculthorpe married quarters.

For several months the situation continued happily enough for Marymont; his wife, back at Sculthorpe with the children, had not an inkling that her husband's frequent visits to London and thereabouts were not entirely confined to Air Force business but also literally embraced an extra-marital diversion.

Marymont and Mrs Taylor became familiar in and around Maidenhead. To her friends and neighbours the tall, good-looking American airman with the pencil-thin moustache was introduced first as a friend and later as her fiancé. To keep up this pretence, Marymont bought Cynthia a diamond and sapphire ring.

It was in 1957 that events started to go wrong. By this time Marymont was completely besotted with Mrs Taylor and was correspondingly disenchanted with his marriage and home life. Now, in addition to his visits to the south of England on official business, when he was able to avail himself of the opportunity to visit Mrs Taylor, he was making excuses to travel down to Maidenhead specifically to be with her. The affaire, although not common knowledge at his base, was beginning to be talked about by colleagues and neighbours. In September 1956 Marymont travelled to Dorset with a fellow NCO in whom he had confided, and both men stayed overnight at Mrs Taylor's home; thenceforth word had started to spread.

During 1957 Mary Helen Marymont suffered a number of gastric upsets; these were later seized upon when it was suggested that they might have had a sinister connotation.

In early spring the same year Cynthia Taylor told Marymont that she was expecting a baby, and in October she gave birth to a son. Whether it was this event that prompted Marymont to spend Christmas with her rather than with his family in Norfolk is unclear, but thereafter events had the inevitability and momentum of a torrent nearing a cascade.

The situation was further complicated for Marymont by increasing financial pressure. Although he was well paid, the upkeep of his home, together with socializing at the base and the need to maintain appearances with Cynthia and their friends was overstretching his resources. He started borrowing from fellow NCOs, a futile expedient which only exacerbated the situation.

Before winter surrendered to spring in 1958, word of Marymont's philandering eventually reached his wife. Poor Mary Helen: not wanting to believe it, let alone confront her husband with her fears and suspicions, she prepared a number of written questions concerning her mistrust of his behaviour. This she presented to him one evening at home. Marymont laughed off her fears, gave her a reassuring hug and threw the piece of paper into the fire. Notwithstanding his apparent insouciance, the episode worried him; it may not have been only the stress of the situation that induced the vomiting attacks in his wife that made her visit the base hospital for medication ...

A few weeks later there occurred the event that precipitated Mary Helen Marymont's death. She had never felt completely reassured by her husband's response to her questionnaire, so it was with only a slight twinge of guilt that one morning, as she was tidying up, she ran her hands quickly through one of his jacket pockets. What she found confirmed her lingering fear and suspicion: an unsealed letter addressed to Cynthia Taylor, couched in affectionate terms, which Marymont had forgotten to post. It left Mary Helen stunned and in no doubt as to where her husband's affections lay. Nevertheless, after the ailing woman (she was still suffering periodic bouts of sickness and diarrhoea) had recovered from the shock, she determined, if only for the sake of their children, to try to salvage what remained of her marriage.

Later in the day she confronted Marymont with the

incriminating letter. As he looked at his wife, her face white with fury and despair, he could not deny the letter; the best he could hope for was to minimize its effect and prevent her taking any precipitate action that would have civil or military repercussions. At the same time Marymont knew that he would have to prepare now to take the irrevocable step that would resolve the situation and leave him unhindered to pursue his affaire with Cynthia.

According to Marymont's later testimony, after his wife had said that she still loved him, although adding a rider that she would find it difficult in future to trust him, they discussed the situation and agreed for the sake of their children to stay together and to try to resolve the problem. That evening Mrs Marymont had another vomiting attack.

A couple of weeks later two civilian cleaners working late in the chemical laboratory at the base were surprised when at 10.30 an Air Force master sergeant entered the room. James Twite from the nearby village of East Rudham said later that after scanning the various bottles containing powders and solutions on the shelves the sergeant asked, 'Don't they lock this stuff up?' Twite's companion, Charles Waterson, replied in the negative, whereupon the newcomer remarked, 'They ought to. There's a lot of chemicals on these shelves; even arsenic.'

Mrs Marymont continued to be unwell; she was suffering intermittent bouts of vomiting and diarrhoea and on 11 May was confined to bed, where she was visited by Mrs Teresa Dunning, a neighbour, who thought she was a 'funny colour'. Although she had been seen by doctors at the base hospital, she did not seem to be responding to medication.

Friday 23 May was Cynthia Taylor's birthday. Marymont drove down to Maidenhead and arrived at her home in Sylvester Road at 10 p.m. He stayed with her until the Sunday, and it was either prior to seeing her on Friday or on the following day, when they went shopping for her birthday present, that he called into a chemist's shop in Maidenhead and enquired whether arsenic was stocked. The chemist confirmed that this was so but told Marymont that he would require a permit if he wanted to purchase some, whereupon the airman left his premises. It was an incident that Bernard Sampson, the pharmacist, was to recall when he was interviewed a few weeks later by Detective Constable Gordon from Maidenhead CID.

Back at Sculthorpe, Marcus Marymont spent a disturbed night looking after his wife, who had apparently been taken ill the previous evening. He called at the base hospital and obtained some medication for her, after which there seemed to be a slight improvement in her condition. In the morning Mrs Marymont refused to let her husband fetch a doctor, and later her condition worsened, her eyes rolling and her lips and hands turning blue. By the early afternoon, nearly seventeen hours after the onset of her illness, Marymont decided that it was imperative that she enter hospital, for her death at home could lead to some awkward questions. Shortly before two o'clock on Monday afternoon an ambulance arrived in response to his summons and conveyed his wife to the base hospital.

Captain Max Buchfuhrer was the first doctor to examine Mrs Marymont at the hospital. He saw immediately that she was 'in severe shock and just about dead'. Nevertheless, Buchfuhrer and two other doctors fought for almost eight hours to save the critically sick woman. Their combined efforts were to no avail, and Mary Helen Marymont eventually died at 9.47 p.m.

Marymont's behaviour and reaction whilst at the hospital with his wife had surprised some of the staff. Captain Buchfuhrer, when discussing with Marymont his wife's symptoms and the critical nature of her illness, had been nonplussed when the airman had confided in him his sexual inadequacy with his wife. 'I felt at that time that it was extraordinary and out of context,' Buchfuhrer later said.

Assisting Buchfuhrer at the hospital was Dr Albert Cook, an obstetrician who had previously treated Mrs Marymont; he considered her husband's reaction to be normal, noticing tears in his eyes when he discussed his wife's case. Likewise, after Mrs Marymont had died, Captain Janet Hyde, a staff nurse, and Captain John Rayford, another doctor present, both noticed that Marymont was crying and upset as he was helped from the treatment room.

Whatever his reaction, there was already suspicion lurking as to the cause of his wife's death. Dr Cook in particular harboured doubts. For several months he had been treating Mrs Marymont for gastric ulcers and had earlier diagnosed an inflammation of the pancreas. Cook had already voiced his disquiet to Max Buchfuhrer, and on the night their patient died he told a gathering of his medical colleagues that he thought she might have been poisoned.

Although Cook's suspicions were not universally shared, there was sufficient doubt as to the cause of Mrs Marymont's death to justify a post-mortem. Marymont was appalled at this development; when first approached, he had little choice but to consent to the examination, but he subsequently visited Dr Cook late at night to ask if the decision could be reversed, on the grounds that his children did not like the idea of their mother's body being cut up. Cook was unmoved and told Marymont that the autopsy was necessary.

With the post-mortem decided, Marymont set about enlisting the sympathy of others. In apparent distress he called at the NCOs' club, where he met his wife's friend Teresa Dunning. He told her that rumour had it that he had poisoned Mary Helen. Mrs Dunning laughed.

'Oh, Mark, no!' she said. 'They must be kidding. Why do they say that?'

'Because I threw the medicine out and also a bottle that was in the ice-box,' he told her.

Despite the ominous developments, Marymont still appears to have been planning in the long term. The day after his wife died he applied for a six-month extension of overseas duty, '... because my wife has just passed away' and such a lengthening of his stay would enable him to make the necessary arrangements for the well-being of his children. Circumstances would dictate that his request was never fully processed, but in the meantime he was granted one month's immediate leave. According to Marymont, he had not wanted to leave his children, but friends and neighbours persuaded him that he should go away for a time, while they would look after them.

Master Sergeant Marcus Marymont then made the decision that, although in retrospect predictable, later prejudiced others overwhelmingly against him. Four days after his wife had died agonizingly in hospital, he drove down to Mrs Taylor's home at Maidenhead. Before leaving Sculthorpe, an insurance representative had called upon him, and as he reflected on their discussion on his way to Maidenhead, there occurred to him a possible explanation he might suggest should it be revealed, as now seemed likely, that his wife had died from the effects of poison – that it had been self-administered.

Having him arrive at two o'clock on a Saturday morning was disturbing enough, but when Marymont announced that his wife had died, Mrs Taylor could only ask him, 'In America?'

His reply bewildered her: 'No, here in England. She came over with me.'

'But you told me you were divorced.'

'Yes, I know,' Marymont admitted.

Marymont stayed with Mrs Taylor until the early hours of Monday morning. It must have been one of the unhappiest weekends the couple had spent together, and by the time they parted their relationship had taken on a new dimension. Cynthia's feelings for the American, and her hopes and expectations for their future together, had been dented by his revelations and by the knowledge that for two years he had lied to her about his own situation.

Similarly for Marymont: he knew that his affaire with Cynthia had suffered a setback, but he had done his best to retrieve the situation and convince her that their future still lay together. Currently more worrying were developments back at Sculthorpe, particularly the post-mortem examination on his wife.

The American authorities had enlisted the services of two of Britain's most eminent men in the field of forensic medicine/ science to investigate the cause of Mrs Marymont's death. The Home Office pathologist Dr Francis Camps carried out the post-mortem, while Dr L.C. Nickolls, director of the Metropolitan Police laboratory, examined various of Mrs Marymont's organs sent to him by Camps. The pathologist, who had a reputation for performing rapid and precise examinations, first carried out a number of tests aimed primarily at determining whether a recipient of arsenic would be aware of the fact. His subsequent examination confirmed suspicion that Mrs Marymont had died from arsenical poisoning. Dr Nickolls analysed the organs and hair samples and concluded that there were indications not only that Mrs Marymont had imbibed a lethal dose of arsenic within twenty-four hours of her death but that two further doses had been taken previously, one possibly as far back as January.

Returning from Maidenhead, Marymont was soon made aware that, after hearing of his alleged misconduct with a married woman and following a request from the base commander, service investigators had started looking closely into the circumstances surrounding his wife's death.

His first encounter with special agents Eugene Bonner and Hugh Carey, from the office of the special investigation detachment at Sculthorpe, took place on the day he arrived back from Maidenhead. The meeting was confined to apprising Marymont of his rights, telling him why they were enquiring into Mary Helen Marymont's death and informing him that there was a delay in returning her body to the United States. Marymont promised his co-operation.

The following day he contacted Bonner and asked him to call round to his home. This time, after a lengthy interview, Marymont made a written statement. In it he described how he and his wife had 'seemed to get into a rut' after returning to the United States from Japan. He went on to tell of meeting Cynthia Taylor and of their intimate relationship up until the present time. 'I began to feel I was deeply in love with her,' he told Bonner. After referring to his wife's increasing unhappiness following the discovery of his unposted letter to Mrs Taylor, Marymont described her illness prior to being admitted to hospital. He then mentioned some rat poison he had taken home in 1957 to kill mice in the kitchen; he said that his wife had put it in the kitchen cupboard but that, when he had later looked for it to give to a neighbour experiencing a similar problem, it had disappeared. His wife told him that she had thrown it away. This was the first covert suggestion that the poison had been self-administered.

Marymont ended his statement to Bonner: 'Since my wife's death I have experienced tremendous loss and at the same time a sense of guilt even to the point that I may have caused her to take her life .... After considerable thought I am sure I am not responsible for my wife's death, and I am sure I did not give anything by mistake to cause her death.'

For the next three weeks enquiries continued, with witnesses being interviewed and statements taken; after due consideration by the judge advocate general of the Air Force in Washington, Marymont was seen again by Eugene Bonner on Thursday 10 July. Just over four weeks had elapsed since Mrs Marymont's death, and now a grim-faced agent told the Air Force sergeant that from the enquiries he had made and the information obtained, it seemed that he was responsible for his wife's death. Following the post-mortem examination, Marymont had known that analysis of his wife's organs would lead to further investigation into her death. Nevertheless, he appeared shocked and distressed at Bonner's revelation. On this occasion the interview was short, and by the time it ended the status of Marymont was no longer that of a grieving husband but that of a man accused of wife-murder.

His court martial was not to take place until December 1958; in the meantime enquiries and preparations continued. Agreement was reached with the British authorities that the trial of a US serviceman for crimes alleged to have been committed in Britain should be by a United States general court martial rather than in a British criminal court.

The trial of 37-year-old Marcus M. Marymont, of Hobbsville, North Carolina, latterly serving with the 47th Bombardment Wing of the United States Third Air Force, took place between 8 and 18 December 1958, in a former film studio at Denham in Buckinghamshire. The accused man faced two charges: the first that of the premeditated murder of his wife, 43-year-old Mrs Mary Helen Marymont, about 9 June 1956 at RAF Station Sculthorpe, 'by means of administering to her a lethal dose of toxic substance, namely arsenic', the second alleging that of wrongfully having sexual intercourse on various occasions between 20 December 1956 and 31 May, at Maidenhead, with Mrs Cynthia Taylor, a woman not his wife.

The stars and stripes formed the backdrop to the fifteen American officers, with Colonel Albert Snider as court president and with a civilian American law officer as adviser, who were to try the case. The senior prosecuting officer was Major C.J. Lewis, assisted by Captain Ellis R. Dufficy, while Marymont's defence was in the hands of Major William Karr, Captain Neil Kasdan and Lieutenant Trimble. The accused man was an impressive figure, tall, broad and immaculately clad in Air Force uniform, four rows of medal ribbons on his chest bearing testimony to his wartime service. Throughout his trial he was to deport himself with military bearing and dignity.

The case against Marymont had strength in depth. From the testimony of their first witness until the closing speeches of the prosecuting officers, it was apparent that a formidable, albeit circumstantial case had been assembled.

'The motive for the murder was that Marymont was in love with another woman – Cynthia Taylor, a married woman.' Major Lewis was making his opening address to the court. 'This affaire was not the common variety of love affair, but had gone on for over two years and had progressed to the point that marriage had been promised by each to the other.'

After telling of Mrs Marymont's death following her admission to the base hospital on 9 June, Major Lewis pointed out that arsenic was unavailable at the hospital but that the accused had at one time had access to poison in the laboratory of Maryland University in the United States. Before starting to call his witnesses, Lewis told the court of Marymont's weekends with Cynthia Taylor, and of the Christmas he had spent with her in 1957.

Captain Max Buchfuhrer, the doctor who had first seen Mrs Marymont on her final hospital admission in June, told the assistant prosecuting officer, Captain Dufficy, that the clinical picture, together with his observation of Marymont, had led him to suspect the possibility that Mrs Marymont had been poisoned. Marymont's reaction to his wife's condition had astonished Buchfuhrer. After describing their sexual problems, Marymont had gone on to say that his wife had been similarly ill on several occasions during the past year, most recently just six weeks earlier.

Two other doctors followed Max Buchfuhrer to the witness-chair. Captain John Rayford and Dr Albert Cook both confirmed that Mary Helen Marymont had been treated several times in the past for vomiting attacks and apparent gastric upsets. Rayford said that she had been referred to another hospital for investigation, while in answer to Major Lewis, Cook stated that the symptoms accompanying an episode of vomiting in May 1958 '... would indicate that it was arsenical poisoning at that time. She had a good deal of vomiting which might have offset the effect of the poisoning then.' He agreed that other attacks during the year could have been the result of a small degree of arsenical poisoning.

In trials for murder by poisoning, forensic evidence is vital, a fact amply illustrated during the trial of Marcus Marymont. It was Day 3, and Dr L.C. Nickolls, director of the Metropolitan Police laboratory, was giving evidence. 'There was a heavy dose of arsenic in the hair .... This indicated that there had been a dose of arsenic some time prior to death – a minimum of about a month, and possibly two months before. Another similar dose had possibly been ingested up to about six months prior to death ....' Nickolls explained to Colonel Snider that, as hair grew, it retained traces of arsenic, and the further those traces were from the scalp, the longer the time since it had been ingested. When invited by Captain Kasdan, for Marymont, to say how small a dose of arsenic a person could recover from, the witness replied drily, 'One has very little experience of doses from which people recover. They don't come to me.'

The testimony of Dr Francis Camps, the pathologist who had carried out the post-mortem on Mary Marymont, was even more damaging than that of Nickolls. Although an acknowledged expert on arsenic, Camps had nonetheless previously tasted some diluted arsenic without swallowing it, so that he could later explain its effect to the court. He stated that, although he had experienced a burning sensation in his mouth, a lethal dose of the poison could be disguised in a strong-tasting drink such as coffee. He went on to say that his analysis of Mrs Marymont's organs, and his findings in her nails and hair, indicated that she had imbibed two doses of arsenic, a non-fatal one and that from which she had died. He concluded: The clinical picture of this case, accompanied by the chemical findings, make it beyond any reasonable doubt that this woman died from arsenical poisoning [and] ... clearly indicate that it was taken by mouth.'

The prosecution had established the motive for Mrs Marymont's death, the method by which it had been achieved and the likely means of administration.

All heads turned as Cynthia, stylishly dressed and with a fur slung round her shoulders, entered the courtroom on Day 4.

After taking her seat in the witness-chair, she glanced round at the imposing row of uniformed officers, the spectators, counsel and court officials, before finally looking at Marymont, seated a few feet away behind a table next to Major Karr. Their eyes met but neither showed a sign of either recognition or emotion.

When Major Lewis stepped forward to begin his examination-in-chief of Mrs Taylor, her nervousness was apparent to all present as she sat with clenched hands in the witness-chair. She told Lewis that she had known Marymont for over two years.

'I thought he was divorced. He told me he was,' she said.

'Did the accused promise to marry you?' asked Lewis.

'Yes, when I got my divorce,' Cynthia replied. She denied having received an engagement ring from Marymont – 'I am not divorced yet, so how could I receive an engagement ring?' But she agreed that he had bought her a diamond and sapphire ring either as a birthday present the previous May or at Christmas 1957, she could not remember which.

'To your knowledge has he any children?' enquired Major Lewis.

'Yes, three,' replied Mrs Taylor.

After telling the court that they had spent Christmas 1957 together, the witness went on to say that since she had known Marymont he had bought her the ring, a pair of shoes and a fur.

'Will you describe the fur?' asked Major Lewis.

'I will show it to you,' replied Cynthia, slipping the fur she was wearing from around her shoulders.

The questioning continued, with the aim of establishing the depth of the couple's relationship.

'How was the accused known to your friends and neighbours?' enquired Lewis.

'As a friend,' Cynthia replied.

'Have you ever been introduced as Mrs Marymont?'

'As his fiancée,' she told him.

When referring to a television set she had bought, Mrs Taylor was asked if Marymont had assisted her financially: 'No, I am purchasing that myself …. I used to give him money in cash and he paid by cheque.'

If the early questioning had been painful, albeit fairly innocuous for Cynthia, worse was to follow. To her anguish, a bundle of her letters recovered from Marymont's desk drawer at Sculthorpe was produced. An appeal by the defence counsel that the letters were inadmissible – on the grounds that 'the substantial rights of Marymont had been prejudiced' – was overruled, so Cynthia sat in abject misery and embarrassment as her letters were read by each of the adjudicating officers. She was herself asked to read some of them. After reading one, she protested, 'I am not prepared to answer for this one', a remark followed by the first of several adjournments granted so that she could recover from the outbursts of sobbing that overtook her. After each break the court remorselessly continued with the letters. Marymont sat helplessly, bitterly regretting his neglect in failing to rid himself of the incriminating documents.

After thirty-two of the letters had been circulated and read, Mrs Taylor collapsed in a final paroxysm of sobbing, whereupon Colonel Snider decided to adjourn the proceedings until the next day. There were few present who did not feel sympathy for the distraught woman as she was helped from the room by a nurse, to be driven away, her head shrouded in a blanket.

Cynthia Taylor's ordeal was not over. The next day she returned to court, where her suffering continued as thirty-seven more of her letters were perused. Finally, after she had spent altogether 6¾ hours in the witness-chair, her nightmare ended and she was again hurried from the building.

After the wretchedness that had been evident when Mrs Taylor had been in court, the laconic, matter-of-fact testimony of special agent Eugene Bonner came as a relief. Bonner said that he had interviewed Marymont for ten hours, '... but we had several breaks ...', after which the airman had signed a statement. The defence objected to the admission of this on the grounds that, when questioned, Marymont had not been advised that he was a suspect. The court deferred its decision over the weekend and on Monday ruled that the statement be allowed. As it was read out by Captain Dufficy, it seemed that Marymont's denial of the lesser charge of adultery was inconsistent with the defence strategy. His love-affair with Cynthia, the discovery by his wife of the unposted letter, Mrs Marymont's final illness and the carefully veiled suggestion that her death might have been attributable to self-administered rat poison indicated that the defence tactic was to admit as much as was prudent and capable of proof, in the hope that Marymont's denial of murder would appear credible.

For the rest of Monday and into Tuesday, secondary prosecution witnesses testified. Major G.L. Fletcher, chief of the intelligence unit at Sculthorpe, and Captain William Arrondondo, Marymont's immediate chief, had both had conversations with him about his affaire with Mrs Taylor. Arrondondo had warned him that he would '...get tangled up over here. You will not be able to pay alimony and child support ....' Major Fletcher stated that he had discussed the situation with Marymont, whom he described as '... one of the finest non-commissioned officers I have had working for me. He was a very brilliant man in his field – very popular.' At Christmas 1957 Marymont '... was all mixed up as to whether he should spend Christmas with his family at Sculthorpe or with Cynthia Taylor .... I advised him to straighten out his family situation before he got himself into another ....'

After former neighbours of the Marymonts had described the state of affairs during the months preceding her death, and cleaners Twite and Waterson had told of Marymont's unexpected evening visit to the chemical laboratory, an officer and an NCO employed at the chemistry school in which the laboratory was situated testified as to the easy availability of poison.

The final prosecution witness was Bernard Sampson, a Maidenhead chemist. After explaining to the court the legal requirements pertaining to the sale of arsenic, he told of Marymont's brief visit to his shop the previous May. Major Lewis asked Sampson if he was positive that it was Marymont who had come into his shop.

'To my own mind, yes,' he replied. Asked how he was so sure, the chemist said, 'Because he made such an odd request, and he spoke such good English with an American accent.'

It was on Wednesday 17 December, the eighth day of his trial, that Marcus M. Marymont walked across the courtroom to the witness-chair to speak in his own defence. He looked relaxed as his counsel, Major William Karr, prepared to question him. First Karr produced the thick bundle of letters which Marymont agreed were those sent to him by Cynthia Taylor. He went on to explain that he had left his children to visit Mrs Taylor soon after his wife's death, as he felt that, after having displayed little emotion at news of their mother's death, they did not need him. Before leaving them he had applied to stay in Britain so that his children could continue their education there, and to give himself time to readjust after his wife's death.

'Have you at any time purchased arsenic while stationed in the United Kingdom?' asked Major Karr.

'No, I have not,' Marymont replied.

'Have you at any time in any way administered or attempted to administer arsenic to your wife?'

'No, sir, I have not.'

'Are you deeply in love with Cynthia Taylor?' – It was the turn of Major Lewis.

'During the past two years I would say I was in love with Mrs Taylor,' Marymont agreed.

'Do you admit committing adultery with Mrs Taylor from Christmas 1956 up to May this year?'

'Yes, I do.'

'Would it be fair to say that you promised marriage to Mrs Taylor?' asked Lewis.

'No, it would not,' replied Marymont. 'We merely discussed it on the basis of her obtaining her freedom.'

The prosecutor changed tack. 'Did you have any feeling of love and affection for your wife and family?' he asked.

'Yes, I did,' said Marymont clearly.

'Yet you spent Christmas 1957 with Cynthia Taylor, leaving your wife and children to spend Christmas alone?'

'Yes, I did,' Marymont repeated.

This was a damaging admission. Taken with his earlier statement that soon after their mother's death he had left his children to go to Cynthia Taylor, it suggested that, despite his assertions to the contrary, Marymont in fact cared little for the welfare or feelings of his family.

Lewis moved on to the letter Mary Helen Marymont had found in her husband's pocket. 'Would it be fair to say that in spite of this letter your wife was determined to keep the family together?' he asked.

'We discussed it and we thought we could work this problem out together … we came to an agreement mutually in discussion,' Marymont replied.

The accused man was then questioned by Lewis regarding his movements after his wife had died. He said that friends and neighbours had recommended that he take a trip, while his children were looked after. This provoked Lewis into asking stingingly, 'Did they urge you to go and stay with Mrs Taylor for the weekend?'

'No, they did not …,' replied Marymont tightly.

The prosecutor pursued the theme. 'What ages are your children?' he enquired.

'A set of twins just past fourteen and a boy of nine,' Marymont told him.

'Did they not need you at this time?'

'They did not seem to need anybody. They had not shown any reaction so far' – another reply that did nothing to help the defence case.

'Would you not say that she [Mrs Taylor] was fully expecting to be your wife?' – Lewis was nearing the end of his cross-examination.

'Yes, she was, because she was not aware of my true marital situation,' Marymont told him.

Before returning to his seat next to Major Karr, Marymont told a member of the court that he had informed his children of their mother's death upon his return from the base hospital. In reply to a question from Colonel Snider, he denied ever having gone into the chemist's shop at Maidenhead, and ever having had arsenic in his house or quarters. He did admit, however, to the identification by the cleaners James Twite and Charles Waterson: 'I would say the testimony these men gave was correct,' he agreed.

For over two hours the Air Force master sergeant had sat in the witness-chair. Although remaining outwardly unruffled, he had made a number of damaging statements and admissions.

The trial was reaching its final stages. There remained only the closing speeches of the prosecuting and defending officers before the court would consider its verdict.

The defence address was shared by Major Karr and Captain Kasdan. Both played down the intensity of the relationship between Marymont and Cynthia Taylor. Karr maintained that Mrs Taylor's most recent letters '... show a marked cooling in the affection of Mrs Taylor for Marymont. They were ordinary letters from people who had no particular affection for each other ... if you have a girl friend and that is enough to convict a man of murder, then God help the greatest portion of our society ....' Karr went on to argue that, 'The probability of suicide or accident is just as great, if not greater, than that of murder ....'

'It is anybody's guess whose liver was analysed by Dr Nickolls ....' After Captain Kasdan's barely concealed slur on the professionalism of the highly qualified and respected forensic experts, he went on to disparage the fatal affaire: 'a sordid little romance of the type that breaks up thousands of families every year'.

It seemed that counsel on both sides aimed to denigrate Marymont, albeit with a different objective.

As with the defence, responsibility for the final prosecution address was split between Lewis and his assistant, Captain Dufficy. After saying that, 'Any man who would leave three children at Christmas, which is the children's time, is cool, calculating and without scruples. He is a man who would do anything,' Dufficy said that it was Marymont's egoism that had induced him to retain Mrs Taylor's letters. 'This man decides he must dispose of his wife,' continued the assistant prosecutor. 'She has been sick for a year under the care of a doctor, and there enters his diabolical mind that, as everybody knows she is sick, what kind of poison gives the same symptoms ...?' Thus had Marymont hoped to deceive her doctor, friends and others who knew her.

After conceding that the murder evidence was circumstantial, Major Lewis discounted the possibility that Mrs Marymont had died by accident or from natural causes. 'There exists the most compelling reason for the accused to kill his wife – his love for another woman.' It was a cogent argument; it remained only to be seen whether or not the adjudicating officers were convinced.

It took them 5½ hours to reach their decision, and it was dark outside by the time they re-entered the courtroom. Marymont stood rigidly to attention, his face pale, as the verdict was announced by Colonel Snider. Guilty of murdering his wife, and guilty of committing adultery with Mrs Cynthia Taylor. As Marymont turned without a word and marched smartly with his escort from the courtroom, the only other sound was muffled sobbing, coming not from Mrs Taylor but from the prisoner's mother, Gertrude Marymont, flown over from America for her son's trial. Marymont was driven from Denham to spend the longest night of his life in the detention barracks at nearby Bushey, Hertfordshire.

Unlike British courts, in which sentencing normally follows immediately after the verdict is announced, the American system entailed a delay before Marymont would know his fate. There were only two sentencing options available to the court, death or life imprisonment, which meant literally what it said.

When the court martial reconvened for the last time the next morning, it listened first to Captain Kasdan make a speech in mitigation before pleading for Marymont's life to be spared: 'I say in all sincerity there are possibilities of innocence in this case. There might just remain some lingering doubts .... If this is so, I ask you to give him the benefit of that doubt and bring in the lesser sentence of life imprisonment.'

Some of the adjudicating officers at least were swayed by Captain Kasdan's plea, as there was not the unanimity required to invoke the death penalty. Marymont listened unmoved as Colonel Snider sentenced him to hard labour for life. It was also ordered that he be dishonourably discharged from the American Air Force and forfeit all pay and allowances.

Before being taken away, Marymont spoke briefly to reporters: 'Every single thing I said in the court was the truth. I did not murder my wife .... When she became ill, I did everything a husband could be expected to do.'

His mother added: 'He was always a good boy. We never had any trouble with him .... He is my only child ....'

Gertrude Marymont's was by no means the final word. While

her son prepared to fly back to the United States to start his sentence in Fort Leavenworth, Kansas, Captain Kasdan was announcing that at the automatic review of the case it was proposed to draw attention to errors both in law and in fact. The verdict and the sentence were subject to three reviews in the United Kingdom and Washington.

Mr William Mars Jones QC appeared for Marymont before the staff judge advocate of the United States Air Force at Denham. It seems that an English lawyer was retained because a significant element of Marymont's appeal centred on a supposed infringement of Cynthia Taylor's rights that had influenced the result of the trial. 'She should never have been compelled to give evidence against him [Marymont],' insisted Mr Mars Jones. 'As a British subject, she had the right not to give evidence on matters that might incriminate her ... she was entitled to the same immunities and privileges as if she had been a witness in the High Court of England.' Mars Jones maintained that the American law officer advising the court martial had 'completely disregarded such right', as a result of which, 'The whole thing became a travesty ....' He further submitted that a letter written by Gertrude Marymont saying that her daughter-in-law had threatened to 'take something first', if ever she thought she had cancer, should have been introduced at the trial.

Although the barrister's arguments were initially rejected and Marymont's conviction was confirmed by the judge advocate general in Washington, in 1960 the United States Court of Military Appeals, the highest appellate body in American military justice, dismissed the charge of adultery and reduced Marymont's sentence to one of thirty-five years.

Did Marcus Marymont kill his wife? The evidence of Doctors Camps and Nickolls confirmed that arsenic *had* been ingested by Mary Helen Marymont for weeks before she died.

What of the defence suggestions that the poison had been self-administered? Not only was the theory discounted by Dr Camps, but it should be borne in mind also that arsenical poisoning is a singularly unpleasant and painful manner of dying, thus rendering it even more unlikely that prolonged self-administration is a feasible hypothesis. Similarly the accidental ingestion of the poison by Mrs Marymont was unsupported by any credible evidence.

One is left with only one conclusion, that Master Sergeant Marcus M. Marymont, USAF deliberately killed his wife to enable him to continue unhindered his love-affair with the woman with whom he had become infatuated.

– 11 –
A Question of Identification
1972

'We are all prone to make mistakes about identification ....'
Never were the words of Mr Hamilton John Leonard QC more
graphically illustrated than during the investigation and
subsequent trials of a man who was placed in double jeopardy
following a particularly brutal shooting which took place during
the early hours of Guy Fawkes Day 1972.

Two muffled shots climaxed the robbery from a large
detached house lying fifty yards behind a rambling single-
storeyed building called the Barn Restaurant at Braintree in
Essex. Minutes earlier another shot, fired through a velvet-
covered cushion, had fatally injured the 51-year-old wife of the
restaurant's owner. Now he and their daughter were the
gunman's target. Shortly after the last shot, a blue Volkswagen
estate containing two men was driven rapidly out of the
car-park and disappeared in the direction of Great Dunmow.

The evening of Saturday 4 November 1972 had followed its
regular pattern at the Barn Restaurant. Three hundred people,
many of whom had travelled up from the East End of London,
enjoyed a dinner, dance and cabaret. The short, tubby figure of
Robert Patience, the Barn's owner, circulated among the tables,
greeting old customers and welcoming new ones.

Patience, an ex-RAF air-gunner, married, with two children,
epitomized the successful, self-made entrepreneur. From selling
firewood, logs and second-hand furniture, he had expanded his
interests in the late 1950s by purchasing a small night club in
Ilford. However, after a fracas in which a man had died, he sold
this establishment and in 1962 bought some modest tea-rooms
at Braintree. Over the next ten years these grew into a
flourishing restaurant and nightspot. The Barn Restaurant
became a well-known Essex rendezvous, its growth bringing
with it a prosperous and comfortable lifestyle for its owner and

159

his family. A Mercedes saloon, family holidays abroad and a collection of antiques testified to Bob Patience's success. He also had a reputation as a philanthropist known to have helped several local charities financially.

The business was very much a family concern. Muriel Patience, an attractive blonde woman devoted to her family, and the ideal partner for her extrovert husband, was able to exercise a cautionary and restraining influence upon his occasionally over-ambitious and speculative ideas but was equally supportive and encouraging of his more carefully thought-out ventures. That Saturday evening she was working in the restaurant alongside her 20-year-old daughter, Beverley. Not far away, Beverley's elder brother David had spent most of the evening at the cash desk. Everything appeared normal …

Beverley Patience screamed. Confronting her in the kitchen of her home were two men, one of whom was pointing a gun. Instinctively she stepped back into the doorway, bumping into her mother, who was behind her. The man with the gun stepped quickly across the room. 'Be quiet. It's not you we want,' he said.

Muriel Patience and her daughter had arrived home just before 2 a.m., having left the restaurant a few minutes earlier as the entertainment was winding down and customers were starting to depart. It was raw and bitterly cold, and the two women had hurried across the car-park towards the warmth of Sun Lido House.

Beverley would never forget the nightmarish events that took place during the next half-hour. In response to the gunman's directions, she and her mother, who by now was hysterical, went into the lounge and sat down side by side on the settee. The two men followed and sat opposite them. They asked the women for the safe keys; Beverley, while attempting to reassure her sobbing mother, tried stalling by saying that the keys were in the restaurant.

With mixed feelings she heard her father arrive home. While confident that he would know how to handle the situation, she was nevertheless apprehensive lest his volatile temperament place them in even greater peril. (Robert Patience had driven a couple of the restaurant staff home before following his wife and daughter to the house.) As he entered the lounge, he immediately took in the situation: Muriel and Beverley huddled together on the settee, and two men, one holding a gun, facing them. Patience did as he was told when ordered to sit in an armchair, but when the man with the gun asked for the keys to the safe in the hall, he, like his daughter, tried to prevaricate: there was no money in the safe; the keys were at the restaurant; the staff had to be paid. The gunman was unimpressed, repeating his demand that Patience hand over the safe keys and emphasizing it with a menacing, all-embracing motion with his gun. Patience, still refusing to be intimidated, continued to deny that he had the keys.

Suddenly the man with the gun came to a decision. Pressing the weapon into a cushion he was holding, he pointed it first at Muriel Patience and then at Beverley, saying ominously to Bob Patience, 'Your wife or your daughter?' The shot, when it came, was unexpected; with the words 'Your wife, I think', he squeezed the trigger. There was a muffled crack, a shower of feathers, and Muriel Patience jerked back with a cry before slumping forward, a .32-calibre bullet lodged in her brain. For a moment there was silence, then with a cry of anguish Bob Patience leapt to his feet as though to hurl himself at the other man. A jerk of the gun brought him up short. 'The keys!' the gunman demanded.

With his bluff savagely called, Patience delayed no longer but retrieved the safe keys from a vase nearby. With a look of grim satisfaction, his captor ordered him into the hall and told him to open the safe. Patience complied and gave the other man two bank bags containing about £900 in cash, along with cheques and credit-card slips, before slamming the safe door on a further £7,000 in cash that the robber had overlooked.

Meanwhile, in response to Beverley's pleadings, the second man had gone into the kitchen and fetched a towel with which he attempted to staunch the bleeding from Muriel Patience's wound. When his companion returned to the lounge, the two men had a brief conversation, ending with the second man's collecting from the kitchen some plastic clothes-line and two neckties, which he used to tie up and gag Beverley and her father, leaving them both lying face downwards on the floor.

Then came a cold-blooded attempt to execute father and daughter. Bending first over Beverley, the man with the gun placed the cushion over her back and fired through it. She screamed and lapsed into unconsciousness. Moving to her father, he put the cushion against the side of his head before firing. Without a word, the gunman and his accomplice – who throughout had spoken only briefly – left the house.

Miraculously Bob Patience and his daughter survived. An instant before the bullet exploded into his brain, Patience had moved his head fractionally, enough for the round to be diverted so that, instead of penetrating his skull, it inflicted only a minor injury to his right ear. Although deeply shocked, he managed to reach an internal telephone and free himself sufficiently to alert his son, who was still at the restaurant. David Patience immediately called the police before dashing across the car-park to Sun Lido House. On the way he was passed by his Estate car with two men in it.

Police and an ambulance were soon at the scene. Both women were critically injured: Muriel Patience was unconscious, her daughter now conscious but in great pain. The bullet had entered her back and passed through her body, inflicting severe but non-fatal injuries to several internal organs during its progress. The round had lodged in her clothing, from which it was later recovered. Her mother was less fortunate: the brain-damage was irremediable, despite her having been immediately transferred from Black Notley Hospital at Braintree to the neurological unit at Oldchurch Hospital, thirty miles away in Romford.

Back at Sun Lido House, the first uniformed policemen to arrive had recovered two cartridge cases, one of which had dropped from Muriel Patience's dress before she was placed in the ambulance. These were handed to Detective Chief Inspector Derek Wyatt of Colchester CID who had driven immediately to the scene. After arranging for the attendance of fingerprint experts and photographers and having made preliminary arrangements for a police major incident room to be set up in the restaurant, Wyatt continued to Black Notley Hospital. Meanwhile other detectives started interviewing those who had earlier been at the restaurant, and taking written statements. A description of David Patience's Volkswagen Estate was also circulated, in the hope that it would soon be found.

At the hospital Wyatt was able to have a brief chat with Bob Patience, after which the detective arranged for him, his wife and daughter to be given armed protection. By 4 a.m., barely two hours after the first shot had been fired, the police investigation was well under way.

Later that Sunday morning Detective Chief Superintendent Cecil Leonard (Len) White, head of Essex Police CID took charge. His enquiry was conducted along conventional and well-proven lines. Over sixty detectives from Essex and the Metropolitan Police Force were eventually assigned to the case. In addition to the measures already in hand, White directed that passengers at sea – and airports be scrutinized, to prevent the wanted men leaving the country. Details of the fracas outside Robert Patience's Ilford club ten years before were recalled, in case there was a possible connection, and detectives later investigated suggestions that the Barn Restaurant had been deliberately targeted for a robbery.

Soon after 8 a.m. on Sunday morning, a farmworker found David Patience's Volkswagen in a field alongside the A120. The vehicle was removed to Braintree police station, where fingerprint and forensic examination failed to give a lead as to its most recent occupants.

The next day, Monday 6 November, police efforts concentrated on obtaining descriptions of the wanted men. In the morning Detective Chief Inspector Wyatt visited Beverley Patience in hospital and recorded an interview in which she briefly described the events that had taken place. More importantly, she gave an excellent description of the two intruders. This supplemented a photofit picture based on her father's recollection which had been compiled by Detective Sergeant Rampling.

The gunman was apparently in his early thirties, about five feet eight inches tall, with short, sandy hair combed forward. His eyes, described as 'very blue', were set in a sallow-complexioned face. He had been wearing a beige mackintosh and brown buckled shoes. His younger companion, who was estimated to be in his late twenties, was slightly over six feet tall, of slim build, with dark hair worn slightly longer than the other man's. He had been dressed in a light tweed suit and had been carrying a briefcase.

Following newspaper reports of the shootings and publication of the photofits, a number of people contacted the police. Among them were some public house regulars from the village of Felstead who on the Thursday before the robbery had noticed two strangers in the bar, and a witness named Jonathan Ridley who, on Saturday 4 November in Braintree, had been approached by two men who had asked for directions to Rayne Road in which the Barn Restaurant was situated. The witnesses' descriptions all roughly tallied with the photofit pictures.

The detectives were quietly satisfied with the early progress of their investigation: witnesses were beginning to come forward, and they had a good description of the suspects. Their enquiry assumed a new dimension when on the Wednesday afternoon, in Oldchurch Hospital, Muriel Patience died without ever having regained consciousness. Now it was a murder case.

Earlier that day Robert Patience had left Black Notley Hospital vowing, 'If it takes all the money I have, I will see justice done to these two fanatical and despicable men.' He offered a reward of £2,000 for help in bringing them to justice, and a fund set up by the *Colchester Evening Gazette* attracted another £10,000 from

Essex licensees. Detective Chief Superintendent White reinforced the financial inducement by appealing to the 'underworld' for information. As a result of the combined encouragement police received hundreds of telephoned tip-offs; one of these, sent not to the Murder Squad in Essex but to Scotland Yard's Serious Crimes Squad, named George Ince as the man detectives were seeking.

Thirty-five-year-old George Henry Ince was a thoroughbred East Ender. Apart from two years during the war when he had been evacuated, he had grown up within the tight-knit community off the Bow Road. His family was poor, and George was the second youngest of James and Minnie Ince's eight children. Their shared hardships had bonded the children close together, and throughout George's forthcoming ordeal their support never wavered.

Although he was a contemporary of the criminal Kray twins and their older brother Charles, George was never in the same league – that is, until May 1972. He was certainly no friend of the Krays, having entered into a hazardous relationship with Charlie Kray's wife, Dolly. Despite some imaginative attempts on Kray's part to dissuade him, which included firing a shotgun down the front of his trousers (without hitting its intended target), the affaire continued. After the Krays had been gaoled in 1968, the way was clear and the romance flourished unhindered.

In May 1972 things began to go wrong for George Ince. It started when he became involved in a plan with several other men to hijack a bullion lorry in transit from the City of London to the east-coast port of Harwich. The potential proceeds from the robbery had been £400,000 worth of silver ingots, but unfortunately for the gang a quick-witted milkman who was passing the scene frustrated their efforts and they succeeded in getting away with only £40,000 worth of the bullion.

Within three hours of the robbery one of the gang was captured. The others, including George Ince, whose fingerprints were later found in a get-away vehicle, escaped. With two of his companions he made his way to a small hotel at Margate, where they stayed for a few weeks before moving to a caravan near Whitstable. If the hunt for George Ince in connection with the bullion hijack had been intensive, it was nothing compared to that which followed the tip-off that he was involved in the Barn murder.

According to Ince, it was not until he telephoned his mother's home from Kent on Wednesday 22 November, and spoke to his sister Phyllis, that he became aware that police were seeking him in connection with the Braintree killing. If this was true, he was almost certainly the last member of his family to know of the situation. Following the tip-off his council flat had been visited by a posse of armed policemen; police also called at the homes of his sister Rose and Doris Gray (formerly Kray), his mother's flat and addresses of other members of his family, friends and acquaintances. Nothing was found to connect him with the Barn murder, nor was there any indication as to his present whereabouts.

Meanwhile a series of photographs, which included one of Ince, was shown to Beverley as she lay in her hospital bed. From them she identified him as the gunman. Not so her father: when he was shown the line-up of photographs, he failed to pick out Ince.

By now relations between Bob Patience and the investigating officers were strained. Since his discharge from Black Notley Hospital, he had spoken freely to reporters; early on, he had told them that, when holidaying abroad the previous summer, he had been warned that his restaurant was a likely target for a robbery. The police felt that his revealing such information hampered their enquiry, and they were even more vexed when Patience, after leaking George Ince's name to the pressmen, revealed that he proposed to sell his story to a Sunday newspaper.

After a private talk between Patience and Chief Superintendent Len White, police transferred their incident room from the Barn Restaurant to Braintree police station. One of the first communications they received at their new headquarters was a letter from Patience enclosing a bill for £240 for the refreshments which had been supplied to the officers on the enquiry during the time they had been based at the restaurant.

While five carloads of mourners attended the funeral service of Muriel Patience at St Michael's Church, Braintree, and her subsequent cremation at Chelmsford, Len White and his team pressed on with the investigation. The witnesses from Felstead and elsewhere were interviewed and statements obtained; Beverley Patience was again seen in hospital and for the second time identified George Ince from photographs; members of Ince's family were revisited.

Eventually, on 20 November, police allowed details of their suspect, still without naming him, to appear in the press. There was no doubt from the description that the wanted man was George Ince, who did not see the newspaper report but who two days later telephoned his mother …

Ince was dumbfounded. He would not have been surprised had Phyllis told him that the police were seeking him in connection with the bullion hijack, but as a murder suspect, that was a far more serious matter. He pondered the situation over the weekend and came to the conclusion that his best course was to surrender to the police. He had an alibi for the night of Saturday 4/Sunday 5 November, having spent it in bed with Doris Gray. Ince telephoned her, and she agreed to call into his solicitor's to make a statement verifying this before he went to the police. He went to see Mr Stanley, his solicitor, on Friday 24 November, where he made a statement denying any involvement in the Barn murder and putting his alibi on record.

After spending the weekend with friends in East London, on Monday morning Ince and Mr Stanley drove to Epping police station. Their arrival was not entirely unexpected, as a colleague of Stanley's had telephoned Essex police in advance and told them whom to expect. The murder squad detectives were elated. During the weekend Beverley Patience had yet again identified Ince from a photograph she was shown – now he had surrendered himself. Their satisfaction was increased by a sense of relief that his apprehension had not involved a gun battle with the police.

Ince was transferred from Epping to Braintree police station, and it was there, during the late afternoon, that he was formally interviewed by Detective Chief Superintendent White in the presence of Detective Superintendent George Harris, Chief Inspector Wyatt and Mr Stanley. When asked specifically about the shootings, Ince said, 'I'm absolutely innocent and that's what I have come to see you about.'

White read the statements made by Ince and Doris Gray. After being assured that her true identity would not be recorded in the interview, and with Ince's permission, Mr Stanley told White that Doris Gray was better known as Dolly Kray, the wife of Charlie, who was currently serving ten years. The detective then questioned Ince in embarrassing detail about the night he said he had spent with Mrs Gray.

'Were you both intimate that night?' he asked.

'Yes,' replied Ince.

'What time roughly?'

'I couldn't say to be truthful. It could have been 11.30 p.m. to 12.30 a.m. I don't really know ...'

'What did you wear in bed?' enquired White.

'Nothing.'

'And her?'

'Nothing,' Ince not surprisingly replied.

At the end of the interview arrangements were made for him to be taken to Colchester for an identification parade.

The subsequent trials of George Ince centred to a large extent on the identification parades that were held at Colchester police station on Monday 27 and Wednesday 29 November 1972. A total of eight witnesses attended the parades, of whom the most vital from everyone's point of view were Beverley Patience and her father. Both had had ample opportunity of seeing the robbers and could therefore reasonably be expected to have a good idea of what they looked like.

So it seemed with Beverley; she was in no doubt and picked Ince out almost immediately. It should be remembered, however, that she had earlier identified him as her mother's killer on three separate occasions from photographs shown to her by the police. Her father was not as positive. After studying each man on the parade individually, pausing long and contemplatively in front of Ince, he finally indicated another man on the line-up. Yet after the parade was over Patience made a statement saying that he had made a mistake and that he should have pointed to the man wearing the green shirt – George Ince. It was only during Ince's second trial that it emerged that he had donned the green shirt, his second shirt-change during the parade, only *after* Patience had left the room.

The next witness, David Patience, tentatively identified Ince as the man he had seen driving out of the Barn car-park in his Volkswagen Estate. The penultimate witness on the Monday evening parade was Jonathan Ridley, who had been asked directions in Braintree on the eve of the murder; he was unable to identify anyone. Not so a lorry-driver named Layzell, who unhesitatingly picked out Ince as one of the men he had seen in the hotel bar in Felstead on the Thursday before the murder.

It was enough for the police. After a further brief interview with Chief Superintendent White, Ince was taken back to Braintree police station and charged with the murder of Muriel Patience. For George Ince, his intention of clearing himself of suspicion had gone disastrously wrong.

A few hours later he made his first appearance before a specially convened court at Braintree. Security in the courtroom was tight as the accused man stood in the dock, dressed neatly in a grey suit, white shirt and a blue tie. After pleading 'not guilty' to the murder of Muriel Patience, he was remanded by the chairman of the bench, Mr David Douglas-Hughes, into police custody for three days.

The following afternoon Ince was put up on another

identification parade. Three more witnesses were present, of whom only one, Harry Leverett, who had been in the public house with Layzell, identified him.

Now that Ince was in custody, police efforts were concentrated on tracking down the second Barn robber. Three of Ince's hijack accomplices gave themselves up after they had been featured in the press and on television as being wanted for questioning in connection with the murder. Their feelings were mixed when, after being eliminated from the Barn inquiry, they were detained and later charged with the bullion robbery.

Similarly with another hijack suspect, John Brett. He too, accompanied by a solicitor, surrendered to the police with the aim of clearing himself of complicity in the Braintree shooting. Unlike Ince, Brett was identified by only one of seven witnesses and escaped a possible murder charge. However, he also was later convicted for his part in the bullion robbery. The hunt for the second Barn robber continued.

Meanwhile Ince was regularly appearing at Braintree magistrates' court. In early December he was additionally charged with attempting to murder Robert and Beverley Patience; he was to be tried later for his part in the bullion hijack, but for the time being he was preoccupied with the approaching murder trial. On 9 March 1973 Mr Douglas-Hughes committed him for trial at Chelmsford Crown Court on the murder indictment, after which he was to remain in custody for almost two months waiting for his trial to begin.

May 1973 was a watershed for George Ince. Until then he had been a small-time East End crook suspected of having committed a singularly cold-blooded murder. Attendant publicity had already prematurely convinced many people of his guilt, but, by the end of the month the events in Chelmsford Crown Court were to make sensational, nationwide headlines.

George Ince's first trial opened on Wednesday 2 May. Due to the immense interest in the case, a long queue had formed several hours before the Shire Hall doors were opened to the public. Prominent among the spectators later admitted to the public gallery were Ince's mother and five sisters. Throughout the hearing their acerbic but often ribald comments frequently enlivened the proceedings.

Even before the trial started, there had been developments behind the scenes. In common with many of the criminal fraternity, Ince had decided views on the merits and shortcomings of any particular judge. Mr Justice Melford Stevenson, who was to preside at his trial, was low down in his mental league-table of judges. Ince well knew of his punitive reputation – he had sent the Kray twins and their accomplices to prison for a total of 142 years. Of equal concern to Ince was his conviction that Melford Stevenson would be prejudiced against him, a feeling that increased as the trial progressed. His lawyers, in a bid to avert what they foresaw as a future source of difficulty, applied to have another judge appointed. Predictably their request was refused, so at 10 a.m. on 2 May Judge Melford Stevenson and George Ince faced each other across the courtroom.

Mr Victor Durand QC, a vastly experienced and accomplished barrister, assisted by Mr Robert Flach, defended Ince, while prosecuting was Mr Hamilton John Leonard QC, forty-eight years old and with over twenty years experience at the bar.

'The shots fired at Beverley and Mr Patience were shots of execution deliberately fired and intended to cause the death of these two people.' So did Mr Leonard in his opening address describe the shooting that had taken place at Sun Lido House during the night of 4/5 November the previous year. He went on to tell the court that at first Robert Patience had thought the intruders were bluffing, but he was soon cruelly disillusioned when his wife was shot. 'That shot entered her brain and some days later caused her death ...,' he said. After telling the jury of the evidence they would hear, Mr Leonard called his first witness.

Most of the evidence given at the first hearing and repeated at Ince's re-trial varied only in detail, the main difference being that a crucial witness testified on the second occasion who was not called initially. Additionally during the first trial, proceedings were frequently interrupted by the accused disagreeing with a witness's testimony and by heated exchanges between him and the judge. Victor Durand also clashed verbally on several occasions with Mr Justice Melford Stevenson, persuading Ince even more of the judge's bias.

'Why don't you tell the truth? You know I wasn't the one that done it.' This outburst from Ince, directed at Robert Patience, who had pointed to him as 'the man who shot my wife', was the first of several and did nothing to endear him to Mr Justice Melford Stevenson. Patience continued by describing his attempts to stall the gunman before he had suddenly approached Muriel Patience and shot her.

The court listened in silence as the witness told how, after he had handed over some money from the safe to the man with the gun, the accomplice had tied up Beverley and himself. After his daughter had been shot, Patience recalled the cushion's being placed over his head: 'I endeavoured to make some movement, there was a report and I remember crying out.'

After Patience had finished telling of the events on the night of 4/5 November, the remainder of his testimony was devoted to the less dramatic but even more critical question of identification. Of the first identification parade held on 27 November at Colchester police station, Mr Leonard asked him, 'The person you picked out was not the defendant; that is right, is it not?'

'After great meditation, no,' replied Patience. 'Finally I went to the end of the line again to the person on the extreme right and touched him on the shoulder.'

After saying that immediately following the parade he had decided that he had picked out the wrong man, the witness was asked by Mr Leonard, 'Did you come to any conclusion as to whether a man ought to have been picked out on the parade or not?'

'I did.'

'Who was that?'

'The man with the green shirt, the accused,' replied Patience.

Although later the green shirt was to assume vital importance, during the first trial its significance was not recognized by the defence, and Mr Durand made no mention of it during his cross-examination. Instead he concentrated on the photographs Patience had been shown by police before the identification parade on 27 November.

'You have seen photographs of this man many times, have you not?' said counsel.

'This man, Mr Ince, the name of Ince was never mentioned to me,' Patience replied abstrusely.

'I will put it again,' said Mr Durand. 'This man Ince, you have been shown by the police many photographs from November 6 to November 27, is that correct?'

'I have only been shown photographs with this man Ince among them.'

'On Saturday 11 November had you been shown Mr Ince's passport photograph separately?' the witness was asked.

'Possibly it was among several photographs I was shown but the name Ince was never mentioned.'

'I put it to you that on Saturday the eleventh you pointed to Ince's passport photograph and the least you could say was "The face seems a bit familiar"?'

'I most probably said it,' Patience admitted.

'Were you not picking out any subject from a photograph when you went on the parade?'

'I was picking out the man who shot my wife,' Patience insisted.

Beverley Patience showed no signs of her earlier ordeal as she walked briskly round the court into the witness-box. 'He put a cushion over my back and then he shot me. I had my head turned to the left and I could see. The gun went into the cushion. I screamed "No, don't," then he fired.'

After describing the events that had led up to the shooting of her mother, Beverley was now telling of the moment at which she herself thought she was going to die. The court listened attentively as she hesitantly recalled the unforgettable events of that night.

Her cross-examination by Mr Durand again concentrated on identification. Her insistence that Ince was the man who had shot first her mother and then her father and herself prompted another explosion of anger from the man in the dock.

'Why don't you tell the truth?' Ince yelled across at Beverley, who immediately burst into tears. Ince regretted his interruption and attempted to apologize from the dock, but Mr Justice Melford Stevenson had lost patience with him, and after granting a short adjournment to enable Beverley to recover, he announced, 'I am not going to risk an outburst of the kind to which we have been subjected on two occasions in this very important trial ... take the defendant downstairs.'

After Ince had gone, Mr Durand continued his cross-examination. In reply to his question as to how many photographs of Ince she had been shown prior to the 27 November identification parade, Beverley replied, 'I can definitely say some were shown to me before the parade but I cannot remember all of them. I cannot say.' Beverley Patience was a good witness; her obvious efforts to recall truthfully and accurately all that had taken place almost six months earlier won her the sympathy and admiration of most of the people in court.

Ince clearly gave much thought to his situation over the weekend. Monday passed off without incident, but on Tuesday he demanded a change of judge. Melford Stevenson told him he was unable to grant such a request, whereupon Ince promptly sacked his lawyers and turned to leave the dock, saying to the judge, 'This is an unfair and biased trial.' The judge instructed that he be prevented from leaving, so in a gesture of frustrated defiance Ince turned his back on the judicial bench.

Melford Stevenson appeared unperturbed and ordered that the proceedings continue. During the police evidence which followed, Ince occasionally interrupted with caustic remarks but ignored totally anything the judge said to him. At one stage he tried to introduce a new element into British jurisprudence by asking that he be given a truth drug; to no one's surprise the request was turned down.

Finally the moment arrived for Mr Justice Melford Stevenson to sum up. For 2½ hours during which time he was continually interrupted by the man in the dock, he spoke to the jury. His remarks were lucid, fair and objective, a splendid reflection on the British judiciary's wisdom and tolerance. Throughout his discourse Melford Stevenson made only passing reference to Ince's behaviour during the trial, and he warned the jury against being prejudiced towards the accused by anything he had said or done.

The jury had difficulty in reaching a verdict; twice they returned to seek guidance from the judge, who at 6.30 p.m. told them that he would accept a 10–2 majority verdict. After three more hours had elapsed, by which time they had been out for 6½ hours, the jury were fetched back into court. After the foreman had told Mr Justice Melford Stevenson that they were still unable to reach even a majority decision, he told them, '... you tried your best and in these circumstances the whole case will have to be tried again ....'

While this announcement provoked scenes of jubilation among his family and friends in the public gallery, George Ince was led away to await a retrial. As he departed he was unable to resist a final swipe at the trial judge: 'I would like to thank the members of the jury for giving me the chance to state my case and let my case go forward in front of a truthful judge.' Mr Melford Stevenson merely smiled enigmatically.

The second trial of George Ince opened at Chelmsford less than a week later. This time he stood before Mr Justice Eveleigh, a judge of whom he apparently approved. Although there was to be much less verbal crossfire on this occasion, in other ways the retrial was to be even more sensational than its predecessor.

The evidence given by the three members of the Patience family was completed without interruption from the man in the dock. It varied only slightly, but Bob Patience especially was subjected to a searching cross-examination by Mr Durand, who had been reinstated as defence counsel. Despite this, Patience remained adamant that Ince was the man who had shot first his wife and then himself and his daughter. Similarly Beverley Patience, although pressed hard by Mr Durand, insisted that she had correctly identified Ince.

The trial started to lean in George Ince's direction during the police evidence. It turned on the moment at which he had changed into a green shirt on the 27 November identification parade. According to the notes made at the time by Chief Inspector James Gorham, the officer in charge of the parade,

Ince had *twice* exchanged shirts, the first time with Mr Stanley, his solicitor, before the first witness was introduced, the second occasion prior to the last witness's entering the room, when he changed shirts with another man on the parade wearing a green shirt.

When Detective Chief Superintendent Leonard White, who had been present during the identification parade, testified, he stated that Ince had changed his shirt *three* times and had been wearing a green shirt when Bob Patience had been introduced to the parade. White was followed into the witness-box the next day by Chief Inspector Gorham, who said that he had made a mistake and that Ince had after all made *three* shirt-changes and not *two* as he had originally stated.

Gorham was subjected to a rigorous cross-examination by Mr Durand on this vital matter. He seemed confused as to the men with whom Ince had changed shirts, but tried to retrieve the situation by apologizing: 'I can only say I am sorry and I made a mistake, but I am absolutely certain,' he told Mr Durand. Despite this assurance, with the confusion over the shirt-changes, the pendulum swung in George Ince's favour.

The shirt episode was to be resurrected briefly when Howard Huett, who had been standing on the parade, and Mr Stanley, Ince's solicitor, appeared for the defence to support its contention that Ince had been wearing Stanley's beige-coloured shirt until a break towards the end of the proceedings. During cross-examination the solicitor told Mr Leonard, 'I know he [Ince] had my shirt on when the three members of the Patience family saw him.'

This apart, the defence relied on Ince's alibi that he had been in bed with Doris Gray on the night of the murder.

The accused was the first to testify. He acquitted himself well, displaying no sign of the bitterness that had characterized his previous trial. From his reply to Victor Durand's question as to whether he had anything to do with the shootings, 'No, sir, I am completely innocent', until finally in response to a question from the judge he affirmed that he and Mrs Gray were in love with each other, Ince did not falter as questions were put to him by his own counsel and by Mr Leonard. He and Mrs Gray had gone to bed about half-past midnight, he told Mr Durand.

'What time did you get up?'

'Approximately quarter-past eight.'

'During the whole of that time where was Mrs Gray?'

'With me,' replied Ince. He denied Mr Leonard's suggestion that, after having spent only part of the night with Mrs Gray, he had left her to travel to Braintree.

Mr Justice Eveleigh agreed that Mrs Gray's former name should not be disclosed in court, so the mystery surrounding her background added to the prurient anticipation of the spectators. Slender and well dressed, she stood nervously in the witness-box on the morning of Monday 21 May. Although in love with the man in the dock and prepared to testify and bare her soul in public on his behalf, Doris Gray had nonetheless been fervently hoping that the written statement she had made to Mr Stanley would be enough, a wish shared no less keenly by Ince. Such was not to be; nothing other than her personal testimony would suffice, the defence team decided.

In the event she comported herself with dignity, replying in a quiet London accent when asked by Mr Durand, 'Was he [Ince] in bed with you the whole night?', 'Yes, sir, the whole night.'

'Could he have left you during the night?'

'No, not at all.'

Mr Leonard's cross-examination was aimed at discrediting Mrs Gray by drawing attention to the adulterous nature of her relationship with Ince.

'Is it since your husband disappeared from the world of active circulation that you have been intimate with Ince?' he asked at one point.

'In 1969. My husband went away in 1968,' she replied.

Mr Leonard went on to suggest that she had fabricated her evidence to protect Ince. This provoked a heated reply from the witness: 'I am telling the absolute truth. This man never left my side when he came on the Saturday and left on the Sunday .... I am a Catholic, and I will not come here to lie.'

As Doris Gray stepped down from the witness-box when she had finished testifying, there remained only counsels' closing speeches and Mr Justice Eveleigh's summing-up before a jury for the second time would try to decide on George Ince's guilt or innocence.

Mr Leonard unemotionally summarized the Crown case, drawing the jury's attention to its salient points, while Victor Durand focused upon the apparent weaknesses in his opponent's arguments, unashamedly playing on the jury's emotions: 'The action on the court floor has stopped. You, and each one of you, have seen the principal parts played there ... you may well feel, coming out from beneath, a deep sense of unease that something is still hidden.' He continued: 'The prisoner innocent, crying out for the truth to be revealed to you. The heartfelt answer by his lover .... Mrs Gray's call of truth still ringing in your ears. ...Not a single item, fibre or spot of blood from the "room of death" in the Patience home could be identified with George Ince. There were no palmprints or footprints .... There isn't a single link thrown up by science against Ince.'

While agreeing with Mr Durand that, 'There is something funny about the whole thing. The more one looks at it, the more remarkable the story becomes', the jury may well have asked which was the more remarkable story. Which indeed? That of Robert Patience, convinced that Ince was the man who had killed his wife, or that of the accused himself, denying the charges and allowing his lover to suffer the ordeal of testifying to prove his innocence?

Unlike his predecessor Mr Melford Stevenson, Mr Justice Eveleigh was able to complete his summing-up without interruption from Ince. It was Wednesday 23 May and even more people – press and public – had crowded into the court to witness the closing stages of this memorable trial.

Aside from the identification evidence, the judge, mindful that some members of the jury at least probably suspected the identity of Mrs Gray's husband, discreetly warned them against holding such knowledge against her. It was nearly one o'clock by the time Mr Justice Eveleigh finished, and over three hours more were to elapse while the jury was out considering its verdict. Ince waited beneath the court, where he was visited by his sisters. The conversation was stilted, the women trying to encourage and reassure him, while he became more convinced as time passed that the verdict would go against him. Eventually his sisters left him to wait in the Shire Hall foyer.

In the courtroom police, lawyers and reporters chatted inconsequentially while court officials hovered in the background. The tension was palpable. At last came word that the jury was about to return. Everyone either returned to their seats or stood waiting expectantly. The judge re-entered the court, and Ince, looking pale and drawn, was brought up from below.

'Not guilty.'

As the foreman of the jury uttered these words, there was uproar and scenes of unmitigated joy among Ince's friends and relatives. As the words were repeated in respect of the other charges, Mr Justice Eveleigh and court officials strove to restore order, while Ince could be heard shouting abuse at the police officers in the case. He was hustled away and taken back to prison to await trial for his part in the bullion robbery.

The detectives, while remaining tight-lipped over the result, were thoroughly dejected. Months of hard and patient slog spent gathering evidence, tracing and interviewing witnesses and preparing the case for trial counted for little with Ince's acquittal. Notwithstanding their personal feelings about the result, the hunt for the killer of Muriel Patience would now have to start again.

Robert and Beverley Patience were devastated at the verdict. They realized that the jury had rejected their evidence and accepted that they might have been mistaken in their identification. Both nonetheless remained convinced that they had been right. If anyone else was ever brought to trial for the Barn shootings, the prosecution's two leading witnesses in the Ince proceedings could hardly be asked to try to identify the accused after having already been so positive that George Ince was the man. For everyone recently involved in the prosecution case against Ince, it was a depressing situation.

'NEW MOVE BY POLICE': the stark black headline in the *Colchester Evening Gazette* of Wednesday 20 June 1973, exactly four weeks after George Ince's acquittal, presaged a report saying that Detective Chief Superintendent Len White and six of his colleagues had travelled up to the Lake District in what were described as 'sensational new moves in the Braintree Barn murder case'.

As has frequently been the case in major police investigations, the breakthrough that led to the final solving of the Barn case came from a totally unexpected source. On Thursday 14 June, 300 miles away from Braintree on the southern fringe of the Lake District, a young, small-time criminal named Peter Hanson had walked into Kendal police station to admit to a break-in he had carried out in neighbouring Westmorland. Whilst being interviewed, Hanson, possibly hoping to ingratiate himself with the detectives, casually mentioned a man with whom he had worked at an Ambleside hotel, who had shown him a small pistol with which he boasted he had shot the Patience family in Essex.

Hanson's startling disclosure prompted a swift response by the Cumbrian officers. Within twenty-four hours they had traced his former room-mate to a Bowness-on-Windermere restaurant, where they arrested him. They later found hidden in his room nearby a Beretta pistol and fourteen rounds of ammunition.

The man was John Brook, thirty years old and with a formidable list of convictions stretching back to his youth. Familiar with police interrogations, Brook at first denied ownership of the gun, but eventually he admitted to Detective Constable Tony Crellin that he had bought the weapon the previous October, a few days after having been released from Pentonville Prison, where he had been on the prison hostel scheme serving out the end of a three-year sentence for assault.

The Cumbrian police had prima facie evidence that Brook was unlawfully in possession of the firearm and ammunition and charged him accordingly. Additionally, on the strength of Hanson's statement and their deepening suspicion that Brook might have been involved in the Barn affair, the local police notified their Essex colleagues of the developments. Meanwhile the Beretta and ammunition were sent for examination to the Home Office forensic science laboratory in Nottingham.

The effect of the information from the Cumbrian police on Chief Superintendent White and his team at Chelmsford was immediate. For weeks they had fruitlessly been seeking new leads to the Barn robbers; now it seemed that their luck might have changed. White and two other detectives set off for Kendal the following morning, while Detective Sergeant Peter Douglas and Detective Constable John Kelly drove to Nottingham, taking with them the rounds of ammunition recovered from the Barn shooting for comparison with the gun and ammunition seized in Cumbria. The subsequent result largely removed any doubt White and the other detectives had regarding Brook's involvement in the Braintree shootings, for tests proved that the bullets recovered at the scene had been fired from Brook's gun.

The net was closing around Brook, but his ownership of the murder weapon at the material time, and Hanson's statement, was still not enough to warrant his being charged with murder. This time there must be no mistake; White was determined that the second man involved should be found, and with this objective he questioned Brook. The interrogation was lengthy and probing, but Brook admitted nothing. When told by White that he was suspected of having been the gunman at Sun Lido House, he replied, 'How can I be when Ince was picked out as the man?'

'Your gun was used at the Barn,' White pointed out.

'It doesn't mean that I was the one to have it that night,' Brook countered. He admitted to having heard of Bob Patience and suggested at one point that it might have been a revenge shooting, adding, 'I didn't do it.' His diary for 1972 had been discovered, with 5 November circled. 'It could have been the day I intended to go to my grandmother's,' he explained woodenly.

While Chief Superintendent White interviewed the obdurate suspect, other detectives sought additional witnesses, hoping thereby to corroborate Peter Hanson's statement. Two aides to

CID (probationer detectives) were given the less salubrious task of searching through a rubbish tip at Convent Lane on the outskirts of Braintree in an effort to retrieve exhibits, including the cushions through which the shots had been fired. After the Ince retrial these and other items had been returned to Robert Patience, who had immediately thrown them away. The young detectives succeeded in their quest – one hopes to the enhancement of their future careers.

Sheer determination and detective ability were eventually rewarded in the search for the second man. By meticulously checking on former friends and acquaintances of John Brook, both in and outside prison, they arrived at a man who appeared to have been associated with him more closely than most. Nicholas St Clare Johnson had struck up a friendship with Brook while in prison and had worked with him on the Pentonville hostel scheme. When it was learnt that Johnson had been on home leave during the weekend of 4/5 November 1972, suspicion against him increased.

It did not take long for Johnson's whereabouts to be established: he was in custody at Southampton awaiting trial on a theft charge. Chief Superintendent White promptly returned to Chelmsford on Wednesday 20 June, before continuing the next day to the south-coast port accompanied by Superintendent George Harris. At the central police station in Southampton the two men came face to face with Nicholas St Clare Johnson.

Johnson was more co-operative than John Brook. A less ruthless criminal than the other man, he had nonetheless spent a considerable number of his twenty-nine years in prison. His interview with White and Harris culminated in his making a lengthy written statement in which he implicated Brook and confirmed his own participation in the Barn affair but at the same time revealed himself as the more compassionate of the two men.

After being cautioned he said, 'I am ashamed of what happened .... Why he had to try and kill the other two I don't know.'

'Did you have a gun yourself?' asked White.

'No ...'

'Did you intend there to be a killing?'

'No.'

'Did John?'

'No ... I got in too deep.'

In his written account, after telling how he and Brook had first met, he described what had taken place at Sun Lido House during the night of 4/5 November 1972.

After breaking in through a rear bedroom window, he had

admitted Brook through the back door. They had been surprised by the arrival of Muriel Patience and her daughter, and later when Bob Patience had returned home they had demanded the keys to the safe. According to Johnson, as the restaurant-owner prevaricated he had said to him, 'Aren't you being foolish with your wife and daughter?' He still thought that Patience had been 'an incredibly stupid man' by refusing to produce the keys, and attributed Muriel Patience's death – an 'accident', he termed it – directly to her husband's intransigence.

He said that after she had been shot he had '... got a towel and tried to do what I could for Mrs Patience. I lifted her back onto the settee .... I think I put a cushion under her head.' After tying up Beverley and her father, Johnson said he had grabbed the car keys and money bags and left the house. Outside he '... heard two further shots ....'

Johnson had still not finished. After telling of their getaway, he was asked by Chief Superintendent White if he had known that John Brook was armed.

'Yes I did,' he replied, '... and for that reason I should have tried to prevent its use ....' As though in atonement, Nicholas St Clare Johnson accepted entire responsibility for what had happened and concluded his statement by saying, '... the whole episode should never have been.'

During the next six weeks police efforts never flagged. Both men were interviewed again. When confronted with Johnson's statement, Brook made one cross-allegation that the other man had been the gunman, a familiar ploy when two men are suspected of complicity in a murder. He even suggested that it was 'Ince and Johnson' who had committed the Barn robbery.

When Johnson was seen again in Winchester Prison, he clarified certain points he had made earlier, in particular telling Superintendent Harris that, although he had known earlier that Brook had a gun, he was unaware that he had taken it with him to the Barn. 'As far as Brook's statement is concerned, most of this is lies ...,' he added.

Detectives also recovered the bank bags from where they had been buried in a Second World War concrete pillbox in which Brook and Johnson had sheltered when fleeing from the scene. Three schoolboys who had already uncovered from the same pillbox a table lighter and screwdriver taken from Sun Lido House were also traced. Finally, after the director of public prosecutions had recommended that proceedings should go ahead, Brook and Johnson were brought back to Braintree police station, where on Wednesday 1 August 1973 they were jointly charged with the murder of Muriel Patience. Johnson faced an alternative charge of manslaughter and one of robbery. Brook also was to be indicted for the robbery, and with the attempted murder of Robert and Beverley Patience. Would there be a different outcome on this occasion? Only time would tell …

Some 5½ months were to elapse before the third Barn trial opened before Mr Justice Stocker at Chelmsford Crown Court. A shrewd, kindly man, Sir John Dexter Stocker had served with distinction during the Second World War, during which he had been awarded the MC. Called to the bar in 1948, he had been appointed a judge of the Queen's Bench Division in 1973. After all that had gone before, his conduct of the Brook/Johnson trial would be subjected to critical appraisal by layman and lawyer alike.

Public attention meantime was focused on the labour relations and economic problems facing the Heath administration; these included the threat of petrol rationing brought about by a seventy per cent increase in oil prices announced by the Middle East oil-producers.

Among those queueing to gain admittance to the Shire Hall on Tuesday 15 January 1974 were George Ince's sisters Betty and Margaret. When the trial started, they heard Mr John Leonard, prosecuting for the third time, tell the jury that, 'This case does not in any way depend upon identification …' and that the Patience family would be called upon to say only what had actually occurred on the fateful night. Mr Leonard described the circumstances of the shooting and the subsequent course of events, including the police investigation that had culminated in Brook and Johnson's appearing in the dock.

Robert Patience, who was again the first prosecution witness, repeated in essence the account he had given at the previous trials. Brook had Mr Oliver Martin QC defending him, a somewhat histrionic advocate who was soon engaged in a searching cross-examination of the witness.

'Three times on your oath … you swore positively that Ince was the man in your house,' he said.

'Yes, correct,' agreed Patience, adding that the image of the gunman was 'still clear in my mind'. He bridled as Mr Martin remarked, 'Somebody else now, is it? Dear, oh dear.'

Later Brook's counsel made play on the fact that only a relatively small amount of money had been taken: 'There is your safe full of money, jewellery in a holdall, and the robbers make off with two bags full of paper. Then you put the jewellery back in the safe. Didn't that strike you as odd?' he asked.

'No, it didn't strike me as odd. He lost his nerve and couldn't get out quickly enough …,' Patience replied.

After a less rigorous cross-examination from Mr Patrick Back QC on behalf of Johnson, Robert Patience stepped down from the witness-box. His place was taken by his daughter Beverley. Apart from the matter of identification, both she and her brother David largely repeated what they had said at George Ince's trials. Beverley agreed during cross-examination that she no longer maintained that Ince had been the gunman.

A first-time witness, John Knight, was a senior prison officer who had been at Pentonville at the time Brook and Johnson were there. He said that the two men had been 'friendly with each other', later confirming that Brook had been released from the prison in October 1972 and that Johnson had booked out for weekend leave at 5.50 p.m. on Friday 3 November 1972. He agreed with Mr Back that Johnson was 'a friendly sort of individual – very easy going and of a mild nature'.

The second week of the trial opened with the evidence of the young man whose initial statement had led to the arrest of Brook and Johnson. Peter Hanson told of his conversations with Brook in their shared staff-room at the Ambleside hotel, and recalled his room-mate's showing him the gun and telling him that the weapon had been used in the Barn murder.

Although he admitted having made several court appearances, Hanson denied under cross-examination that he had made his statement to win police favour. He also rejected Mr Martin's suggestion that details of the Barn robbery, allegedly told him by Brook, could have been gleaned from the newspapers. He '... told me how he got away and mentioned a few objects that were there,' Hanson told counsel. Mr Martin's penetrating attack on the witness was understandable for, if the jury believed Hanson, conviction for his client loomed ever more strongly.

The next day, after Geoffrey Brunt, a firearms expert, had stated that the rounds found at Sun Lido House had been fired from John Brook's gun, it was the turn of the police.

Detective Chief Superintendent Leonard White spent most of Tuesday and part of Wednesday morning in the witness-box. The early part of his testimony was devoted to his interviews with Brook and Johnson. He said that after he had outlined the events at Sun Lido House, Brook had told him that he thought he had been at his grandmother's house in Leeds at the time. Later, when testifying in his own defence, Brook was to contradict this statement, saying he had been in London during the weekend of the shooting.

The police chief continued giving evidence until Tuesday afternoon, immediately following which Mr Martin rose to cross-examine. In an apparent attempt to discredit other prosecution witnesses, Brook's advocate asked White, 'Did you say Robert Patience was a fence?'

'No, I definitely did not. He was one of the prosecution witnesses,' the policeman replied.

'All prosecution witnesses are not as pure as snow,' Martin pointed out drily.

'There is no shred of evidence to prove this,' White riposted.

The detective stated that at one point he had asked Brook, 'Is it possible you had no intention to kill Mrs Patience and then panicked?' Brook, he said, had ambiguously replied, ' "The punishment would be the same. It would be three consecutive life sentences. Even if I served a third I would still serve life".' This answer, said White, had reinforced his suspicion that Brook had been involved in the Barn shootings.

The chief superintendent's cross-examination by Johnson's counsel, Mr Back, was less probing and revealed Johnson in a more favourable light than Brook.

'He didn't appear to be a man with a hardened nature at all – a gentle type of man,' said the policeman. 'He was friendly, easy to deal with and after the initial denial co-operative and articulate. He wanted to get it completely off his chest,' he continued. The detective said Johnson had told him that he had '... tied Beverley up very slowly and very loosely'. White added that as the result also of Johnson's statement the items from Sun Lido House had been recovered from the pillbox.

Detective Superintendent George Harris stated later that Johnson had said that on the night of the shooting Brook had taken over after Beverley and her mother had entered the house, implying that he had played the lesser role in the proceedings.

Two other prosecution witnesses, Robert Breredon and Robert Quinn, were convicted prisoners who had been on remand in Risley Remand Centre at the same time as Brook. Both men stated that during their time at Risley Brook had confessed to the Barn shooting. Despite rigorously cross-examining both witnesses, Mr Martin failed to make any significant inroads into their testimony.

The prosecution case ended with Robert Quinn's stepping from the witness-box. Mr Martin, however, then requested that Robert Patience be recalled as he had some further matters to raise with him. During this latter questioning of Patience it became apparent that Brook's advocate was endeavouring to raise doubt about his morality. He alluded to the bullion hijack, for his part in which George Ince was now serving fifteen years imprisonment, and suggested to Patience that he might have been asked to store some of the proceeds from the robbery in his disused swimming-pool at the Barn.

'Utterly ridiculous, sir. I have been maligned and discredited in this case throughout .... I have already been cleared by a senior police officer ...' – Patience was seething.

He was later asked by Mr Martin if, following the incident at his former establishment at Ilford when a man had died, he knew the identity of any of the four men who had tried to intimidate him into influencing witnesses.

He replied, 'I do not, sir. There was a mention that the gentleman with the gun, if you can call him a gentleman, was one of the Kray organization but I have never met them ....'

With that Mr Martin had to be satisfied.

As Robert Patience left the witness-box for the last time, he may well have felt that everyone was overlooking the fact that the trials had all come about as the result of his wife's having been murdered. Mr Justice Stocker may well have been understanding of his feelings when he told him, 'I am sorry you were brought back.'

At the start of the trial's third week the defence case opened. Mr Martin again mentioned the name of George Ince during his introductory defence speech on Monday 28 January: 'Our defence is that the evidence shows he might have been there ...' – a remark that demonstrably angered Ince's sisters, who were sitting in the public gallery.

Brook was to prove a brash and defiant witness. He told Mr Martin that he had lent his gun to Johnson, who he understood wanted it for a robbery, but that he was in London at the time of the Barn shooting. Although he had admitted both to Peter Hanson at Ambleside and to Chief Superintendent White that he had heard of Robert Patience, he strongly denied having known or met him. Brook went on to say that White's suspicion of his involvement, after having suggested that perhaps the shooting of Muriel Patience had been accidental, was ill-founded. 'I was in no way admitting I was the gunman,' he said. He further denied admitting the shooting to Breredon or Quinn at Risley: 'I never told Breredon I was at the Barn or did the shooting, or had been there at the time ...,' he avowed.

'Did you have anything whatever to do with the shooting at the Barn on 5 November?' Mr Martin put to him.

'No,' Brook replied.

During his cross-examination by both Mr Back and Mr Leonard, Brook had difficulty at times in restraining himself. When Johnson's counsel suggested to him that his client was 'a man of mild disposition', Brook replied incredulously, 'You're joking, aren't you? .... You want me to say a killer is a gentleman .... I call him a killer ....' Later he said to Mr Back, 'I told you Johnson would say exactly the opposite to me. He has got to, hasn't he?'

There was a measure of desperation in his replies to Mr Leonard. After contradicting the evidence of the firearms expert, he interrupted the Crown counsel to suggest that there had been a deal struck between the prosecution and Johnson whereby the case against the latter had been watered down.

'Throughout these enquiries you have been prepared to tell any lie to divert suspicion from yourself,' Mr Leonard remarked trenchantly.

'Not in relation to the Barn,' Brook replied.

There was an unusual twist to the proceedings when Henry Leverett and Bernard Layzell, the two Felstead witnesses who months before had positively identified George Ince for the prosecution, this time reaffirmed their opinion, but on behalf of John Brook.

Whereas Brook had denied all part in the Barn shooting, his alleged accomplice Nicholas St Clare Johnson, while trying his best to convince the jury that he had been acting entirely under the other man's influence, nonetheless openly admitted his own participation. Dressed in an over-large green suit, he stood in the witness-box and told the court how, he and Brook had first met in prison and their friendship continued after Brook's release.

Johnson said he had agreed with Brook's suggestion that they should rob a safe at Braintree but, 'I had no idea he had a gun .... I would never have agreed if violence had been involved.' He went on to tell how, soon after gaining entry to Sun Lido House, they were suddenly interrupted by the arrival of Mrs Patience and her daughter, and shortly afterwards were joined by Bob Patience. His refusal to hand over the safe keys had, according to Johnson, culminated suddenly in Brook's, '... mumbling something to himself about a "family affair" and there was a bang'.

Johnson claimed that after Muriel Patience had been shot, 'All my concentration was on her .... Beverley put an arm round her mother and asked me for a towel. I got one from the kitchen and gave it to Beverley ....' At the same time, he told Mr Back, he had attempted to reassure the young woman that her mother's wound was not serious. He was prevented from helping further by Brook, who ordered him to "... tie them up". ...I didn't want to do it and I tied them loosely so they could escape and help Mrs Patience. I'd been instructed to do it; he'd just shot somebody. I didn't want to be shot,' Johnson continued. He said that, after they left the scene of the shootings, Brook laughingly told him, "There are no witnesses now," adding, "I shot Beverley through her back to her heart and I shot the man in the head".'

Oliver Martin concentrated on nullifying Johnson's account, accusing him of being a 'Walter Mitty' character, prone to fantasizing about himself. This prompted Johnson to insist that, despite having been seen by psychiatrists when in prison, 'I know when I am telling a lie and when I am not.' He also strongly repudiated Mr Martin's suggestion that, '... you got the gun from Brook and carried it off to your master. Brook was framed and the *real killer* got away' (author's italics).

While acknowledging Johnson's concern for Mrs Patience after she had been shot, Mr Leonard maintained that he was just as culpable as Brook: 'I suggest you either had a gun yourself, or pretended you had.'

'No, sir.'

'Your account has been directed at whitewashing your position. This was a work of fiction ....'

'No, it is not, sir.'

Johnson certainly came across as a less abrasive witness than Brook, but was he more truthful? That was the question the jury would have to decide.

When Hamilton John Leonard stood up on Tuesday 5 February, the sixteenth day of the trial, to recapitulate on the prosecution case, it signalled entry to the closing phase of the proceedings. The witnesses had been heard, and both the accused had testified; it now remained only for counsel to make their closing speeches and for the judge to sum up. Interest – which had gradually diminished as the trial had dragged on – revived, and a lengthy queue, mainly of women, was again to be seen in the mornings outside the Shire Hall.

Mr Leonard said little to minimize Johnson's complicity: '... why does he obey the instructions from this terrible gunman? ... he could have run away and raised the alarm,' the prosecutor said. He did give some credence to Johnson's testimony in relation to Brook: 'It is difficult to see a motive for him saying it was Brook, if it was somebody else with him,' he said.

The Crown counsel dismissed Brook's explanations: '... you have the inherent improbability of the version of the matter Brook gives to explain how the gun came to be used for the shootings,' he told the jury. At one point in his speech Mr Leonard was interrupted by Brook's shouting from the dock: 'I thought I was being tried for the Barn, not the gun ...' and later voicing his opinion that the advocate's address was 'rubbish'.

Oliver Martin drew upon all his rhetorical skill when it was time for him to address the jury. He refused to exculpate George Ince, describing his trial as a '... spectre which hangs like the albatross around the neck of the Ancient Mariner .... You have got to look at the evidence against Ince and take it into account when you come to deal with the case against Brook.' A theme of Mr Martin's speech was that Johnson had substituted Brook for his true accomplice – by inference George Ince: 'How can three people identify George Ince as the gunman on 5 November and each one had to be completely wrong about it?' he asked.

Mr Back soon counter-attacked on his client's behalf. He would vindicate Johnson, he said, and cautioned the jury against being misled by prosecution insinuations and 'Brook's counsel's invective': 'I am not putting him [Johnson] before you as an angel ... but as a man who would not willingly embark on such an enterprise as armed robbery.' After disparaging Brook's defence, he said of Johnson: 'They call this man the author of fiction, but it is fact, fact, fact that he told the police.' Mr Back's was a forceful and persuasive speech aimed at convincing the jury of Johnson's lesser involvement in the Sun Lido House robbery and shooting.

During the last three days of the trial Mr Justice Stocker spoke altogether for 7½ hours. His summing-up analysed the evidence and submissions of both the prosecution and defence, shrewdly defining their respective strengths and weaknesses. The judge also referred to the earlier investigation surrounding George Ince: had Robert and Beverley Patience been correct after all in their original identification, he asked. The present jury needed to consider this suggestion carefully: '... if that identity was right, it would follow the present case against Brook must be wrong,' he pointed out.

Later the jury were invited by the judge to decide whether the discovery of the gun had added a new dimension to the case. Had Brook lent his gun to Johnson? If so, the former could not have been at Sun Lido House, as he would not have had the gun. 'If you do not believe that story of the gun ... it is capable of corroborating Johnson's story ....' Mr Justice Stocker reminded the jury, however, that it was not Brook who had to prove anything. The onus of proof remained with the prosecution.

When the eleven men and one woman of the jury retired at the end of Mr Justice Stocker's marathon summing-up, they took with them photographs of George Ince and John Brook, with an invitation from the judge to examine other exhibits if they so wished.

Neither Brook nor Johnson betrayed any emotion as the jury

foreman stood up, two hours and twenty-five minutes later, to announce the verdicts.

Brook: guilty of murdering Muriel Patience; guilty of attempting to murder Robert and Beverley Patience; guilty of robbery.

Johnson: not guilty of murder but guilty of the alternative charge of manslaughter; guilty of robbery.

As the foreman sat down, the tension in court gave way to an atmosphere of almost tangible relief. At last, fifteen months after Muriel Patience, her husband and daughter had been shot, the perpetrators had been brought to book.

Mr Justice Stocker first turned to John Brook: '... the sentence I pass on you is mandatory. It is that you go to prison for life ....' Two further life sentences followed for the attempted murders, with twelve years concurrent imprisonment for the robbery.

After Mr Back had spoken in mitigation, the judge turned his attention to Nicholas St Clare Johnson. Telling him that the gravity of his offence was much less than that of Brook, he said that he was nonetheless '... bound to reflect the horror that anybody must feel even at the degree of complicity which I accept was your part in this outrage'. Sir John Stocker then sent Johnson to prison for ten years for the manslaughter, with a concurrent seven-year sentence for robbery.

Both the police and the Ince family felt vindicated. Despite the criticism that had been levelled at them from various quarters during and after the Ince trials, Detective Chief Superintendent Len White and his team had determinedly pursued the inquiry through to a successful conclusion. The Ince family were satisfied, as it had at last been proved that George had been telling the truth.

It was neither the detectives' thoroughness nor their investigative methods that should have been questioned, but the identification procedures upon which they had had to rely during the Ince enquiry. Several noteworthy cases in the past have revolved around the question of identification, and it is accepted by many people that, prior to the abolition of capital punishment, innocent men were wrongly executed after having been mistakenly identified. George Ince had not been on trial for his life, but the prospect of being sentenced to life imprisonment as a result of being wrongly identified was daunting enough.

During the past fifteen years the advent of increasingly sophisticated forensic science equipment and techniques has enormously reduced the likelihood of error. These developments have been of invaluable help and reassurance to those charged with investigating major crimes, while those contemplating such deeds are aware that the armoury of those whose job it will be to bring them to justice is being continually strengthened.

One cannot help but feel sympathy for Robert Patience and his daughter Beverley. After Muriel Patience had been cold-bloodedly shot before their eyes, they had been subjected to a fearsome ordeal that only by pure fluke they had survived. Each was certain of the identification of George Ince, having been in the gunman's presence for almost half an hour and having had ample opportunity to study the features, build and clothing of both him and his companion. There was, furthermore, a strong overall resemblance between George Ince and John Brook. Who could doubt their identification of Ince as one of the men who had been in Sun Lido House that night? Certainly not the police; they were sure that Ince had been one of the intruders and were initially dejected when he was acquitted. But wrong Patience and his daughter proved to be, thereby dramatically illustrating the fallibility of identification evidence.

After the furore at the end of the case had died down, Robert Patience and his surviving family tried to resume a normal life. The Barn Restaurant – 'a monument to my wife's memory', as Patience referred to it – continued to thrive, its notoriety attracting the curious among its more usual clientele. Eventually, in 1977, Patience sold the restaurant for a rumoured £300,000.

He lived until April 1983, dying from natural causes at his Bocking home a little over ten years after the tragic events that had thrust him and his family into the limelight. His death was the final sad postscript to one of the most contentious cases ever to have been investigated in the region.

Appendix:
Scenes of the Crimes

In giving the Ordnance Survey grid references of the cases mentioned in this book, I have endeavoured to be as accurate as possible. In those cases where it has not been possible to identify the location precisely, I have shown the grid reference of the nearest village or town.

BNG = British National Grid

OS = Ordnance Survey.

William Sheward: Tabernacle Street (now Bishopgate), Norwich, Norfolk OS sheet no. 134. BNG ref. TG238090

Louis Thain: Denmark Road, Lowestoft, Suffolk. OS sheet no. 134. BNG ref. TG524074

Marcus Marymont: Sculthorpe, Norfolk. OS sheet no. 132. BNG ref. TF845317

Alice East: Girton, Cambridgeshire. OS sheet no. 154. BNG ref. TL422624

William Corder: Polstead, Suffolk. OS sheet no. 155. BNG ref. TL994383

Henry Jones: Abberton, Essex. OS sheet no. 168. BNG ref. TL005190

Albert Schule: Regent Street, Cambridge. OS sheet no. 154. BNG ref. 454580

John Ducker: Halesworth, Suffolk. OS sheet no. 156. BNG ref. TM384774

Samuel Yarham: Howard Street South, Great Yarmouth, Norfolk OS sheet no. 134. BNG ref. TG524074

Herbert Tebbutt: Hills Avenue, Cambridge. OS sheet no. 154. BNG ref. TL466562

John Brook/Nicholas St Clare Johnson: Rayne Road, Braintree, Essex. OS sheet no. 167. BNG ref. TL738228

Bibliography

Cole, Peter, and Pringle, Peter, *Can You Positively Identify this Man?* (Andre Deutsch, 1974)

Curtis, J., *Maria Marten* (Geoffrey Bles, 1928; reprinted from the original edition published by Thomas Kelly, 1828)

Deary, Terry, 'The Real Maria Marten' (*East Anglian*, 1973)

Fielder, Michael, and Steele, Peter, *Alibi at Midnight* (Everest Books, 1974)

Furneaux, Rupert, *Famous Criminal Cases (6)* (Odhams Press, 1960)

Gaute, J.H.H., and Odell, Robin, *The Murderers Who's Who* (Geo. G. Harrap, 1979)

Haining, Peter, *Buried Passions* (Neville Spearman, 1980)

Huson, Richard ed., *Sixty Famous Trials* (*Daily Express*, 1939)

Jackson, Robert, *Francis Camps* (Hart-Davis MacGibbon, 1975)

Newby, J.W., *The Patrick Stead Hospital (Halesworth 1824-64)* (Newby Publicity Organisations, 1964)

Simpson, Keith, *Forty Years of Murder* (Geo. G. Harrap, 1978)

Smith-Hughes, Jack, *Unfair Comment* (Cassell, 1951).

Totterdell, G.H., *Country Copper* (Geo. G. Harrap, 1956)

Wilson, Colin, and Pitman, Patricia, *Encyclopaedia of Murder* (Arthur Barker, 1961)

Other Sources

Famous Crimes Past and Present Published in the 1890s as a weekly penny newsheet

Mackie, Charles, *Norfolk Annals*, Vol. I, 1801-50, and Vol. II, 1851-1900 (compiled from the files of the *Norfolk Chronicle*, 1901)

Norfolk Fair, September 1972 and January 1973 issues (R.F. County Magazine Group)

Prosecution Brief, *The Queen Against John Ducker, 1863*

East Suffolk Police charge book (Petty Sessional Division of Lowestoft), 1913

Index